Implementing Continuous Quality Improvement in Health Care

A Global Casebook

Curtis P. McLaughlin, DBA
Professor Emeritus of Business Administration
Kenan-Flagler Business School
Senior Research Fellow Emeritus
Cecil B. Sheps Center for Health Services Research
University of North Carolina at Chapel Hill
Chapel Hill, North Carolina

Julie K. Johnson, MSPH, PhD
Associate Professor in the Faculty of Medicine
Deputy Director of the Centre for Clinical Governance Research
University of New South Wales
Sydney, NSW, Australia

William A. Sollecito, DrPH
Clinical Professor, Public Health Leadership Program
Director, Online Global Health Certificate Program
Gillings School of Global Public Health
University of North Carolina at Chapel Hill
Chapel Hill, North Carolina

JONES & BARTLETT
L E A R N I N G

World Headquarters

Jones & Bartlett Learning
40 Tall Pine Drive
Sudbury, MA 01776
978-443-5000
info@jblearning.com
www.jblearning.com

Jones & Bartlett Learning
Canada
6339 Ormindale Way
Mississauga, Ontario L5V 1J2
Canada

Jones & Bartlett Learning
International
Barb House, Barb Mews
London W6 7PA
United Kingdom

Jones & Bartlett Learning books and products are available through most bookstores and online booksellers. To contact Jones & Bartlett Learning directly, call 800-832-0034, fax 978-443-8000, or visit our website, www.jblearning.com.

This publication is designed to provide accurate and authoritative information in regard to the Subject Matter covered. It is sold with the understanding that the publisher is not engaged in rendering legal, accounting, or other professional service. If legal advice or other expert assistance is required, the service of a competent professional person should be sought.

Production Credits

Publisher: Michael Brown
Associate Editor: Maro Gartside
Editorial Assistant: Teresa Reilly
Production Assistant: Rebekah Linga
Senior Marketing Manager: Sophie Fleck
Manufacturing and Inventory Control
  Supervisor: Amy Bacus

Composition: Shepherd, Inc.
Cover Design: Scott Moden
Cover Image: ©gualtiero boffi/
  ShutterStock, Inc.
Printing and Binding: Malloy, Inc.
Cover printing: Malloy, Inc.

Library of Congress Cataloging-in-Publication Data
McLaughlin, Curtis P.
   Implementing continuous quality improvement in health care: a global casebook / Curt McLaughlin, Julie K. Johnson, and William A. Sollecito.
      p. ; cm.
   Includes bibliographical references and index.
   ISBN-13: 978-0-7637-9536-8 (pbk.)
   ISBN-10: 0-7637-9536-4 (pbk.)
      1. Medical care—Quality control—Case studies. 2. Total quality management—Case studies. I. Johnson, Julie K. II. Sollecito, William A. III. Title.
   [DNLM: 1. Quality Assurance, Health Care—methods. 2. Delivery of Health Care—organization & administration. 3. Organizational Case Studies. W 84.4]
   RA399.A3M35 2012
   362.1068—dc22

                                                                                    2010049156
6048

Printed in the United States of America
15 14 13 12 11 10 9 8 7 6 5 4 3 2 1

Dedication

To our families, home academic institutions, and contributing colleagues
with many thanks.

Table of Contents

Preface

This book has its origins in the first three editions of Curtis P. McLaughlin and Arnold D. Kaluzny's *Continuous Quality Improvement in Health Care*. Each edition contained a number of cases under the "illustrations" rubric. However, when we began considering the fourth edition, it was clear that the book would be too long if it included the cases. The field of quality improvement has experienced an evolution across multiple fields, within and outside health care, and geographically as well. It has grown by leaps and bounds, and a single textbook cannot continue to fully address all the relevant issues. So in discussions with our publisher at Jones & Bartlett Learning, Mike Brown, we suggested two independent yet coordinated books. Furthermore, we realized that one could develop a much more robust educational experience centered on cases, if given the opportunity. We have split the teaching material into two volumes so the case approach stands on its own for those instructors who want more of a case approach, or it can be used in tandem with the fourth edition of *Continuous Quality Improvement in Health Care*. The cases are intended to be the basis for classroom discussion and not a judgment of either good or bad management. They have been selected to show an aspect of quality improvement in health care in the current environment. Each case has a section called "Case Analysis" that explains the primary themes and our pedagogical intentions for its use.

One new aspect of these cases is that some take place outside the United States, just as continuous quality improvement started in the United States, flourished in Japanese manufacturing, and has now moved around the world in all economic sectors. Increasingly, we have seen that the application of continuous quality improvement is driven by the funders of health care, whether they are national health insurance schemes, employers, or government administrations. In the developing world, donor agencies have been drivers as well. These efforts have generated a "quality-in-health-care industry" with its own vendors, evaluators, think tanks, agencies, and gurus. These are also linked to the current support for expanded investments in information technology, especially electronic health records, and pay-for-performance systems.

We have watched this field evolve for two decades now and the literature related to quality improvement has grown exponentially. The book's initial case features Paul Batalden's pioneering work at HCA. From Lucian Leape's seminal publication on medical error in 1994 through the Institute of Medicine reports on quality and safety opportunities and more pioneering by Wennberg and Batalden at Dartmouth, Berwick at Harvard, and James at Intermountain Healthcare, we have witnessed more interest, more disciples, even more interest, and more activity. The next generation of quality czars and czarinas are on the way. The trick will be to be able to stick with approaches that are simple, effective, and participatory, instead of professionalized and ritualistic, with an emphasis on the philosophy as well as the processes of quality improvement.

STRUCTURE

The book is organized into five parts, each with a central theme. The allocation of cases to each part has been based on a pedagogical purpose, but most cases can easily service multiple purposes. For example, Case 3 about Clemson's Nursing Home was placed in Part I because it illustrates the application of basic continuous quality improvement tools in the workshop it describes. It might just as easily have gone into Part III because it involves an educational intervention by the state's Quality Improvement Organization or in Part IV on assessment, incentives, and regulation because the intervention was triggered by an assessment based on data mining of the mandated reporting of restraint use in the Minimum Data Set for nursing homes receiving payments through Medicare or Medicaid. Similarly, Case 4 about CQI in the malaria program of Ghana went into Part I because it fully describes the effort there using tools such as flowcharts and fishbone diagrams to plan interventions in a number of district programs. However, it could certainly have gone into Part V because the interventions were part of a research project looking in a very preliminary way at the potential of using CQI in Ghana.

Each case is accompanied by three aids: (1) a case analysis, which is written by the editors to prompt your thinking about one or more salient points for analyzing the case; (2) assignment questions; and (3) a class exercise, which encourages further digging into the topic that the instructor may or may not assign. Usually the latter exercise can be accomplished on the Web. Completing the case studies along with the relevant chapters in the textbook will provide the student with a rich educational overview of the theory of quality improvement and its local application.

GLOBALIZATION

Four cases have a major international component. They introduce issues of limited resource availability and brain drain of health professionals in many countries. They also deal with evidence-based decision making in single-payer systems. Cultural and political differences become evident in these cases in various ways. Differences include the use of quality adjusted life years in the United Kingdom, religious preferences, medical tourism, and the potential clashes between continuous quality improvement and the trickle-down management philosophies of many health sector bureaucracies. For resource-poor countries with a large presence of external charitable or government-to-government donors with their own concepts of continuous improvement, there are also issues of national autonomy and reasonably expected responsiveness.

FEEDBACK TO THE AUTHORS

As always, we welcome your feedback about the book so that it can be improved in subsequent printings or editions. We suggest that you address your queries or suggestions to Dr. Sollecito at the University of North Carolina at Chapel Hill, Gillings School of Global Public Health.

Curtis P. McLaughlin
Julie K. Johnson
William A. Sollecito

Contributing Authors

Irene A. Agyepong, MBChB, DrPH
Greater Accra Regional Director of Health Services
Ghana Health Service
Accra, Ghana

Paul Barach, MD, MPH
Professor (Visiting)
Department of Anesthesia and Center for Patient Safety
Utrecht Medical Center
Utrecht, The Netherlands

Carol E. Breland, MPH, RRT, RCP
Project Manager
Chiltern International, Ltd.
Slough, Berkshire, England, UK
(Local Field Office: Winston-Salem, NC, USA)

Richard B. Colletti, MD
Professor and Vice-Chair, Department of Pediatrics
Associate Chief, Vermont Children's Hospital
University of Vermont College of Medicine
Burlington, Vermont, USA

Mary V. Davis, DrPH, MSPH
Director, Evaluation Services
North Carolina Institute for Public Health
Lecturer, Department of Health Behavior & Health Education
Gillings School of Global Public Health
University of North Carolina at Chapel Hill
Chapel Hill, North Carolina, USA

Thomas E. Harvey Jr., FAIA, FACHA, MPH, LEED
Senior Vice President
HKS, Inc.
Dallas, Texas, USA

Helen Haskell, MA
President, Mothers Against Medical Error
Columbia, South Carolina, USA

William Q. Judge, PhD
E.V. Williams Chair of Strategic Leadership
Professor of Strategic Management
Old Dominion University
Norfolk, Virginia, USA

Karen E. Koch, PharmD, MSHA
Patient Focused Improvement Department Director
North Mississippi Health Services
Tupelo, Mississippi, USA

Cheryll D. Lesneski, DrPH
Clinical Assistant Professor
Public Health Leadership Program
Gillings School of Global Public Health
University of North Carolina at Chapel Hill
Chapel Hill, North Carolina, USA

Peter A. Margolis, MD, PhD
Professor of Pediatrics
University of Cincinnati College of Medicine
Co-director, Center for Health Care Quality
Cincinnati Children's Hospital Medical Center
Cincinnati, Ohio, USA

Jill A. McArdle, RN, MSPH
Director of Federal Programs and Service
The Carolinas Center for Medical Excellence
Cary, North Carolina, USA

Craig D. McLaughlin, MJ
Executive Director
Washington State Board of Health
Olympia, Washington, USA

Gwenn E. McLaughlin, MD, MPH
Chief Quality and Safety Officer
Holtz Children's Hospital
Professor of Clinical Pediatrics
Leonard M. Miller School of Medicine
University of Miami
Miami, Florida, USA

Paul V. Miles, MD, FAAP
Senior Vice President
Director of Quality Improvement and Practice Assessment Programs
American Board of Pediatrics
Chapel Hill, North Carolina, USA

Debajyoti Pati, PhD, MASA, FIIA, LEED, AP
Director of Research
HKS, Inc.
Dallas, Texas, USA

Robert Perelman, MD
Deputy Executive Director
Director, Department of Education
American Academy of Pediatrics
Elk Grove Village, Illinois, USA

Lloyd P. Provost, PhD
Improvement Advisor
Associates in Process Improvement
Austin, Texas, USA

Franziska Rokoske, PT, MS
Manager of Research Programs
The Carolinas Center for Medical Excellence
Cary, North Carolina, USA

Lucy A. Savitz, PhD, MBA
Director of Research and Education
Institute for Health Care Delivery Research
Intermountain Healthcare
Associate Professor, Clinical Epidemiology
Director, CCTS Community Engagement Core
University of Utah
Salt Lake City, Utah, USA

Anna P. Schenck, PhD, MSPH
Professor of the Practice and Director
Public Health Leadership Program
Gillings School of Global Public Health
University of North Carolina at Chapel Hill
Chapel Hill, North Carolina, USA

David Stone, MS
Accreditation Administrator
NC Local Health Department Accreditation
NC Institute for Public Health
Gillings School of Global Public Health
University of North Carolina at Chapel Hill
Chapel Hill, North Carolina, USA

Joseph G. Van Matre, PhD
Professor
School of Business
University of Alabama at Birmingham
Birmingham, Alabama, USA

Roswitha M. Wolfram, MD
Interim Medical Director
Prince Court Medical Centre
Kuala Lampur, Malaysia
Professor of Angiology and Internal Medicine
Department of Internal Medicine/Angiology
Medical University
Vienna, Austria

About the Authors

Curtis P. McLaughlin, DBA, is Professor Emeritus and Adjunct Professor in the Kenan-Flagler Business School and Senior Research Fellow Emeritus of the Cecil B. Sheps Center for Health Services Research at the University of North Carolina at Chapel Hill. At the time of his retirement, he was also Professor of Health Policy and Administration in the School of Public Health. He is coeditor with A. D. Kaluzny of *Quality Improvement in Health Care*, now entering its fourth edition. He received his BA in chemistry from Wesleyan University and his MBA and DBA from Harvard Business School, where he participated in the initial interdisciplinary program in healthcare economics and management. He then taught in that program for the School of Public Health, while an Assistant Professor at the Business School. He is an author or coauthor of more than 200 publications and has conducted many executive training programs and consultations.

Julie K. Johnson, MSPH, PhD, is Associate Professor in the Faculty of Medicine and Deputy Director of the Centre for Clinical Governance Research at the University of New South Wales in Sydney, Australia. Her career interests involve building a series of collaborative relationships to improve the quality and safety of health care through teaching, research, and clinical improvement. She uses qualitative research methods to study processes of care with the ultimate goal of translating theory into practice while generating new knowledge about the best models for improving care. She has a master's degree in health policy and administration from the University of North Carolina School of Public Health and a PhD in evaluative clinical sciences from Dartmouth College in Hanover, New Hampshire. As a teacher, Dr. Johnson has a special interest in developing and using serious games as a way to engage learners around important concepts related to understanding and improving the quality and safety of health care.

William A. Sollecito, DrPH, is Clinical Professor in the Public Health Leadership Program and Director of the Online Global Health Certificate Curriculum in the Gillings School of Global Public Health at the University of North Carolina at Chapel Hill. Prior to being appointed as a faculty member at UNC, he worked in the private sector, most recently at Quintiles Transnational Corporation, where he served as president of their Americas Division, overseeing all clinical operations in the United States, Canada, and South America. He has been a practitioner of Continuous Quality Improvement throughout his career, implementing CQI in multiple settings in academia and private industry. This experience is reflected in his publications, which span a broad array of topics including biostatistics and clinical research as well as CQI. He received his BBA in statistics from the Baruch College of the City University of New York, an MS(hyg) in biostatistics from the Graduate School of Public Health of the University of Pittsburgh, and a DrPH in biostatistics from the School of Public Health of the University of North Carolina at Chapel Hill.

Frequently Used Acronyms

AHRQ	Agency for Healthcare Research and Quality (USA)
ALOS	Average Length of Stay
CDC	Centers for Disease Control and Prevention (USA)
CMS	Centers for Medicare and Medicaid Services (USA)
CPOE	Computerized Physician Order Entry
CQI	Continuous Quality Improvement
DHHS	Department of Health and Human Services (USA)
ETOH	Ethanol
FQHC	Federally Qualified Health Centers
HCFA	Health Care Financing Administration, now known as CMS (USA)
IHI	Institute for Healthcare Improvement (USA)
IOM	Institute of Medicine (USA)
ITN	Insecticide Treated Nets
JIT	Just in Time
KQC	Key Quality
MOH	Ministry of Health
NCQA	National Committee for Quality Assurance
NHS	National Health Service (UK)
NHSN	National Healthcare Safety Network
NICE	National Institute for Health and Clinical Excellence (UK)
O&G	Obstetrics and Gynecology
OPD	Outpatient Department
PDSA	Plan Do Study Act
QI	Quality Improvement
QIO	Quality Improvement Organization
STG	Staff Training Guide (Ghana)
TQM	Total Quality Management
WHO	World Health Organization

CONTINUOUS QUALITY IMPROVEMENT USING PLAN, DO, STUDY/CHECK, ACT (PDSA/PDCA) AND QUALITY-IMPROVEMENT TOOLS

Part I presents four cases that illustrate the basic techniques of Continuous Quality Improvement (CQI) under quite varied circumstances. Each organization formed teams, defined improvement opportunities, collected and analyzed data, then modified its processes based on internal and external evidence, assessed the results of these experiments, and then acted on those results. They differ, however, in terms of the type of institution, type of service, cultural setting, impetus for change, staff leadership, and top management leadership. They also represent a range of economic and global diversity, with the first three cases taking place in the United States and the fourth in a resource poor setting in Ghana.

The first case, West Florida Regional Hospital, presents a very early and very straightforward example of the methodology that Dr. Paul Batalden and his associates at Hospital Corporation of America (HCA) developed in the early 1980s. Dr. Batalden has been a strong influence on the work of Dr. Brent James and Intermountain Healthcare, on editors of this casebook, and on many other healthcare leaders. Case 1 displays the core of his early approach, which emphasized participation in Quality 101 by all

1

participating leaders and the use of a quality council to prioritize and motivate the efforts of teams of volunteers.

Holtz Children's Hospital (Case 2) is a contemporary case illustrating how much has changed attitudinally since 2000–2002 when the Institute of Medicine published its influential studies of the problem of medical errors in the United States. What had once been a local and often *ad hoc* application of a set of techniques by the management and staff of a delivery site has become a major focus of professional groups, governments, payer groups, accrediting agencies, and patient advocacy groups. In response, many hospitals have a quality and safety staff group. They are required to report publicly certain key clinical quality indicators and have many available guidelines, checklists, and protocols that are widely accepted. Central line infections, once considered a natural consequence of care, are now considered a medical error and have become a condition for which payers are balking at covering the costs of treatment. This case presents how the team researched the causes of central line infections, implemented changes, and rapidly reduced their incidence.

Case 3 shows the use of externally-induced process improvement based on data mining of payer-required status reports. The U.S. Center for Medicare and Medicaid (CMS) has funded a series of Quality Improvement Organizations (QIOs) to work with providers on process improvement. Clemson's Nursing Home had been identified as an outlier in terms of the use of restraints and received a request to participate in a workshop to develop a continuous-improvement approach to the problem. While this is a voluntary program, any operator in a highly-regulated industry puts a high priority on conforming to the expectations of the regulators. This case illustrates, again, the set of tools that those called on to improve processes tend to use.

Case 4 illustrates the use of CQI in the malaria control program of one region of Ghana. It is one of four international cases in this casebook. In Ghana the lack of resources—human and financial—often block the righteous spiral of improvement reported elsewhere. The focus of the case is on an experiment conducted in 2002–2003 that was relatively inconclusive, but which touches on the ongoing discussion about measuring process vs. outcome and the relative strengths and weaknesses of observational study designs in assessing the impact of CQI initiatives. The case also follows up on the status of the malaria program a number of years later. There have been many changes in the national healthcare environment, but the institutionalization of CQI is not one of them, although there remain both domestic and foreign-aid champions of the approach.

West Florida Regional Medical Center

Curtis P. McLaughlin

INTRODUCTION

West Florida Regional Medical Center (WFRMC) is a Hospital Corporation of America (HCA)-owned and operated, for-profit hospital complex on the north side of Pensacola, Florida. Licensed for 547 beds, it operated approximately 325 beds in December 1991, plus the 89-bed psychiatric Pavilion and the 58-bed Rehabilitation Institute of West Florida. The 11-story office building of the Medical Center Clinic, P.A., was attached to the hospital facility, and a new cancer center was under construction.

The 130 doctors practicing at the Medical Center Clinic and its satellite clinics admitted mostly to WFRMC, whereas most of the other doctors in this city of 150,000 practiced at both Sacred Heart and Baptist Hospitals downtown. Competition for patients was intense, and in 1992, as many as 90% to 95% of patients in the hospital were admitted subject to discounted prices, mostly Medicare for the elderly, CHAMPUS for military dependents, and Blue Cross/Blue Shield of Florida for the employed and their dependents.

The continuous quality improvement (CQI) effort had had some real successes over the previous four years, especially in the areas where package prices for services were required. All of the management team had been trained in quality improvement techniques according to HCA's Deming-based approach, and some 25 task forces were operating. The experiment with departmental self-assessments, using the Baldrige Award criteria and an instrument developed by HCA headquarters, had spurred department heads to become further involved and begin to apply quality improvement techniques within their own work units. Yet John Kausch, the Center's CEO, and his senior leadership sensed some loss of interest among some managers, whereas others who had not bought into the idea at first were now enthusiasts.

THE HCA CQI PROCESS

John Kausch had been in the first group of HCA CEOs trained in CQI techniques in 1987 by Paul Batalden, M.D., Corporate Vice President for Medical Care. John had become a member of the steering committee for HCA's overall quality effort. The HCA approach was dependent on the active and continued participation of top local management and on the Plan-Do-Check-Act (PDCA) cycle of Deming. Figure 1–1 shows that process as presented to company employees. Dr. Batalden told the case writer that he did not work with a hospital administrator until he was convinced that that individual was fully committed to the concept and was ready to lead the process at his or her own institution—a responsibility that included being the one to teach the Quality 101 course on site to his or her own managers. John Kausch also took members of his management team to visit other quality exemplars, such as Florida Power and Light and local plants of Westinghouse and Monsanto.

In 1991, John Kausch became actively involved in the Total Quality Council of the Pensacola Area Chamber of Commerce (PATQC) when a group of Pensacola area leaders in business, government, military, education, and health care began meeting informally to share ideas in productivity and quality improvement. From this informal group emerged the PATQC under the sponsorship of the Chamber of Commerce. The vision of PATQC was "helping the Pensacola area develop into a total quality community by promoting productivity and quality in all area organizations, public and private, and by promoting economic development through aiding existing business and attracting new business development." The primary employer in Pensacola, the U.S. Navy, was using the total quality management (TQM) approach extensively, was quite satisfied with the results, and supported the Chamber of Commerce program. In fact, the first 1992 one-day seminar presented by Mr. George F. Butts,

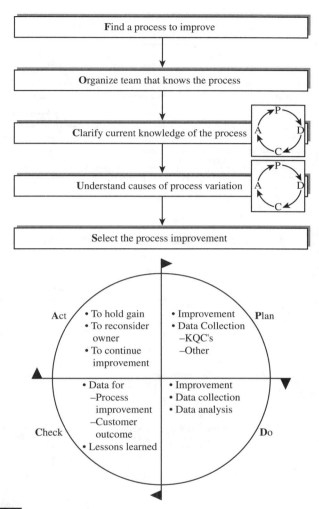

Figure 1-1 HCA's FOCUS–PDCA Cycle

consultant and retired Chrysler Vice President for Quality and Produc-tivity, was held at the Naval Air Station's Mustin Beach Officer's Club. Celanese Corporation, a Monsanto division, and the largest nongovern-mental employer in the area, also supported PATQC.

The CQI staffing at WFRMC was quite small, in keeping with HCA practice. The only program employee was Ms. Bette Gulsby, M.Ed.,

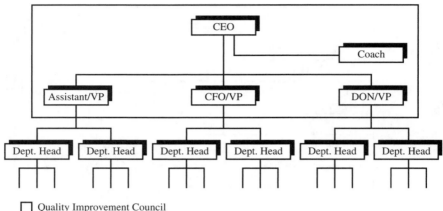

Figure 1–2   Organization Chart with Quality Improvement Council

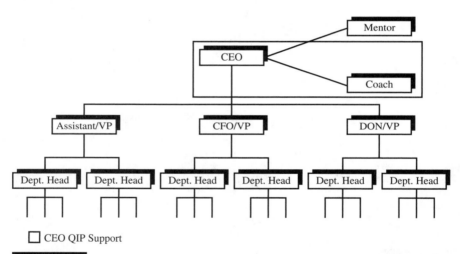

Figure 1–3   Organization Chart with CEO QIP Support Mentor

Director of Quality Improvement Resources, who served as staff and "coach" to Mr. Kausch and as a member of the quality improvement council. Figures 1–2 and 1–3 show the organization of the council and the staffing for Quality Improvement Program (QIP) support. The "mentor" was provided by headquarters staff, and in the case of WFRMC, was Dr. Batalden himself. The planning process had been careful and detailed. Exhibit 1–1 shows excerpts from the planning processes used in the early years of the program.

EXHIBIT 1–1

Planning Chronology for CQI

Initiation Plan—3 to 6 months, starting May 25, 1988

May 25: Develop initial working definition of quality for WFRMC.

May 25: Define the purpose of the Quality Improvement Council (QIC) and set schedule for 2–4 PM every Tuesday and Thursday.

May 25: Integrate Health Quality Trends (HQT) into continuous improvement cycle and hold initial review.

June 2: Start several multifunctional teams with their core from those completing the Leadership Workshop with topics selected by the Quality Improvement Council using surveys, experience, and group techniques.

June 2: Department Heads complete "CEO assessment" to identify customers and expectations, determine training needs, and identify department opportunities. To be discussed with assistant administrators on June 15.

June 16: Present to QIC the Task Force report on elements and recommendations on organizational elements to guide and monitor QIP.

June 20: Division meetings to gain consensus on Department plans and set priorities. QIC reviews and consolidates on June 21. Final assignments to Department Heads on June 22.

June 27: Draft initial Statement of Purpose for WFRMC and present to QIC.

June 29–July 1:Conduct first Facilitator's Training Workshop for 16.

July 1: Task Force reports on additional QIP education and training requirements for:
- Team training and team members' handbook
- Head nurses
- Employee orientation (new and current)
- Integration of community resources (colleges and industry)
- Use of HCA network resources for Medical Staff, Board of Trustees

(continues)

EXHIBIT 1-1

July 19: Task Force report on communications program to support awareness, education, and feedback from employees, vendors, medical staff, local business, colleges and universities, and HCA.
August 1: Complete the organization of the QIC.

Quality Improvement Implementation Plan to June 30, 1989

Fall: Pilot and evaluate "Patient Comment Card System."
Oct. 21: QIC input to draft policies—guidelines regarding forming teams, quality responsibility, and guidelines for multifunctional teams. Brainstorm at Oct. 27 meeting, have revisions for Nov. 10 meeting, and distribute to employees by November 15.
Oct. 27: Review proposals for communicating QIP to employees to heighten awareness and understanding, communicate on HCA and WFRMC commitments; key definitions, policies, guidelines; HQT; QIP; teams and improvements to date; responsibility and opportunities for individual employees; initiate ASAP.
Nov. 15: Prepare statements "On further consideration of HCA's Quality Guidelines;" discuss with department heads, hospital staff, employee orientation; use to identify barriers to Quality Improvement (QI) and opportunities for QI. Develop specific action plan and discuss with QIC.
Dec. 1: Identify and evaluate community sources for QI assistance—statistical and operational—including colleges, companies, and the Navy. Make recommendations.
Early Dec.: Conduct Quality 102 course for remaining Dept. Heads. Conduct Quality 101 course for head nurses and several new Dept. Heads.
Jan. 1, 1989: Develop and implement a suggestion program consistent with our HCA Quality Guidelines, providing quick and easy ways to become involved in making suggestions/identifying situations needing improvement, providing quick feedback and recognition; and interfacing with identifying opportunities for QIP.

(continues)

EXHIBIT 1–1

QIP Implementation Plan, July 1989–June 1990

Aug. 1: Survey Department Heads to identify priorities for additional education and training.

Sept. 14–15: Conduct a management workshop to sharpen and practice QI methods. To include practice methods; to increase management/staff confidence, comfort; to develop a model for departmental implementation; to develop process assessment/QIP implementation tool; to start Quality Team Review.

September: Develop a standardized team orientation program to cover QI tools and group process rules.

Fall: Expand use of HQTs and integrate into Health Quality Improvement Process (HQIP)—improve communication of results and integration of quality improvement action plans. Psychiatric Pavilion to evaluate and implement HQT recommendations from "Patient Comment Card System"—evaluate and pilot.

October: Incorporate QIP implementation into existing management/communication structure. Establish division "steering committee functions" to guide and facilitate departmental implementation. Identify QI project for each Department Head/Assistant Administrator.

Establish regular Quality Reviews into Department Manager meetings.

December: Evaluate effectiveness of existing policies, guidelines, and practices for sanctioning, supporting, and guiding QI teams. Include Opportunity Form/Cross Functional Team Sanctioning; Team leader and Facilitator responsibilities; Team progress monitoring/guiding; Standardized team presentation format (storyboard). Demonstrate measurable improvement through Baxter QI team.

Monthly: Monitor and improve the suggestion program.

January: Pilot the Clinical Process Improvement methodology.

All year: In all communications, written and verbal, maintain constant message regarding WFRMC commitment to HQIP; report successes of teams and suggestions; and continue to educate about principles and practices of HQIP strategy.

(continues)

EXHIBIT 1–1

January: Successfully demonstrate measurable improvement from focused QIP in one department (Medical Records).
Spring: Expand use of HQTs and integrate into HQIP.
  • Pilot HQT in Rehab Center.
  • Evaluate and implement Physicians' HQT.
  • Pilot Ambulatory Care HQT.
Summer: Expand use of HQTs and integrate into HQIP.
  • Human Resources—Pilot HQT.
  • Payers—Pilot HQT.

WFRMC has been one of several HCA hospitals to work with a self-assessment tool for department heads. Exhibit 1–2 shows the cover letter sent to all department heads. Exhibit 1–3 shows the Scoring Matrix for Self-Assessment. Exhibit 1–4 shows the Scoring Guidelines, and Exhibit 1–5 displays the five assessment categories used.

FOUR EXAMPLES OF TEAMS

IV Documentation

The nursing department originated the IV Documentation Team in September 1990 after receiving documentation from the pharmacy department that over a 58-day period there had been $16,800 in lost charges related to the administration of intravenous (IV) solutions. The pharmacy attributed the loss to the nursing staff's recordkeeping. This was the first time that the nursing department was aware of a problem or that the pharmacy department had been tracking this variable. There were other lost charges, not yet quantified, due to recording errors in the oral administration of pharmaceuticals as well.

The team formed to look at this problem found that there were some 15 possible reasons why the errors occurred, but that the primary one was that documentation of the administration of the IV solution was not entered into the medication administration record (MAR). The MAR was

EXHIBIT 1–2

Departmental Quality Improvement Assessment

In an effort to continue to monitor and implement elements of improvement and innovation within our organization, it will become more and more necessary to find methods which will describe our level of QI implementation.

The assessment or review of a quality initiative is only as good as the thought processes which have been triggered during the actual assessment. Last year (1990) the Quality Improvement Council prepared for and participated in a quality review. This exercise was extremely beneficial to the overall understanding of what was being done and the results that have been accomplished utilizing various quality techniques and tools.

The Departmental Implementation of QI has been somewhat varied throughout the organization and although the variation is certainly within the range of acceptability, it is the intent of the QIC to better understand each department's implementation road map and furthermore to provide advice/coaching on the next steps for each department.

Attached please find a scoring matrix for self-assessment. This matrix is followed by five category ratings (to be completed by each department head). The use of this type of tool reinforces the self-evaluation which is consistent with continuous improvement and meeting the vision of West Florida Regional Medical Center.

Please read and review the attachment describing the scoring instructions and then score your department category standings, relative to the approach, deployment, and effects. This information will be forwarded to Bette Gulsby by April 19, 1991, and following a preliminary assessment by the QIC, an appointment will be scheduled for your departmental review.

The review will be conducted by John Kausch and Bette Gulsby, along with your administrative director. Please take the time to review the attachments and begin your self-assessment scoring. You will be notified of the date and time of your review.

This information will be utilized for preparing for the next Department Head retreat, scheduled for May 29 and 30, 1991 at the Perdido Beach Hilton.

12   CASE 1   WEST FLORIDA REGIONAL MEDICAL CENTER

EXHIBIT 1–3

A Scoring Matrix for Self-Assessment

APPROACH	DEPLOYMENT (Implementation)	EFFECTS (Results)
• HQIP design includes all eight dimensions* • Integration across dimensions of HQIP and areas of operation	• Breadth of implementation (areas or functions) • Depth of implementation (awareness, knowledge, understanding, and applications)	• Quality of measurable results

*The eight dimensions of HQIP are: leadership constancy, employee mindedness, customer mindedness, process focused, statistical thinking, PDCA driven, innovativeness, and regulatory proactiveness.

	APPROACH	DEPLOYMENT	EFFECTS
100%	• World-class approach: sound, systematic, effective HQIP based, continuously evaluated, refined, and improved. • Total interaction across all functions. • Repeated cycles of innovation/improvement.	• Fully in all areas and functions. • Ingrained in the culture.	• Exceptional, world-class, superior to all competition in all areas. • Sustained (3 to 5 years), clearly caused by the approach.
80%	• Well-developed and tested, HQIP-based. • Excellent integration.	• In almost all areas and functions. • Evident in the culture of all groups.	• Excellent, sustained in all areas with improving competitive advantage. • Much evidence that they are caused by the approach.
60%	• Well planned, documented, sound, systematic. HQIP-based, all aspects addressed. • Good integration	• In most areas and functions. • Evident in the culture of most groups.	• Solid, with positive trends in most areas. • Some evidence that they are caused by the approach.
40%	• Beginning of sound, systematic, HQIP-based; not all aspects addressed. • Fair integration	• Begun in many areas and functions. • Evident in the culture of some groups.	• Some success in major areas. • Not much evidence that they are caused by the approach.
20%	• Beginning of HQIP awareness. • No integration across functions.	• Beginning in some areas and functions. • Not part of the culture.	• Few or no results. • Little or no evidence that any results are caused by the approach.
0%			

EXHIBIT 1–4

Departmental Quality Improvement Assessment Scoring Guidelines

In order to determine your department's score in each of the five categories, please review the Scoring Matrix for self-assessment. The operational definitions for Approach, Deployment, and Effects are listed in the small boxes on the top of the scoring matrix. Each criteria is divided into per-centage of progress–implementation (i.e., 0% to 100%). For example, you may determine that your departmental score on category 3.0 (QI Practice) is:

APPROACH	DEPLOYMENT	EFFECTS
20%	20%	20%

This means that your departmental approach has fair integra-tion of QIP practice, your departmental deployment is evident in the culture of some of your groups, and your departmental effects are not actually evidence that they are caused by the approach.

Please remember that this is a self-assessment and only you know your departmental progress. This assessment is not a tool to generate documentation. However, if you would like to bring any particular document(s) to your review, please do so. This is only meant to provide a forum for you to showcase your progress and receive recognition and feedback on such.

Remember, review each of the self-assessment criteria of approach, deployment, and effects and become familiar with the levels or percentages described. You have three scores for each Departmental QI Assessment Category (categories 1.0–5.0)

kept at the patient bedside, and each time that a medication was admin-istered the nurse was to enter documentation into this record.

The team had to come to understand some terms as they went along. According to the way the pharmacy kept its books, anything that was sent to the floors but not billed within 48 to 72 hours was considered a "lost charge." If an inquiry was sent to the floor about the material and what happened and a correction was made, the entry was classified as

EXHIBIT 1–5

Departmental QI Assessment Categories

1.0 Departmental QI Framework Development

The Departmental QI Framework Development category examines how the departmental quality values have been developed, how they are applied to projects in a consistent manner, and how adoption of the values throughout the department is assessed and reinforced.

Examples of areas to address:
- Department Mission
- Departmental Quality Definition
- Departmental Employee Performance Feedback Review
- Departmental QI Plan
- QI Methods

APPROACH	DEPLOYMENT	EFFECTS
_____%	_____%	_____%

2.0 Customer Knowledge Development

The Customer Knowledge Deployment category examines how the departmental leadership has involved and utilized various facets of customer-mindedness to guide the quality effort.

Examples of areas to address:
- HQT Family of Measures (patient, employee, etc.)
- Departmental Customer Identification
- Identification of Customer Needs and Expectations
- Customer Feedback/Data Review

APPROACH	DEPLOYMENT	EFFECTS
_____%	_____%	_____%

3.0 Quality Improvement Practice

The Quality Improvement Practice category examines the effectiveness of the department's efforts to develop and realize the full potential of the work force, including management, and the

(continues)

EXHIBIT 1–5

methods to maintain an environment conducive to full participation, quality leadership, and personal and organizational growth.
Examples of areas to address:
- Process Improvement Practice
- Meeting Skills
- QI Storyboards
- QI in Daily Work Life (individual use of QI tools, i.e., flow chart, run chart, Pareto chart)
- Practice Quality Management Guidelines
- Departmental Data Review
- Plans to Incorporate QI in Daily Clinical Operations
- Identification of Key Physician Leaders

APPROACH	DEPLOYMENT	EFFECTS
_____%	_____%	_____%

4.0 Quality Awareness Building

The Quality Awareness Building category examines how the department decides what quality education and training is needed by employees and how it utilizes the knowledge and skills acquired. It also examines what has been done to communicate QI to the department and how QI is addressed in departmental staff meetings.
Examples of areas to address:
- JIT Training
- Employee Orientation
- Creating Employee Awareness
- Communication of QI Results

APPROACH	DEPLOYMENT	EFFECTS
_____%	_____%	_____%

(continues)

EXHIBIT 1–5

5.0 QA/QI Linkage

The QA/QI Linkage category examines how the department has connected QA data and information to the QI process improvement strategy. Also examined is the utilization of QI data-gathering and decision-making tools to document and analyze data. (How the department relates the ongoing QA activities to QI process improvement activities.) Examples of areas to address:

- QA Process Identification
- FOCUS-PDCA Process Improvement
- Regulatory/Accreditation Connection (The Joint Commission)

APPROACH	DEPLOYMENT	EFFECTS
_____%	_____%	_____%

"revenue recovered." Thus, the core issue was not so much one of lost revenue as one of unnecessary rework in the pharmacy and on the nursing floors.

The team developed Pareto charts showing the reasons for the documentation errors. The most common ones were procedural—for example, "patient moved to the operating room," or "patient already discharged." Following the HCA model, these procedural problems were dealt with one at a time to correct the accounting for unused materials. The next step in the usual procedure was to develop a run chart to show what was happening over time to the lost charges on IVs. Here, the team determined that the best quality indicator would be the ratio of lost charges to total charges issued. At this point, pharmacy management realized that it lacked the denominator figure and that its lack of computerization led to the lack of that information. Therefore, the task force was inactive for three months, while the pharmacy implemented a computer system that could provide the denominator.

Ms. Debbie Koenig, Assistant Director of Nursing, who was responsible for the team, said that the next step would be to look at situations where the MAR was not at the patient bedside but perhaps at the nursing station so that a nurse could not make the entry at the appropriate time. This was an especially bothersome rework problem because of nurses working various shifts and because, occasionally, an agency nurse had been on duty and was not available to consult when the pharmacy asked why documentation was not present for an IV dose of medication.

Universal Charting

There was evidence that a number of ancillary services results, "loose reports," were not getting into the patients' medical records in a timely fashion. This was irritating to physicians and sometimes resulted in delays in a patient's discharge, which under DRGs (diagnosis-related groups) meant higher costs without higher reimbursement. One employee filed a suggestion that a single system be developed to avoid people running over other people on the floor doing the "charting." A CQI team was developed and led by Ms. Debbie Wroten, Medical Records Director. The 12-member team included supervisors and directors from the laboratory, the pulmonary lab, the EKG lab, medical records, radiology, and nursing. They developed the following "Opportunity Statement":

> At present six departments are utilizing nine full-time equivalents 92 hours per week for charting separate ancillary reports. Rework is created in the form of repulling of inhouse patient records creating an ever-increasing demand of chart accessibility. All parties affected by this process are frustrated because the current process increases the opportunity for lost documentation, chart unavailability, increased traffic on units creating congestion, prolonged charting times, and provides for untimely availability of clinical reports for patient care. Therefore, an opportunity exists to improve the current charting practice for all departments involved to allow for the efficiency, timeliness, and accuracy of charting loose reports.

The team met, assessed, and flow-charted the current charting processes of the five departments involved. Key variables were defined as follows:

- Charting timeliness—number of charting times per day, consistency of charting, and reports not charted per charting round.

- Report availability—indicated by the number of telephone calls per department asking for reports not yet charted.

Table 1-1 Charting Log					
	Mean Records		**Mean Hours**		
Department	**Per Day**	**Range**	**Per Day**	**Range**	**Comments**
Medical Records	77.3	20–40	1.6	0.6–2.5	Daily
Pulmonary Lab	50.3	37–55	1.0	0.7–1.5	MWF
Clinical Lab	244.7	163–305	3.2	1.9–5.4	Daily
EKG Lab	40.2	35–48	0.8	0.1–1.0	Weekdays
Microbiology	106.9	3–197	1.4	0.1–2.2	Daily
Radiology	87.1	6–163	1.5	0.1–2.9	Daily

- Chart availability—chart is accessible at the nurses' station without interruption.

- Resource utilization—personnel hours and number of hours per day of charting.

Each department was asked to use a common "charting log" track for several weeks of the number of records charted, who did the charting, when it was done, the preparation time, the number of reports charted, the number of reports not charted (missed), and the personnel hours consumed in charting. Some of these results are shown in Table 1–1.

These data gave the team considerable insight into the nature of the problem. Not every department was picking up the materials every day. Two people could cover the whole hospital in three-quarters of an hour each or one person in 1.5 hours. The clinical chemistry laboratory, medical records, and radiology were making two trips per day, whereas other departments were only able to chart every other day and failed to chart over the weekends.

The processes used by all the groups were similar. The printed or typed reports had to be sorted by floors, given room numbers if missing, taken to the floors, and inserted into patient charts. If the chart was not available, they had to be held until the next round. A further problem identified was that when the clerical person assigned to these rounds was not available, a technical person, who was paid considerably more and was often in short supply, had to be sent to do the job.

A smaller team of supervisors who actually knew and owned the charting efforts in the larger departments (medical records, radiology, and clinical chemistry) was set up to design and assess the pilot experiment. The overall team meetings were used only to brief the department heads to gain their feedback and support. A pilot experiment was run in which these three departments took turns doing the runs for each other. The results were favorable. The pilot increased timeliness and chart availability by charting four times per day on weekdays and three times per day on weekends. Report availability was improved, and there were fewer phone calls. Nursing staff, physicians, and participating departments specifically asked for the process to be continued. The hours of labor dropped from 92 weekly to less than 45, using less highly paid labor.

Therefore, the team decided that the issues were important enough that they should consider setting up a separate Universal Charting Team to meet the needs of the entire hospital. However, an unanticipated hospital census decline made impractical the possibility of requesting additional staffing, etc. Consequently, the group reevaluated the possibility of continuing the arrangement developed for the pilot using the charting hours of the smaller departments on a volume basis. It was discovered that this had the effect of freeing the professional staff of the smaller departments from charting activities and a very minimal allocation of hours floated to the larger departments. It also increased the availability of charters in the larger departments for other activities.

The payroll department was then asked to develop a system for allocating the hours that floated from one department to another. That proved cumbersome, so the group decided to allocate charting hours on the basis of each department's volume. "In the event that one or more departments experiences a significant increase/decrease in charting needs, the group will reconvene and the hourly allocation will be adjusted."

The resulting schedule has the lab making rounds at 6:00 AM and 9:00 AM and radiology at 4:00 PM and 9:30 PM Monday through Friday, and Medical Records at 6:00 AM, 1:00 PM, and 8:00 PM on Saturday and Sunday. Continuing statistics were kept on the process, which is shown in Exhibit 1–6. The system continued to work effectively.

Labor, Delivery, Recovery, Postpartum (LDRP) Nursing

Competition for young families needing maternity services had become quite intense in Pensacola. WFRMC Obstetrical (OB) Services offered very traditional services in 1989 in three separate units—labor and delivery, nursery, and postpartum—and operated considerably below capacity.

EXHIBIT 1-6

Universal Charting Team FOCUS–PDCA Outline

F Opportunity Statement:

At present, six departments are utilizing 9 full-time equivalents 92 hours a week for charting separate ancillary reports. Rework is created in the form of repulling of inhouse patient records creating an ever-increasing demand of chart accessibility. All parties affected by this process are frustrated because the current process increases the opportunity for lost documentation, chart unavailability, increased traffic on units creating congestion, prolonged charting times, and provides for untimely availability of clinical reports for patient care.

Therefore, an opportunity exists to improve the current charting practice for all departments involved to allow for the efficiency, timeliness, and accuracy of charting loose reports.

O Team members include:
Debbie Wroten, Medical Records Director—Leader
Bernie Grappe, Marketing Director—Facilitator
Joan Simmons, Laboratory Director
Mary Gunter, Laboratory Patient Services Coordinator
Al Clarke, Pulmonary Services Director
Carol Riley, Pulmonary Services Assistant Director
Marlene Rodrigues, EKG Supervisor
Patti Travis, EKG
Debra Wright, Medical Records Transcription Supervisor
Mike West, Radiology Director
Lori Mikesell, Radiology Transcription Supervisor
Debbie Fernandez, Head Nurse

C Assessed and flow-charted current charting practices of departments. Clarified and defined key quality characteristics of the charting process:

Charting Timeliness—number of charting times per day, consistency of charting, and reports not charted per charting round.

(continues)

EXHIBIT 1–6

Report Availability—indicated by the number of telephone calls per department asking for reports not yet charted.

Chart Availability—chart is accessible at nurses' station for charting without interruption.

Resource Utilization—manhours and number of hours per day of charting.

U Gathered data on departments charting volumes and time spent on charting.

Department: Charting Log							
Date	Charting Tech vs. Clk.	Prep Time	# Reports Charted	# Reports Not Charted	Charting Time (amt)	Hour of Day	Comment

S Data gained through the pilot indicated that significant gains were available through the effort to S justify proceeding with the development of a Universal Charting Team (UCT).

(continues)

EXHIBIT 1–6

P The team developed a flow chart of the charting process using a UCT rather than previous arrangements. In order to pilot the improvement, the group decided to set up a UCT using current charters from the three major charting departments-medical records, laboratory, and radiology. The team also developed written instructions for both the charters and participating departments. A subgroup of the team actually conducted a one-day pilot before beginning extensive education to ensure that the UCT would work as planned and to be sure that the charters from each of the large departments were well versed on possible situations that might occur during the pilot.

D Piloted proposed using current charting personnel from radiology, laboratory, and medical records to chart for all departments.

C Pilot results were positive and indicated that the UCT concept offered significant advantages over the previous charting arrangements. Results were:

Timeliness/Chart Availability—Pilot reduced daily charting to four scheduled charting times daily for all departments. Smaller departments did not chart daily prior to pilot. The charting team also reduced the number of occasions that charters from different departments were on the nursing unit needing the same chart.

Report Availability—Telephone calls were reduced and nursing staff, physicians, and participating departments specifically asked for UCT following the pilot.

Resource Utilization—Number of manhours spent charting and preparing to chart was reduced from 92 hours weekly to less than 45 hours. The improvement also allowed the use of less expensive staff for charting.

(continues)

EXHIBIT 1–6

A The group reached consensus that the easiest configuration for the UCT would be to set up a separate UCT that would serve the needs of the entire hospital. This was to be proposed to administration by the team as the conclusion of their efforts. However, an unanticipated hospital census decline made impractical the possibility of requesting additional staffing, etc. Consequently, the group reevaluated the possibility of continuing the arrangement developed for the pilot using the charting hours of the smaller departments on a volume basis. It was discovered that this had the effect of freeing the professional staff in the smaller departments from charting responsibilities while a very minimal allocation of hours floated to the larger departments, and it increased the availability of charters in the larger departments for other activities. The payroll department was then involved in order to develop the proper mechanism and procedure for floating hours.

This modification of the previous pilot was piloted for a month with continued good results. Streamlining of the hours floating process may be necessary to place less burden on the payroll department.

Since no major changes were required following the pilot, the group has elected to adopt the piloted UCT format. Allocation of charting hours is based on a monthly review of charting volumes for each department. In the event that one or more departments experiences a significant increase/decrease in charting needs, the group will reconvene and the hourly allocation will be adjusted.

Lessons Learned

Because of the size and the makeup of the team, which included a number of department heads, it was found helpful to set up a smaller team of three supervisors who actually knew and owned the charting efforts in the major departments. This group designed and assessed the initial pilot and actually piloted the pilot before bringing departmental charters into the process. As a result, overall team meetings were used primarily to brief department heads and gain their feedback and consensus.

A consultant was hired to evaluate the potential growth of obstetrical services, the value of current services offered by WFRMC, customers' desires, competitors' services, and opportunities for improvement. Focus group interviews with young couples (past and potential customers) indicated that they wanted safe medical care in a warm, homelike setting with the least possible number of rules. Most mothers were in their thirties, planning small families with the possibility of only one child. Fathers wanted to be "actively involved" in the birth process. The message came back, "We want to be actively involved in this experience, and we want to make the decisions." The consultant challenged the staff to develop their own vision for the department based on the focus group responses, customer feedback, and national trends.

It became clear that there was a demand for a system in which a family-centered birth experience could occur. That system needed to revolve around the customers' preferences rather than making the customers follow a rigid traditional routine. Customers wanted all aspects of a normal delivery to happen in the same room. The new service would allow the mother, father, and baby to remain together throughout the hospital stay, now as short as 24 hours. Friends and families would be allowed and encouraged to visit and participate as much as the new parents desired. The main goals were to be responsive to the customer's needs and to provide safe, quality medical care.

The hospital administration and the six obstetricians practicing there were eager to see obstetrical services grow. They were open to trying and supporting the new concept. The pediatricians accepted the changes, but without great enthusiasm. The anesthesiologists were opposed to the change. The OB supervisor and two of the three nursing head nurses were also opposed to any change. They wanted to continue operations in the traditional manner. When the hospital decided to adopt the new LDRP concept, it was clear that patients and families liked it but that the nursing staff, especially management, did not. The OB nursing supervisor retired, one head nurse resigned, one was terminated, and the third opted to move from her management position to a staff nurse role. Ms. Cynthia Ayres, RN, Administrative Director, responsible for the psychiatric and cardiovascular services, was assigned to implement the LDRP transition until nursing management could be replaced.

One of the issues involved in the transition was clarification of the charge structure. Previously each unit charged separately for services and supplies. Now that the care was provided in a single central area, the old charge structure was unnecessarily complex. Duplication of charges was occurring, and some charges were being missed because no one was assuming responsibility.

Ms. Ayres decided to use the CQI process to develop a new charge process and to evaluate the costs and resource consumption of the service. Ms. Ayres had not been a strong supporter of the CQI process when it was first introduced into the organization. She had felt that the process was too slow and rigid, and that data collection was difficult and cumbersome. Several teams were organized and assigned to look at specific areas of the LDRP process.

To reach a simplified charge process, as well as a competitive price, all aspects of the process had to be analyzed. Meetings were held with the nursing and medical staff. Management of OB patient and physician preferences in terms of supplies and practices were analyzed. A number of consensus conferences were held to discuss observed variations. For example, each of the six obstetricians specified a different analgesic for pain control. All of these drugs appeared effective for pain control, but their cost per dose ranged from $10 to $75. The physicians agreed that the $10 product was acceptable since the outcome was the same.

Another standard practice was sending placentas to the pathology laboratory for analysis after every normal delivery. This involved labor time, lab charges, and a pathologist's fee for review. The total procedure cost $196. When questioned about the practice, the current medical staff did not feel it was necessary medically nor the current practice nationally, but felt that they were just following the rules. Upon investigation, the team found that an incident involving a placenta had occurred 15 years ago that had led the service chief (since retired) to order all placentas sent to the lab. The obstetricians developed criteria for when it was medically necessary for the lab review of a placenta. This new rule decreased the number of reviews by 95%, resulting in cost savings to the hospital and to patients.

The team reviewed all OB charges for a one-year period. They found that in 80% of the normal deliveries, 14 items were consistently used. The other items were due to variations in physician preferences. The teams and the physicians met and agreed on which items were the basic requirements for a normal delivery. These items became the basic charges for package pricing.

The team met weekly for at least one hour for over a year. Some meetings went as long as five hours. Initially, there was a great deal of resistance and defensiveness. Everyone wanted to focus on issues that did not affect him or herself. The physicians objected that they were being forced to practice "cookbook medicine," and that the real problem was "the hospital's big markup." Hospital staff continued to provide data on actual hospital charges, resource consumption, and practice patterns. The hospital personnel continued to emphasize repeatedly that the physicians were responsible for determining care. The hospital's concern was to be consistent and to decrease variation.

Another CQI team, the Documentation Team, was responsible for reviewing forms utilized previously by the three separate units. The total number of forms used had been 30. The nursing staff was documenting vital signs an average of five times each time care was provided. Through review of policies, standards, documentation, and care standards, the number of forms was reduced to 20. Nurses were now required to enter each care item only one time. The amount of time spent by nurses on documentation was reduced 50%, as was the cost of forms. Data entry errors were also reduced.

The excess costs that were removed were not all physician-related. Many had to do with administrative and nursing policies. Many were due to old, comfortable, traditional ways of doing things. When asked why a practice was followed, the typical response was, "I don't know; that's just the way we've always done it." The OB staff became comfortable with the use of CQI. They recognized that, although it requires time and effort, it does produce measurable results. The OB staff continued to review their practices and operations to identify opportunities to streamline services and decrease variation.

Pharmacy and Therapeutics Team

In late 1987, a CQI team was formed jointly between the hospital's Pharmacy and Therapeutics (P&T) Committee and the pharmacy leadership. The first topic of concern was the rapidly rising costs of inpatient drugs, especially antibiotics, which were then costing the hospital about $1.3 million per year. The team decided to study the process by which antibiotics were selected and began by asking physicians how they selected antibiotics for treatment. Most of the time physicians ordered a culture of the organism believed to be causing the infection from the

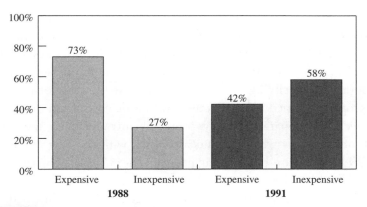

Figure 1–4 Antibiotic Utilization Ratio, Expensive: Inexpensive Doses
Dispensed (expensive ≈ $10.00 per dose)

microbiology lab. A microbiology lab report came back identifying the
organism and the antibiotics to which it was sensitive and those to which
it was resistant. Some physicians reported that they would look down the
list (which was in alphabetical order) until they came to an antibiotic to
which the organism was sensitive and order that. A study of antibiotic utilization showed a high correlation between use and alphabetical position,
confirming the anecdotal reports. Therefore, the team recommended to
the P&T committee that the form be changed to list the antibiotics in
order of increasing cost per average daily dose. The doses used would be
based on current local prescribing patterns rather than recommended
dosages. The P&T committee, which included attending physicians,
approved the change and reported it in their annual report to the medical
staff. Figure 1–4 shows what happened to the utilization of "expensive"
antibiotics (more than $10 per dose) from 1988 to 1991. These costs
were not adjusted at all for inflation in drug prices during this period. The
estimated annual saving was $200,000.

Given this success, in 1989 the team went on to deal with the problem
of the length of treatment using antibiotics. Inpatients did not get a prescription for ten days' supply. Their IM and IV antibiotics were continued until the physician stopped the order. If a physician went away for the
weekend and the patient improved, colleagues were very reluctant to alter
the medication until he or she returned. The team wrestled with how to
encourage the appropriate ending of the course of treatment without has-
sling the physicians or risking undue legal liability problems. They settled

on a sticker that was placed in the chart at the end of three days stating that the treatment had gone on for three days at that point and that an ending date should be specified if possible. The hospital newsletter and the P&T committee annual report noted that the physician could avoid this notice by specifying a termination date at the time of prescribing. This program seemed to be effective. Antibiotic costs again dropped, and there were no apparent quality problems introduced as measured by length of stay or by adverse events associated with the new system.

In 1990, the team began an aggressive Drug Usage Evaluation (DUE) program and hired an assistant director of pharmacy clinical services to administer it. The position had to be rigorously cost-justified. DUE involved a review of cases to determine whether the selection and scheduling of powerful drugs matched the clinical picture presented. For example, if the physician prescribed one of three types of antibiotics known to represent a risk of kidney damage in 3% to 5% of cases, the DUE administrator ordered lab tests to study serum creatinine levels and warn the physician if they rose, indicating kidney involvement. There was a sharp decline in the adverse effects due to the use of these drugs. This program was expanded further to incorporate looking at other critical lab values and relating them to pharmacy activities beyond antibiotics, for example, use of IV solutions and potassium levels. By 1991, the unadjusted antibiotic costs for roughly the same number of admissions had dropped to less than $900,000.

LOOKING AHEAD

One of the things that had concerned John Kausch during 1991 was the fact that implementation had varied from department to department. Although he had written in his annual CQI report that the variation had certainly been within the range of acceptability, he was still concerned about how much variation in implementation was appropriate. If maintaining enthusiasm was a concern, forcing people to conform too tightly might become a demotivator for some staff. This issue and the four mentioned at the beginning of this case study should all be addressed in the coming year.

CASE ANALYSIS

This is a hospital with a large group of physicians closely tied to it, both economically and geographically. It is also operating in an area of intense competition and tight cost controls. The fact that 90% to 95% of the hospital's compensation is case-based (DRGs) and not procedure-based has a profound impact on management motivation. Intense support for the CQI implementation was provided by Dr. Batalden and his staff at HCA corporate headquarters.

ASSIGNMENT QUESTIONS

1. What were the strategic reasons behind West Florida Regional Medical Center's (WFRMC's) decision to invest heavily in TQM?

2. How did the program undertaken at WFRMC reflect this strategic impetus?

3. What were the strengths and weaknesses of the TQM program as it was implemented here?

4. What were the influences of corporate headquarters in this effort?

5. What effort has been made to measure the impact of the program on the hospital, especially in terms of supporting its strategic directions?

6. What effort has been made to use TQM to support tactical programs within the hospital?

7. What should John Kausch do next in dealing with continuous improvement?

8. If West Florida Regional Medical Center was to introduce an internal medicine residency program, how would the concepts of microsystems be incorporated into its current quality efforts?

CLASS EXERCISE

Visit a large local health delivery institution. Document how they are motivating participation in continuous improvement by various types of clinical and administrative staff. Compare and contrast their approach with the former HCA approach outlined in the WFRMC case.

CASE **2**

Holtz Children's Hospital: Reducing Central Line Infections

Gwenn E. McLaughlin

INTRODUCTION

Holtz Children's Hospital (HCH) is one of five hospitals in the Jackson Health System. The hospital is affiliated with the University of Miami's Leonard M. Miller School of Medicine's Department of Pediatrics and has more than 110 attending physicians and specialists. With 254 licensed beds, it is among the largest pediatric teaching hospitals and research centers in the country.

Holtz Children's Hospital shares a campus with Jackson Memorial Hospital. First opened in 1918, Jackson Memorial Hospital is an accredited, tax-assisted, tertiary teaching hospital with more than 1,000 licensed beds located in Miami's urban center. The Jackson Health System provides a wide range of patient services, educational programs, a clinical setting for research activities, and a number of health-related community services county-wide. It is governed by the Public Health Trust, a team of citizen volunteers acting on behalf of the Miami–Dade County Board of County Commissioners, tasked to ensure that all residents of Miami–Dade County receive a high standard of care regardless of their ability to pay.

Background

The 100,000 Lives Campaign launched by the Institute for Healthcare Improvement (IHI) insisted that central vascular line infections could be substantially reduced to levels approaching zero. "Vascular catheter-associated blood infection" was one of the 11 complications for which Medicare would no longer make incremental payments after October 1, 2008. The state Medicaid programs were expected to adopt the same rule, and a number of private insurers were also following suit. Holtz Children's Hospital was heavily dependent on Medicaid payments.

Although pediatric settings historically had higher infection rates, many institutions believed, despite sparse literature to support the notion, that these settings were also an area for potential improvement. The National Association of Children's Hospitals and Related Institutions (NACHRI) launched Phase I of its catheter associated–blood stream infection (CA-BSI) prevention intervention in October 2006. In two years, the 27 institutions involved reduced the rate of infections per 1000 catheter days by 45% (from 5.9 to 2.3), far better than the 6.6 infections per 1000 catheter days previously reported as the pooled national rate between 1995 and 2003 (NHSN).

Quality Improvement in the Pediatric Intensive Care Unit (PICU)

The HCH PICU quality-improvement team had been tracking and attempting to reduce catheter-associated blood stream infections for a number of years. It already taught, although did not monitor, compliance with sterile insertion techniques and used Biopatch® antimicrobial devices on all central lines. In addition, either betadine or alcohol and nonsterile gloves were used during catheter entry. The PICU had created its own central line database and collected blood culture and tip culture results for years and adopted other approaches recommended in the literature, such as discussing each episode of catheter-related bacteremia as a sentinel event, to reduce catheter-associated bacteremia.

Despite these efforts, the Infection Control Surveillance program required by The Joint Commission reported a catheter-associated blood-stream infection rate in the PICU for the fourth quarter of 2007 as 9.1 episodes for 1000 line days, virtually at the 90% percentile of CDC's National Healthcare Safety Network (NHSN) pooled survey for such units. As pediatric critical care division's director of quality improvement, Dr. Gwenn McLaughlin, an intensivist and professor of clinical pediatrics, was frustrated with this lack of improvement but had heard through her colleagues at other institutions of Cincinnati Children's Hospital's initial success and its planned expansion through NACHRI. In order to participate in the NACHRI Phase 1 project, hospitals were expected to:

1. Commit a senior leader—who may be the same person as the physician champion—to support and promote the team working on the collaborative improvement project.

2. Send two (required) or three (recommended) team members who have authority to drive change, including the physician champion and, ideally, a nurse and/or infection control professional to learning workshops (travel costs are covered by the hospital).

3. Provide resources and support to the hospital's team (includes attending workshops, devoting time to data entry, testing and implementing changes in the PICU, and promoting active senior leadership).

4. Work to involve all of their staff as appropriate with the aim of helping the multidisciplinary clinical team become competent in safety and quality improvement.

5. Perform prework activities to prepare for the workshop.

6. Connect project goals to the broader patient safety work in the hospital.

7. Implement the standardized database collection tool to track patients and their care and submit at least monthly.

8. Agree to implement central line insertion bundle in a uniform approach and test changes in at least two areas related to maintaining central lines.

9. Participate in calls and a discussion list to share with and learn from others.

10. Make well-defined measurements at least monthly that relate to their aims, plot them over time for the duration of the collaborative

improvement project, and share them with other teams in the collaborative.

11. Share information with collaborative participants to evaluate impact of changes.

12. Maintain responsibility for IRB requirements for a quality-improvement project (with option to publish aggregate data) (NACHRI, 2010).

To encourage participation, the American Board of Pediatrics stated that involvement in the NACHRI project met the standard for "Physician Participation in a QI Project" as required for maintenance of certification. Due to financial constraints, the HCH PICU could not participate in the NACHRI study, but they could use the same approach without NACHRI involvement.

First, the PICUs multidisciplinary quality-improvement team reemphasized through education a commitment to the Institute for Healthcare Improvement's Central Line Bundle. Its key components are:

- Hand Hygiene

- Maximal Barrier Precautions Upon Insertion

- Chlorhexidine Skin Antisepsis

- Optimal Catheter Site Selection, with Avoidance of the Femoral Vein for Central Venous Access in Adult Patients

- Daily Review of Line Necessity with Prompt Removal of Unnecessary Lines

The last item on the checklist was addressed by the HCH PICU through the creation of a "daily goals" checklist to prompt practitioners to evaluate the need for all indwelling catheters on a daily basis.

The Importance of Hand Hygiene

During this period, Dr. McLaughlin, who led the PICU quality-improvement team for several years, became the Hospital's Chief Quality and Safety Officer. To improve her skill set, she attended IHI's Patient Safety Executive Development Program. The IHI approach emphasizes that quality improvement requires identifying the drivers of both good and bad outcomes. Realizing that hand hygiene was key to catheter insertion and maintenance, she began by looking at the available data from the Nursing Department, which showed a 40% compliance rate by all health-care workers with the existing hand-hygiene standard. The medical and nursing staff easily identified the following as barriers to hand-hygiene compliance:

- There were not enough ethanol-based dispensers.

- Available dispensers were often empty.

- There was no venue to educate other disciplines (transporters, technicians, etc.) about the importance of hand hygiene.

The team agreed to implement changes to make sure that the supplies for hand hygiene were adequate and situated appropriately to "make it easier to do the right thing." In the PICU, dispensers were procured and place at the entrance to the units and patient rooms. Everyone, not just housekeeping staff, was given access to hand-sanitizer refills and everyone was expected to restock the dispensers and other supplies. Figure 2–1 shows the availability of supplies during 2008.

At the start of the year, overall availability of gloves near the patient and filled and functional dispensers was around 86%. The team's efforts led to a corresponding compliance figure by the last quarter of the year of 100%. Similarly, overall compliance with hand-hygiene standards improved from 40% to over 70% by the end of the year, as shown in Figure 2–2.

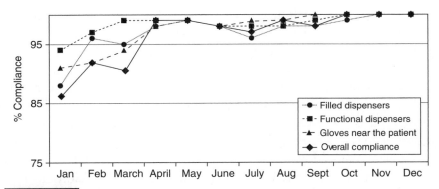

Figure 2–1 Availability of Supplies for Hand Hygiene Over Time

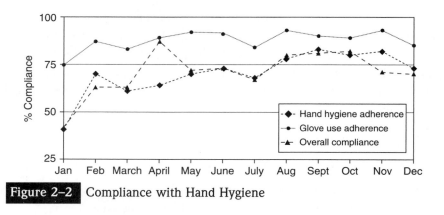

Figure 2–2   Compliance with Hand Hygiene

Scrubbing the Hub

The PICU examined its own surveillance data noting that most central line infections occurred after the first week of hospitalization. Given that the current PICU infections did not seem to occur during the insertion period, the team decided to focus on maintenance practices. Knowing that the NACHRI project was justified by the initial success in reducing catheter-associated bloodstream infections at Cincinnati Children's Hospital, Dr. McLaughlin implemented a similar "scrub the hub" campaign based on policies and procedures from Cincinnati Children's Hospital (http://www.cincinnatichildrens.org/about/measures/system/cvc.htm). These policies emphasized the aseptic technique every time a catheter hub was exposed to the environment. The hub was required to be scrubbed for 15 seconds with 2% Chlorhexidine Gluconate with Isopropyl Alcohol (CHG) impregnated swabs (ChloraPrep™).

In setting "how much by when" objectives, Dr. McLaughlin wanted to achieve 100% compliance with ChloraPrep™ use immediately. Because this was a change that would meet some staff resistance, the team decided to conduct a small experiment and report the results rapidly to educate the staff about the effect of the change in methods. Each pediatric ICU bed had its own small cart, which was stocked with regularly-used equipment, such as gauze, catheters, and ethanol and betadine swabs. To "make it easy to do the right thing," and hard to do the wrong thing, the ethanol swabs were removed from the bedside and replaced with CHG impregnated sponges. The PICU nursing manager, Carrie Feinroth, RN, acquired CHG impregnated sponges already available in the hospital as surgical skin prep and on April 8, 2008 removed the ethanol swabs from

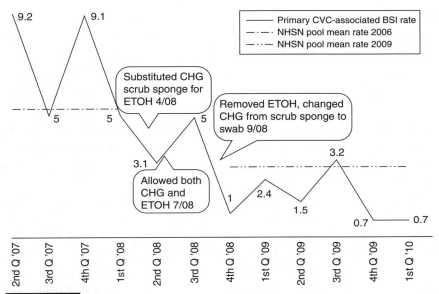

Figure 2–3 CVC-Associated Infection Rate: PICU

the bedside and replaced them with the ChloraPrep™ sponges. The nurses and physicians were instructed to scrub the hub of the catheter for 15 seconds prior to the each hub entry. Some coaching was required to explain that 15 seconds really meant 15 seconds of forceful scrubbing and not a quick wipe. In the next quarter, the infection rate, as determined by the hospital infection control committee, dropped drastically.

This improvement was shared with the nursing staff through posters throughout the PICU. Because the ethanol swabs were still being used to access peripheral IVs and for other tubing access away from the hub, they were returned to the bedside on July 8, 2008. Subsequently, the infection rate rose sharply. Feedback was requested from the nurses about why they might choose ethanol over ChloraPrep™ for hub entry cleaning. The nurses expressed concern that the "scrubbers" would not adequately clean the crevices present in the stopcocks and caps and therefore some were still using the ethanol swabs. After receiving staff feedback, nursing management obtained the CHG swabs and removed the ethanol swabs from the bedside again. As Figure 2–3 shows, the infection rate dropped once again over the following two quarters.

The PICU was able to maintain the levels achieved during the experimental period, and during the second quarter of 2009, had the lowest CA-BSI infection rate of any ICU on the Jackson Memorial Hospital campus.

Spreading Change

After reviewing this data with the staff, the Children's Hospital changed its procedures and manuals to require the CHG swabs on CVC hubs. But changing a policy is much easier than changing a practice. Holtz's large transplantation surgery service also had its own intermediate post-transplant surgical unit (PTSU). This unit had a high infection rate that concerned the PICU QI team because many of these patients required PICU care due to sepsis. Dr. McLaughlin first approached the transplant unit's Nursing Director about this issue and presented the data and the PICU's success. The initial response was that the patients in the PTSU were sicker and that CA-BSI's were unavoidable. Given that there were no published benchmarks for infection rates in pediatric transplant ICUs, it was difficult to argue against this response. However, Dr. McLaughlin enlisted the assistance of the PTSU's new Medical Director, Dr. Lesley Smith, who contacted units outside of the United States with similar patients and obtained data on their rates that were indeed lower than those of the PTSU. Furthermore, the success of the effort in the PICU had made the PTSU Medical Director much more conscious of the opportunities for improvement. After further discussion to acknowledge the work patterns of the existing staff members, the PTSU staff agreed to a number of changes led primarily by one nurse champion and the nurse educator. These included:

- Reducing the frequency of blood drawing.

- The Scrub the Hub procedures using ChloraPrep™ rather than the ethanol swab to promote the concept of scrubbing.

- Selecting a day for dressing changes.

- Having two individuals involved when dressings are changed.

The involvement of two caregivers for dressing changes had been cited in the literature as a way to reduce catheter-related complications and made sense to the PTSU staff because:

- It was much easier to follow all the proper steps with two pairs of hands.

- The site was less likely to become contaminated.

- It was often necessary to handle young patients who, unlike the ICU patients, were not heavily sedated and therefore active.

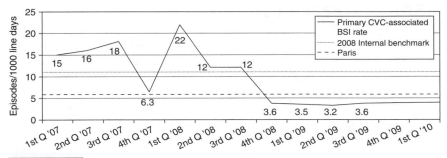

Figure 2–4   CVC-Associated Infection Rates: PTSU

Because this process was more involved than the simple substitution of one product for another, as was the case in the PICU, it took longer to implement. All nurses were reeducated about the procedures involved in dressing changes and evaluated for competency by a nursing educator. Figure 2–4 reports the infection rates in the PTSU during the planning period and after implementation.

Then the team's orientation shifted toward ways to sustain the gains already made and to seek out new alternatives for further improvements.

CASE ANALYSIS

The West Florida case, which precedes this one, is an early example of a quality-improvement system with an informal or "shadow" organizational structure. The Holtz Children's Hospital case shows action by a designated hospital quality and safety officer. You might consider and contrast the two approaches. Using your other knowledge about line- versus staff-management positions in professional-service organizations, consider the possible impacts of three loci of initiative for improvement: a quality council of top managers, a designated staff quality-improvement position, or the line management of the delivery unit. There are also contrasts with the earlier case in terms of the resources available to implement and then institutionalize a quality-improvement program.

ASSIGNMENT QUESTIONS

1. Why would one question whether the well-documented improvement efforts in CA-BSI in adult ICU settings are transferrable to pediatric settings?

2. Why might some PICU staff members resist implementing the central line bundle given its success elsewhere?

3. This case takes place in a resource-constrained environment. What approaches were used to overcome these limitations?

4. What would be your response if the chief of the transplant service had said, "We don't seem to be doing too badly, certainly not any worse than our local competitors."

5. Discuss the relative merits of each of the alternative approaches available for reducing line infections in addition to improved care and maintenance:

   • Discussing each infection as a sentinel event.

   • Using a daily goals checklist.

   • Using insertion practices, such as sterile insertion techniques.

   What factors might lead you to emphasize one over the others?

6. What are the merits of using a forcing tactic, such as removing the ethanol swab materials from the bedside?

CLASS EXERCISE

Use the Internet to follow up on the latest approaches to reducing central line infections in both children and adults. What low levels have organizations been able to maintain? What new wrinkles have been added to motivate continuing improvement?

ACKNOWLEDGMENTS

Many individuals contributed to this successful effort. The author wishes to thank them all. Special gratitude goes to Debbie Whitson, ARNP, MSN and Charlene Schaefer, RN, BSN for their leadership in the hand-hygiene effort, to Carrie Feinroth, RN, MSN and Michael Nares, MD for their leadership on the PICU CA-BSI side, and to Lesley Smith, MD, Evel Michel, RN, BSN, and Jasmine LaLanne, RN for their leadership on the PTSU CA-BSI side.

Clemson's Nursing Home: Working with the State Quality-Improvement Organization's Restraint Reduction Initiative

Franziska Rokoske, Jill A. McArdle, and Anna P. Schenck

INTRODUCTION

Clemson's Nursing Home is situated in the foothills of North Carolina on 20 beautiful rolling acres. It is a 95-bed family-owned facility, which has been a part of the Clemson family for the past 50 years. Marie Clemson Parker, RN, MPH, NHA, the current administrator, grew up in this nursing home and learned the family business from her parents and grandparents. Marie married Tom Parker when she was 25 years old and was then acting Director of Nursing. Tom, a carpenter by trade, abandoned his own contractor business soon after their marriage and came aboard full-time at the nursing home as the director of maintenance and grounds. Three years ago, Marie's parents retired as co-administrators of Clemson's and Marie took over as the administrator, having recently

completed her administrator-in-training program and licensing exam.
Tom and Marie have two children, Rachel and Rodney. Both of the children, like their mother before them, have spent many hours in the nursing home. Since the family lives on the property, the children are very
involved in the day-to-day life of the nursing home.

Marie, like her parents, has always been deeply committed to maintaining a home-like environment for all of Clemson's residents. During
her graduate education at the School of Public Health at the University
of North Carolina at Chapel Hill, Marie studied quality-improvement
methods and tools and took, on her own initiative, the Institute of Medicine's STEEP (Safe, Timely, Efficient, Equitable, & Patient-centered)
course. The biggest challenge at Clemson's Nursing Home, as in many
other nursing homes, has been maintaining a resident-centered perspective with the ever-increasing complexity and acuity of the resident population. When Marie was a child, the most complex resident Clemson's had
to deal with was one who had an occasional need for an intravenous
antibiotic. Times have changed dramatically, however, and residents are
now being admitted to nursing homes older, sicker and with more complex treatment requirements, and there are many more residents with cognitive impairments. In addition to a different resident population, Marie
likes to remind her parents that the regulatory requirements for nursing
homes have gotten increasingly more onerous. It is a common belief
among people working in the nursing home industry that nursing homes
are more highly regulated than the nuclear industry. Marie is the first to
concede that the state and federal government surveyors who perform
onsite audits for regulatory adherence are a "necessary evil," but wishes
there was more "regulatory relief" for facilities that demonstrated ongoing, proactive quality improvement.

Hearing from the State Quality-Improvement Organization

Early one February morning in 2010, Marie was returning from the dining room after assisting with breakfast. Some residents need a bit of extra
help with meals and since this is one of Marie's favorite ways to interact
with both residents and staff, she can usually be found in the dining room
during meal times. Marie, as per her usual weekday routine, stopped by
her mailbox to retrieve the mail that arrived in the late afternoon the day
before. Thumbing through the mail, Marie stopped at a type-written enve-

lope that didn't appear to be familiar. She opened and read a letter of invitation from the state's Quality-Improvement Organization (QIO) to participate in a quality-improvement project focusing on physical restraint reduction. She knew physical restraints were defined as "any manual method or physical or mechanical device, material, or equipment attached or adjacent to the resident's body that the individual cannot remove easily which restricts freedom of movement or normal access to one's body" (http://www.cms.gov/nursinghomequalityinits/20_nhqimds20.asp).

Marie was familiar with the QIO from her graduate school days, and from Clemson's membership with the state's professional nursing home association, which provides regular updates on the QIO activities at their semi-annual meetings and in newsletters. The Carolinas Center for Medical Excellence (CCME), the QIO for North and South Carolina, serves the Medicare program to ensure care is provided in the most appropriate setting and is the highest quality and most cost-effective care possible.

The letter indicated she was receiving this invitation to participate because the publicly reported quality measures showed that Clemson's had a rate of restraint use above the state and national averages. Marie was a bit disappointed to receive the invitation because she felt everyone at Clemson's was always working extremely hard to ensure deficiency-free surveys and a pleasant and safe environment for staff and residents. But there was no denying the data that Clemson's had provided. It was true; their restraint rate was higher than average.

She knew the nationwide reduction of restraints and pressure ulcers were two primary targets for the Medicare QIO program. The data sent by CCME on restraint use as measured from the CMS Minimum Data Set (MDS) reporting system did not look good but was not terrible either. Clemson's restraint rate was 10%, and the state average was about 7% and the national average was 3%. The suggested goal was 1% to 2%. Since the quality measure data are posted on Medicare's Nursing Home Compare Web site (http://www.medicare.gov/NHcompare), Marie knew competitors were certainly aware of Clemson's rate and potential patients and their families would also be looking at these quality measures. Clemson's had followed all of the regulatory requirements associated with the use of restraints so it faced no sanctions associated with having a higher rate. However, Marie realized above average rates would attract unwanted attention from regulators. In addition, she recalled that several staff members had recently expressed an interest in reducing the use of restraints, but no consistent action had occurred. Marie was in favor of the concept of a restraint-free environment, too, but hadn't made it a priority. Maybe now was the right time.

Planning a Response

Marie talked with her Director of Nursing (DON), Karen Sodermeier, and the Medical Director, Dr. Nancy McVayer. Neither seemed terribly concerned about the restraint rate. Karen noted Clemson's was smaller than the average nursing home in the state and therefore had a smaller number of residents who would be included in the measures. This could lead to greater variability in the quality measures. Dr. McVayer reminded Marie that the quality measure was not adjusted for case mix and Clemson's had had an unusually high proportion of patients with dementia. Dr. McVayer said, "Remember the Director of Nursing we had about a year ago who thought we should maximize our reimbursement by admitting lots of patients with Alzheimer's Disease? She left us with a very atypical patient mix. It will take us another year to work our way back to normal." Marie also felt, because people in that region of the state tended to take care of their own folks longer at home, Clemson's patients were more impaired once they were finally admitted by their families. She was also concerned about the consistency of the data Clemson's was submitting through the MDS system. She felt that maybe the team that completed the MDS assessments were too rigid in their adherence to the definition of a restraint or were counting patient-care devices as restraints even when they really shouldn't be.

Marie called a friend who managed a larger, chain-owned nursing home in another part of the state who she knew had worked with CCME previously to reduce restraints in their facility. She asked her friend to describe the approach CCME used to assist in their quality-improvement effort and whether the approach had worked for them. The friend explained CCME's quality-improvement support approach and the positive impact it had made on her nursing home's restraint-use rate. After further discussion with her DON and Medical Director, Marie responded to the invitation to participate in the restraint initiative. Now was the time to make the needed changes. A month later, she, Karen, and a longtime nursing assistant, Amy, were on their way to their first CCME workshop.

Participating in the Workshop

Reviewing Trend Data

After providing a general overview of Continuous Quality-Improvement (CQI) methods at the workshop, CCME provided each nursing home team their facility's restraint rate trend report generated from the MDS data (Figure 3–1). This report also provided state and national data. Marie, Karen, and Amy pored over the graphs, and noticed their restraint rate had been consistently around 10% for at least the last year, while the state and national averages had been dropping steadily. They wondered what it had been before the arrival of the DON who admitted so many patients with severe dementia. They were also provided a graph showing the restraint rates of all the nursing homes in NC working with CCME in the Restraint Reduction Initiative (Figure 3–2). They noted with astonishment they had the fourth highest restraint rate in the group.

Implementing the Model for Improvement

In the workshop, Karen, Marie, and Amy learned about the Model for Improvement (Figure 3–3). This approach to quality improvement required them to first answer three fundamental questions and then work systematically to implement small tests of change (Plan-Do-Study-Act or

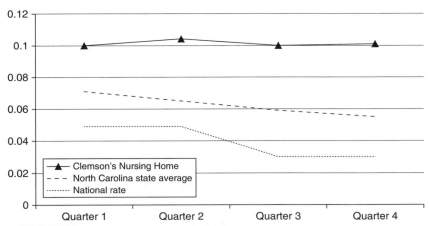

Figure 3–1 Home Restraint Report Time Period Quarter 1 2009–Quarter 4 2009 Trend Graph

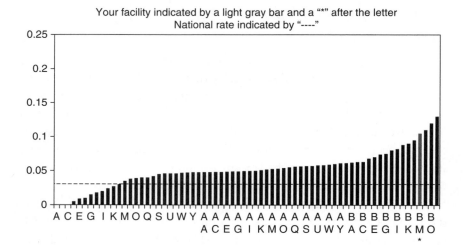

Figure 3–2 Nursing Home Restraint Report Participant Comparison Bar
Chart

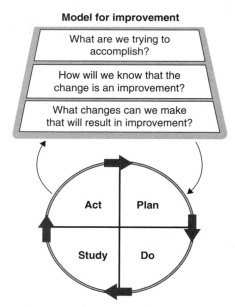

Figure 3–3 Model for Improvement

Source: Copyright by Associates in Process Improvement, 2010. Used with permission.

PDSA cycles) meant to bring about improvement. They began by reviewing and answering the three questions:

1. *What are we trying to accomplish?* Reduce the use of restraints to below the state average.

2. *How will we know that the change is an improvement?* When we see consistently declining restraints quality measures.

3. *What changes can we make that will result in improvement?* Follow the processes presented by CCME to take on small tests of change.

CCME Helps Nursing Home Teams in a Step-Wise Fashion

The Clemson's team was working hard to take in all the information and figure out how to begin reducing restraints. They had so many ideas about what was going on about restraints that they couldn't figure out which one to tackle first. They were relieved when CCME assigned Tom, a Quality-Improvement Consultant (QIC), to work with them. Tom was experienced in QI and had previously been a nurse in a nursing home. Marie, Karen, and Amy immediately felt they could trust him.

Establish the QI Goal

During a breakout session, Tom sat down with the Clemson's team and helped them formulate their specific QI goal. They decided their goal was to reduce their restraint rate to 5% within two months and to 3% within 6 months. They felt this was a logical, achievable, and measurable goal. They could act quickly, capitalizing on the fact that Clemson's was currently fully staffed. They had what they needed to start immediately upon their return. They just needed to focus their energies.

Analyze the Home's Current Process as It Relates to the Prioritized QI Goal

Tom helped Marie, Karen, and Amy think through and map out their current processes related to restraints. They talked through how and under what conditions restraints were ordered and applied, and the weekly Interdisciplinary Team (IDT) meetings where residents were reviewed and Care Plans were updated. In talking through the process, they realized that though they reviewed weekly almost all the residents with a restraint, they rarely planned and implemented any "restraint-reduction trials" that CCME suggested as part of their approach. Why was that? Figuring out the answer to this seemed to be the crux of their problem and the key to the solution.

Their day at the workshop ended with a review of CCME's proposed process for systematically reducing restraints. There were concrete steps such as reviewing all residents weekly and implementing restraint-removal trials with residents. CCME provided the teams with process measures and data-collection tools in spreadsheets. The process measures were designed to help the team identify where their process was falling apart and focus improvement activities and PDSA cycles on those areas. The process measures would help them see all the residents with restraints for whom they had 1) reviewed the restraint device, 2) planned to try an alternative to the device in the next week, and 3) actually completed a restraint-removal trial.

Applying the Workshop Experience

Build a Team

When Marie, Karen, and Amy returned to Clemson's, they immediately realized they were going to have to capitalize on a team approach in order to tackle the many different parts of the processes CCME had laid out to help them get rid of restraints. They approached their Physical Therapist (PT) and Occupational Therapist (OT) and another Certified Nursing Assistant (CNA) who was highly respected by her peers as well as their MDS coordinator—input would be needed from all of them if they were to be successful. At the first meeting of the team, Marie made it clear that removing restraints was now an organizational priority and she was willing to help the team do whatever was needed to be successful.

Conduct Root Cause Analysis

Tom had told them that one of the first things the full team should do is a Root-Cause Analysis (RCA). The RCA would help them figure out WHY certain things were or were not happening in regards to restraints. One approach to RCA is the "Five Whys"—a process in which the team continues to ask "Why?" in an iterative process to discover the root cause. He cautioned them not to jump to conclusions about the Whys—RCA often uncovers unexpected reasons. The question Marie posed to the team was: Why don't we routinely try alternatives to restraints with our residents? She chose this question because their review of their current process related to restraints seemed to show a breakdown at this stage. The IDT was good at reviewing all the residents on the "restraints list" and ensuring valid orders and documentation were in place, but they were not good at thinking through and implementing efforts to remove the restraints. Marie wanted to know why. The responses offered by the team when she asked "why" were as follows:

- *"We don't know the best alternatives to try with residents with severe dementia."*

- *"We are not confident families will agree to us removing the restraints and getting in touch with them to talk through it is very time consuming and difficult."*

- *"We've had bad experiences with restraint removal in the past—residents have sustained injuries."*

- *"We don't have an easy way to communicate about the results of our attempts to remove restraints—to learn from our mistakes and make improvements."*

The team felt these root causes could be addressed systematically through education, family meetings, and the implementation of the tracking processes that CCME recommended.

Choose Changes that Will Result in Improvement

The team reviewed the process laid out by CCME and began by listing all the residents currently coded on the MDS as having a restraint. They noted most, but not all, of the residents with restraints had a diagnosis of dementia. They had learned at the workshop that this is a common finding in nursing homes. The MDS coordinator reviewed all the devices to ensure they weren't "over-coding." She also planned a meeting with the other MDS coder to be sure they were both interpreting and applying the restraint criteria consistently. All the restraints had been coded correctly, and with this fact established, the team applied the CCME process. Working from the list of residents with a restraint, they discussed which ones would most likely succeed in a first attempt to use alternatives to restraints. They then discussed this list at the next IDT meeting and agreed on a resident, Mr. Halvorson, with whom they would try alterna-tives to restraints over the following week. The team knew early success with trying alternatives to restraints would be crucial. Early success would help all of the staff to "buy in" to the efforts that removing restraints would require.

Determine How to Implement Changes

The team decided the best conditions for restraint-removal attempts would happen on the wing of the nursing home where staffing was the most stable and where Clemson's had implemented "consistent staff assignment." Under this staffing model, the same CNA took care of the same resident each day. This allowed the CNA and residents and their families to really get to know one another. This closer bond would hope-fully result in the families cooperating with efforts to remove restraints. Residents and their families would receive information about the plan from Karen, the Director of Nursing.

The PT and OT completed comprehensive assessments of Mr. Halvor-son and created a list of alternatives they thought would be successful with him. He had a diagnosis of dementia and a history of wandering and falls, but had never been injured in a fall. No alternatives to restraints had been tried with him since the implementation of consistent staff assignment. His CNA came to the IDT meeting, and the team made a concrete plan for which alternative to try first and for how long. The PT and OT would be closely involved in the restraint-removal trial as well, helping to monitor Mr. Halvorson's response. Documentation forms provided by CCME allowed for collection of information during the restraint-removal trial including what alternative was tried, what time of the day, resident response to the alternative, and staff observations about the effectiveness of the approach. This would help the team understand the various factors that could impact a restraint-removal trial and learn from their experiences.

Implement the Plan

After the family had been contacted, the CNAs, PT, and OT conducted their first restraint-removal trial with Mr. Halvorson. Instead of using a restraint to keep him from getting up and wandering, his CNA used a personal alarm device and implemented scheduled toileting (one of the main reasons residents try to get up on their own is for toileting—they just can't wait for the CNAs to get to them). She also paid close attention to Mr. Halvorson's behaviors throughout the day, and when he looked restless, she arranged for the restorative aide to help him take a walk around the building.

Evaluate Success of the QI Action Plan

To know whether the approach to removing restraints was successful, Clemson's had to consider multiple perspectives. First, the resident perspective outcome: Was the restraint able to be removed without unintended consequences for the resident? In this case, the restraint-removal trial was successful. Mr. Halvorson did not mind the personal alarm and the scheduled approach to toileting. Second, the staffing perspective outcome: What was the impact of the removal of the restraint on the staff? In this case, his CNA had to bring a heightened awareness of Mr. Halvorson's state throughout the day and had additional charting/tracking to complete. This is a short-term problem since as soon as a successful alternative is found for a resident, the additional tracking stops, and the MDS-mandatory charting about the restraint no longer applies. The CNA also reported feeling personally satisfied that Mr. Halvorson was now restraint-free. She was happy to see him move about more freely. Third, Clemson's had to consider the family's perspective. Although Mr. Halvorson's daughter had initially voiced fears he would fall if not restrained, education on the relative risks of restraints helped her to embrace the idea of removing restraints.

After determining the success of their first PDSA cycle and using the CCME forms to track their process measures (Figure 3–4), the Restraint-Removal Team targeted another resident for restraint removal for the following week. Again, the restraint-removal trial was completed and a safe alternative was found. The Restraint-Removal Team was pleased to see their process measures improving: They were reviewing residents with restraints weekly AND implementing trials of alternatives (often with success). The following week they completed another trial of alternatives with another resident, but were not successful in identifying an alternative. They resolved to continue conducting trials with that resident, and two weeks later, finally were able to remove the restraint. Over the course of their first four weeks in the initiative, they were successful in conducting restraint-removal trials with five residents and successful in removing

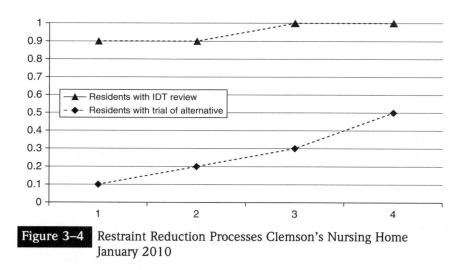

Figure 3-4   Restraint Reduction Processes Clemson's Nursing Home
January 2010

four restraints. They took pride in their improving process measures and could see that following the recommended process was resulting in improved outcomes. They knew that soon their publicly reported data would reflect these changes, too, and they were especially proud they were no longer among the nursing homes with the highest restraint rates.

Ongoing Monitoring

The team continued to try alternatives to restraints systematically and tracking their process measures. If for some reason a resident who was scheduled for a restraint-removal trial didn't complete a trial, the reasons were documented and discussed and another trial was immediately scheduled. They stayed on top of the resident list, making sure all residents were reviewed weekly and trials were implemented. They also made concerted efforts to educate nursing staff and the medical staff to avoid writing orders for positioning or other devices that would have to be coded as a restraint on the MDS. For example, the medical staff frequently ordered lap trays for residents' wheelchairs. They didn't realize that though the lap tray might make it easier for the resident to do some activities while in their wheelchair, it had to be coded as restraint on the MDS. This is because the lap tray typically can't be removed by the resident, and it prevents the resident from being able to get up on their own. They wanted to ensure their hard work to remove restraints would not be undone by the inadvertent application of new restraints!

When the quarterly publicly reported MDS data came out, the Clemson's team was pleased to see their rate had gone down from 10% to 6%. Over the course of the next several months, they achieved their goal of 3%. In addition, Clemson's knew other outcomes might be affected by the use of restraints. For example, reducing restraints is often (erroneously) associated in people's minds with an increase in falls rates. They monitored their fall rates and found no impact. Residents for whom restraints had been removed were not falling regardless of whether they had dementia or not.

Celebrate Success

The team was very pleased with the results they saw in their nursing home. CNAs especially were pleased with the restraint-free environment, and they attributed a lot of the success to their consistent staffing. Families considering admitting a loved one to Clemson's were happy to hear it was a restraint-free facility. To celebrate their success, the Restraint-Removal Team was recognized at the annual staff picnic and received the coveted Team Award. The CNAs who conducted the first few restraint-removal trials were also honored as part of the team.

Marie was proud to be the administrator at Clemson's and proud of her staff. She thought back to what their nursing home was like previously. The staff had always been caring toward the residents, but there obviously had been an opportunity for improvement at Clemson's where restraints were concerned. She was happy she had responded to the invitation from CCME to participate in the initiative. By following their steps, her team had successfully removed all but a few restraint devices.

CASE ANALYSIS

The previous two cases focused on internally generated quality-improvement efforts. In this case, the impetus for the improvement effort came from a government-supported program aimed at providing better services to its beneficiaries. Clemson's Nursing Home was selected through a mandated data-collection process, which was then mined to identify outliers on specific dimensions, apply CQI, and bring them in line with the targets established state-wide and nationally. The program is "voluntary" for nursing homes that are in compliance with current standards, but it is not hard to envision that standards too will change as new levels of perform-ance are proved feasible. However, in the regulatory environment applied to nursing homes one usually is willing to pay almost any price to stay on the good side of the regulators.

ASSIGNMENT QUESTIONS

1. The concept of a Quality-Improvement Organization will be new to many of you. Share your knowledge of what one is and what it does. Is this a regulatory agency?

2. Contrast and compare the approach used in the workshop with that followed in the previous two cases. Here, the facilitator is out-side the organization. How is the team facilitation best handled once the implementation team is formed on site?

3. Clemson's Nursing Home is a relatively small home. How might a chain of five or six nursing homes best respond to the challenges presented by the restraint-reduction initiative?

4. The concept of the QIO is linked to the Medicare program, but it seems to be applicable in other settings. What are some alternatives for external facilitation of continuous improvement across a broad range of care-delivery units?

5. How might one go about making a business case for a restraint-free environment at a national program level? At an individual care-delivery unit level?

CLASS EXERCISE

Research the political history of QIOs and their predecessor organiza-tions. Find out about the types of care-delivery organizations and the quality issues they are dealing with today by accessing the Web site for the American Health Quality Association, their national association.

CQI for Malaria Control in Ghana

Irene A. Agyepong, William A. Sollecito,
and Curtis P. McLaughlin

INTRODUCTION

Despite many highly-publicized programs to fight malaria, involving billions of dollars in unilateral and multilateral aid and non-governmental donor programs (U.S. President's Malaria Initiative (PMI), Roll Back Malaria (RBM), Five Alive!, Clinton Health Access Initiative, Global Fund to Fight AIDS, Tuberculosis, and Malaria, etc.), malaria remains one of the most serious health problems in sub-Saharan Africa. While national rates of infection ebb and flow with economic development and governmental stability, overall progress is slow and uneven (Urbach and Harris, 2008). A significant question is the degree to which continuous quality improvement (CQI) efforts could play a role in attacking the problem and in strengthening local capacity to deliver services effectively.

This case focuses on the malaria situation in Ghana over the past decade, but one can also point to examples of CQI efforts in other sub-Saharan African countries involving malaria, infant and maternal mortality, HIV, and tuberculosis. The public health literature has long emphasized the effectiveness of integrating these services, especially where improved maternal and infant mortality is the objective.

BACKGROUND

The Ministry of Health Ghana, which oversees the various health-sector implementation agencies, has reviewed its mission several times over the last decade in a way that has sometimes been bewildering for frontline staff. However, within these changes has remained the concept of its earlier mission statement:

> [T]he mission of the health Ministries, Departments and Agencies is to improve the health status of all the people living in Ghana through the development and promotion of proactive policies for good health and longevity; the provision of universal access to basic health service and provision of quality health services which are affordable and accessible. These services will be delivered in a humane, efficient, and effective manner by well-trained, friendly, highly motivated and client-oriented personnel.

This is an ambitious goal for this country of approximately 26 million, which had an estimated 2009 gross domestic product (GDP) per capita of US $1500. Ghana is predominantly rural with agriculture, mostly small, independently-owned farms, providing 55% of employment and 35% of the GDP. Its economy is heavily dependent on exports of cocoa and gold and other minerals. As of 2009, life expectancy at birth is about 59 years for males and 60 years for females with infant mortality at 51 per 1000 live births (CIA, 2010). The birth rate is about 4 children born per woman. There are about 15 physicians and 93 nurses per 100,000 persons (WHO, 2010)—4.5% of the country's GDP was spent on health in 2003 (WHO, 2010). International financial and technical assistance is still important, especially in the health sector.

National Health Insurance Replaces Cash-and-Carry

In 2003, Ghana instituted a universal national health insurance scheme (NHIS) and began to develop its insurance infrastructure. This was initiated as the fulfillment by the government at that time of its 2000 election campaign promise to replace the highly unpopular health services user fee system known as "cash-and-carry" that was introduced with World Bank support as part of structural adjustment policies in the 1980s.

EXHIBIT 4–1

Cash-and-Carry System

All working individuals who were not in the Military or the Police were mandated to join the insurance scheme which replaced the "cash-and-carry" system in which the patients had had to pay for each unit of service prior to delivery and many died because of lack of cash or because no family members were there to handle the transaction. The legislation called for NHIS to be financed by a central fund comprising:

- 2.5% of Social Security and National Insurance Trust (SSNIT) pension contributions that are mainly paid by formal sector employees and their employers proportional to income
- An additional 2.5% increase in the Value Added Tax
- Premiums collected from informal sector workers and paid directly to the mutual health insurance schemes and retained locally
- Legislative appropriations

Although the NHIS has been defined as an insurance system, in practice about 70% of the scheme has been tax financed, 24% by social security contributions from formal sector workers, and only about 5% has come from non-SSNIT contributor funds paid directly to the mutual insurance schemes. Each registrant receives a card good for outpatient and inpatient treatment at any primary-care clinic or hospital in the country for the services covered by the benefit package. These services are defined by law and include about 80% to 90% of the most common Outpatient Services, Inpatient Services, Oral Health, and Maternity Care health conditions in Ghana as well as emergencies. A list of medicines related to these conditions that could be paid for under the NHIS has also been defined.

Exclusions are also defined by law for things such as:

- Use of a private ward
- Appliance and prostheses including optical aids, heart aids, orthopedic aids, dentures, etc.
- Assisted reproduction (e.g., artificial insemination) and gynecological hormone replacement therapy.

(continues)

EXHIBIT 4-1

- Echocardiography
- Angiography
- Dialysis for chronic renal (kidney) failure
- Organ transplants
- Drugs not listed on the NHIS list
- Heart and Brain Surgery other than those resulting from accidents
- Cancer treatment other than for breast and cervical cancer

The insurance scheme covers treatment for opportunistic infections in HIV/AIDS but does not cover anti-retroviral drugs for HIV or other treatments already covered under vertical health programs.

Patient bills go to the scheme provider, which then pays the money to the hospital. Prescribed drugs purchased at accredited pharmacies or licensed chemical shops are paid the same way. There have been many complaints from providers about the slowness of payments from the scheme.

The National Health Insurance Act 2003, Act 650, set out three distinct types of health-insurance schemes that can be established and operated in Ghana:

- District mutual health-insurance schemes

- Private commercial health-insurance schemes

- Private mutual health insurance

CONCERN ABOUT MALARIA

Major (retired) Courage Quashigah, the national Health Minister, reported to an annual health summit in Accra in November 2009 that the cost of treating malaria was crippling Ghana's health budget. Spending in 2009 for malaria would amount to US $772 million, an amount equal to the country's entire health budget in 2008 and 10% of the 2006 GDP. He saw this as a serious threat to the National Health Insurance Fund (*Afrol News*, 2009).

As in the rest of Ghana, malaria is endemic in Greater Accra. It was the most frequently reported diagnosis from outpatient clinics all across the region and formed 38% of all diagnoses made. The next most frequently made diagnosis was Acute Upper Respiratory infections as 8% of all diagnoses made. In 2003, malaria was the leading reported cause of death in Achimota Hospital (33% of total deaths) and in Ridge Hospital (20% of total deaths). Malaria was also the most frequently reported cause of admission for all the public sector hospitals in the region and formed 73% of admissions at the Achimota Hospital, which serves a secondary school as well as the general public, and 36% at the PML Children's Hospital, which specializes in malnutrition cases.

On February 24, 2010, Mr. Paul Evans Aidoo, the Western Regional Minister, noted in his address to the Region's 2009 Annual Performance Review that

> Malaria continues to be the number one cause of mortality and morbidity in the region, accounting for 46.2% of OPD attendance, 47.5% of hospital admissions, and 22.6% of hospital deaths. . . . We have to intensify the fight against malaria, by promoting cost-effective interventions against malaria, such as the use of insecticide-treated bed nets, intermittent preventive treatment of malaria in pregnancy.

His talk further emphasized the distribution of free rapid diagnostic tests (RDTS) at the sub-district level and additional funding for integrated malaria-control activities. Dr. Linda Van Otoo, Western Regional Health Director, responded with a 30-minute talk in which she is reported to have declared that the health workers were doing their best and the improvements in the region were due to their efforts. The overwhelming challenges she saw included:

- Lack of accommodations for staff

- Lack of critical staff including midwives, anesthetists, specialists, and technologists

- Deteriorating health infrastructure including uncompleted capital projects in a number of districts

- Aging equipment

- Lack of transport and a poor road network in some districts

- Poor data management

- The huge debts accumulated by the NHIS (Saminu, 2010)

AN EARLY EXPERIMENT WITH CQI IN GHANA

An experiment with the use of CQI in managing malaria control in Ghana was reported in 2003 (Agyepong). This study was an initial early evaluation of CQI that investigated how training and supporting district and Accra Metropolitan sub-district (henceforth called sub-districts and sub-metros respectively) health-management teams in the Greater Accra region could improve the quality of malaria-control-related efforts there. It followed earlier work that developed an implementation model for applying CQI to primary health care in Ghana in general and malaria control in particular (Agyepong, 2000). Despite the fact that CQI is a long-term intervention solution, whose effects are best manifested over 5 to 10 years of implementation, this evaluation, limited to the early impact of the CQI approach on a small scale, was considered useful and necessary before making any recommendations for its wider scale application to malaria control or longer term evaluation of its impact. This limited short-term evaluation also provided a potential baseline for comparison in longer-term evaluations.

The study aimed to:

1. Compare knowledge and understanding of malaria-control objectives and strategies in districts and Accra Metro sub-districts in the region applying CQI to malaria control with those who are not.

2. Compare the design, implementation and management of processes for malaria control in districts and Accra Metro sub-districts in the region applying CQI to malaria control with those who are not.

3. Compare the intermediate outcomes of processes for malaria control in districts and Accra Metro sub-districts in the region applying CQI to malaria control with those who are not.

4. Compare the internal and external customer satisfaction with quality in districts and Accra Metro sub-districts that are implementing CQI with those who are not.

At that time there was not a clearly defined management philosophy or approach in the health system in the Greater Accra region. There was concern about quality assurance, but not quality improvement. Quality assurance had not been specifically applied to malaria control or to the broader managerial issues that influenced the functioning of the health system in the region. It had focused primarily on training for hospital- and clinic-based teams providing clinical care.

Although there had been other managerial models such as the "But Why" approach (Cassels and Janovsky, 1995) sponsored by the Health Systems unit of WHO in the 1980s and early 1990s, these had all been allowed to die out over time.

In assessing outcomes, this two-year study was limited to intermediate outcomes in malaria control such as the quality of clinical-case management of acute fevers and the use of bed nets rather than final program outcomes such as morbidity and mortality. Any attempts to transform the local organizational climate and its influence on health-system functioning and outcomes probably would have taken 5 to 10 years.

Study Design

The study had a quasi-experimental separate sample pre- and post-test control group design. Districts and Accra sub-metros were divided into intervention and control and compared before and after the introduction of CQI training and support for implementation. This design was selected because it had the advantage of dealing with many threats to the study's internal validity. Preintervention status and selected intermediate outcomes of malaria control were assessed in all participating districts and sub-districts in the region using quantitative survey questionnaires with mainly closed- but a few open-ended items.

In the intervention districts and Accra sub-metros, selected members of the health-management teams were trained in CQI and its application to the design, implementation, and management of processes for malaria control. The training was done with manuals developed in the first phase of this work (Agyepong, 2000). Training was done by members of the Dangme West district health-management team who had already gone through CQI training and implementation in 2003 during the preliminary study.

The trained teams were provided with supportive supervision through periodic scheduled visits by members of the Dangme West team in response to the specific needs for assistance expressed by the intervention district and Accra sub-metro teams. In the control districts and Accra sub-metros no such training and supportive supervision was provided. The training of the teams was done with funds provided for implementing the intervention. Beyond that, no special funds were made available to intervention or control teams for malaria control other than that routinely available to districts and sub-metros.

The time frame of the study is outlined in Figure 4–1. It was strictly an early evaluation of the CQI intervention. When the baseline survey was repeated in August 2003, the intervention had been running for approximately 12 months.

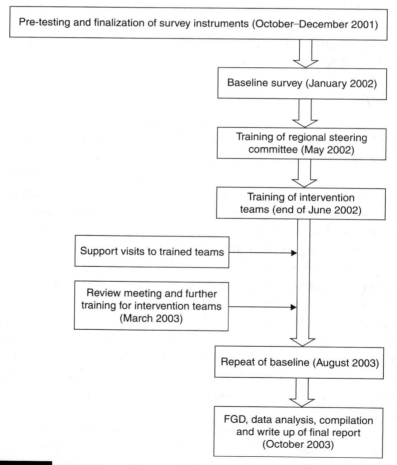

Figure 4–1 Time Frame of the Study

Sampling

The Greater Accra region is one of ten administrative regions of Ghana. It had a population of 2,905,726 in 2000, according to the national population census. It is the most populous region in the country, in part, because it contains the capital city, Accra. Its population density from the 2000 census was 1019 persons per square kilometer. It is the only region in the country where the rural-urban ratio is reversed (20:80). At the time of the study, it was divided into five administrative districts: Accra, Tema, Ga, Dangme East, and Dangme West.

The Accra "district" is an urban metropolis with a total population of 1,658,937 (2000 census) (Ghana Statistical Service, 2005). It is the most densely populated part of the region. At the time of the study it was subdivided in to six sub-metros: Ablekuma, Ashiedu-Keteke, Ayawaso, Kpeshie, Okaikoi, and Osu-Clottey. Each of these sub-metros is treated more or less as an administrative district because of the size of the population and the complexity of the sub-metro health system. Each of these sub-metros is served by a government polyclinic. In addition, there were numerous private clinics and hospitals. There were three government hospitals in the Accra metropolis at the time of the study (Princess Marie Louise (PML) Children's Hospital, Achimota Hospital, Ridge Hospital), and three quasi-government hospitals (Police Hospital, Military Hospital, University Hospital).

All six Accra sub-metros and the other four districts in the Greater Accra region took part in the study; effectively, ten "districts" participated in the study. The six Accra sub-metros were randomly divided equally into intervention and control groups.

The Tema "district," with a population of 506,400, was almost completely urbanized and classified as a municipality at the time of the study. The major seaport in Ghana, Tema Harbor, is part of this municipality. There are, however, several completely rural communities in Tema, especially in the areas where it borders the Dangme West district and the Ga district. Tema had a government hospital, a government polyclinic, three health centers, and numerous private hospitals and clinics.

The Ga district used to be almost entirely rural but had been caught up in the urban spread of the Accra metropolis and Tema municipality and was rapidly urbanizing especially in the areas bordering Accra and Tema. From the 2000 census, it was the most rapidly growing district in the region and had a population of 550,468. There were five health centers and no government hospitals or polyclinics. The lack of health infrastructure was due, in part, to the fact that urban growth had rapidly outstripped an infrastructure that was previously adequate for a sparsely populated rural district. There were, however, numerous private clinics in the urbanized parts.

The Dangme East and West districts were completely rural and typical of rural districts elsewhere in Southern Ghana at the time of the study and remain so. Dangme East had a population of 93,112 and Dangme West 96,809 in the 2000 census. Poverty is widespread, and most of the population are subsistence farmers practicing non-mechanized rain-fed agriculture, and along the coast, fishermen. There were four health centers and no hospital in the Dangme West district. The Dangme East district had four health centers and a hospital that was recently completed and just beginning to function.

Dangme East and West were classified as wholly rural, the Ga district as predominantly rural but with urbanization in the periphery bordering the Accra Metropolis and the Tema municipality, and Tema as predominantly urban but with some rural areas in the periphery bordering the Dangme West district. Dangme East and West were therefore paired as rural and Tema and Ga paired as rural-urban mix. Within each pair one was selected as intervention and the other as control by balloting. However, Dangme East strictly did not have a true match since Dangme West was not considered a part of the study in a strict sense even though evaluation data was also collected in this district.

Dangme West started CQI implementation in 1999 as the district in which the intervention model and the manuals were developed. As an intervention district, it was problematic given that the team doing the regional training was from Dangme West and the Principal Investigator was the district director. It was felt that any evaluation of it as an intervention or as a control district was likely to have more bias than the other districts. Moreover, the added responsibility of providing training for five teams and following up with no new staff or extra staff support restricted the capacity of the Dangme West team to follow up on the CQI interventions in their own district. The ongoing CQI intervention in that district that had focused on improving clinical-case management among other things by using regular support visits and on-the-job feedback actually suffered neglect during the intervention year. Evaluation survey data was collected from this district, but it was neither classified as interven-

Table 4–1 Districts Involved in Study	
Control District/Accra Metro sub-districts	**Intervention Districts/Accra Metro sub-districts**
Ga district	Tema district
Okai-Kwei sub-metro (Kaneshie polyclinic)	Ablekuma sub-metro (Mamprobi polyclinic)
Ayawaso sub-metro (Mamobi polyclinic)	Kpeshie sub-metro (Labadi polyclinic)
Osu Clottey sub-metro (Adabraka polyclinic)	Ashiedu Keteke sub-metro (Ussher polyclinic)
	Dangme East district

tion or control. The intervention and control districts and Accra sub-metros are summarized in Table 4–1.

Survey data was collected from households and from primary-care staff. Household survey data was used to evaluate multiple prevention in malaria control. Within each of the six Accra sub-metros and the four districts, 300 households were selected at random using cluster sampling to give a total of 3000 households in each survey. In each district or Accra sub-metro, a total of 30 clusters were randomly selected proportionate to population using as the sampling frame a list of enumeration areas with their populations based on the 2000 census. Within each cluster, ten households were selected at random by finding the proximate center of the cluster, spinning a pen or a bottle and moving in the direction the tip pointed in from house to house until the ten houses were obtained.

Data on clinical-case management of fever was collected from the major primary-care clinics in the public sector serving each of the districts and Accra sub-metros. Within each clinic, all clients seen daily during the survey period were followed up with until a minimum of 30 fever clients had been seen. Teams of interviewers moved from clinic to clinic during the one-month period of the survey in January 2002 and August 2003, and not more than one week was spent in any one clinic. If within a week the minimum of 30 clients had not been obtained, the team moved on since the project resources could not support more extended time per clinic. Records of clients presenting with fever were reviewed as soon as the client completed the clinic visit and handed in their outpatient medical record at the clinic records office. In the preintervention survey, the clients whose records were reviewed for quality of clinical care were also followed home on the third day after the clinic visit to assess their opinion of the quality of care received. In the postintervention survey, this approach was changed and exit interviews were conducted with the client immediately after the clinic visit. The home visits originally intended to assess adherence to therapy were too resource intensive.

The Intervention

The CQI intervention evaluated in this study tried to empower health teams through training and supportive supervision to identify malaria-control-related processes that needed improvement; analyze and understand those processes; identify variation leading to a defective or reduced quality product; and select process-improvement approaches that would improve the product. The CQI intervention also involved the teams in carefully studying and making decisions on what data were needed for monitoring and how to collect, analyze, and evaluate that information. The teams then planned for continuous monitoring and improvement of the selected malaria-control processes. To facilitate the long-term process of creation and maintenance of a supportive organizational culture and climate for CQI, a regional CQI steering committee made up of top-level regional managers was trained and oriented to the CQI approach and involved as much as possible in the work of the teams so that they could understand and provide the necessary support. The model or process used for the Greater Accra region CQI training and implementation support is summarized in Figure 4–2. The first step in the process was the further briefing of the Regional Director Health Services on the proposed study. He had already been briefed and his permission sought to carry out the study in the region before the proposal was submitted for funding.

During the Regional Steering committee training, the regional team developed a personalized vision statement for the region based on the health-sector vision that read: "Good Health for all People living in Greater Accra." A mission statement was developed that read: "The Ghana Health Service, Greater Accra region will work in collaboration with all partners in the health sector to ensure that every individual, household and community is adequately informed about health, and has access to high quality health and related interventions."

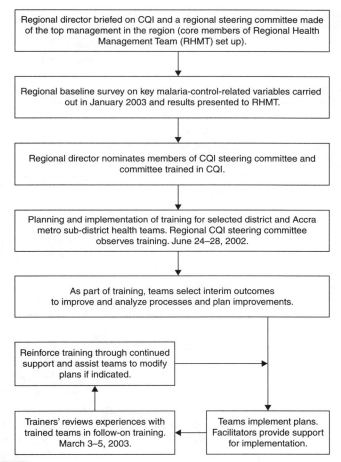

Regional director briefed on CQI and a regional steering committee made of the top management in the region (core members of Regional Health Management Team (RHMT) set up).

Regional baseline survey on key malaria-control-related variables carried out in January 2003 and results presented to RHMT.

Regional director nominates members of CQI steering committee and committee trained in CQI.

Planning and implementation of training for selected district and Accra metro sub-district health teams. Regional CQI steering committee observes training. June 24–28, 2002.

As part of training, teams select interim outcomes to improve and analyze processes and plan improvements.

Reinforce training through continued support and assist teams to modify plans if indicated.

Trainers' reviews experiences with trained teams in follow-on training. March 3–5, 2003.

Teams implement plans. Facilitators provide support for implementation.

Figure 4–2 Summary of Process Used for Implementing CQI in the Greater Accra Region

During their training, the district and sub-district health teams translated this vision and mission specifically to malaria as: "To reduce morbidity (illness) and mortality (death) due to malaria" and "The . . . district or sub-metro health team will work together with all partners to make sure that everybody in the district or sub-metro knows enough about malaria, participates in its control and has access to good quality case management." This vision and mission provided the basis for the selection of malaria-control-related improvement activities. However, each team was given the flexibility to choose an issue that they wanted to

	Concern/Issue Selected for	Aspect of Malaria Control
Team	**Improvement**	**Addressed**
Ablekuma sub-metro (Mamprobi polyclinic)	Use of Insecticide Treated Nets in the sub-metro	Multiple Prevention
Kpeshie sub-metro (La polyclinic)	Time spent in the La polyclinic by clients with fever seeking clinical consultation	Clinical Case management at primary-care facility level of acute uncomplicated episodes (External Customer Satisfaction)
Ashiedu-Keteke sub-metro (Ussher polyclinic)	Use of Insecticide Treated Nets in the sub-metro	Multiple Prevention
Tema Municipality	Time spent in the Tema polyclinic by clients with fever seeking clinical consultation	Clinical Case Management at primary-care facility level of acute uncomplicated episodes (External Customer Satisfaction)
Dangme East district	1. Time spent in the Ada health center by clients with fever seeking clinical consultation 2. Technical Quality of Clinical Case Management for clients with fever	Clinical Case Management at primary-care facility level of acute uncomplicated episodes (External customer satisfaction & Technical quality of care)

Table 4–2 Improvement Focus of the Individual Districts/Sub-metros

address in their locality. The advantage of this was that teams could focus on what they felt was most pressing in their working situation. This is what is expected to happen normally. The disadvantage for evaluation purposes is that since teams selected different products for improvement, it complicated somewhat the analysis and comparison of data from the different sites. The topics selected for improvement by the different teams are summarized in Table 4–2.

Variables and Indicators

Ideal evaluation measurements were initially defined and then reexamined to tease out measurements that were necessary and could be made practically during the study. The defined ideal measurements would enable:

1. Estimation of the malaria burden and the impact of the intervention on the malaria burden.

2. Description and comparison of different management systems:

    a. Describe and compare deployment/communication of knowledge and understanding of malaria-control objectives and strategies by employees of the organization.

    b. Describe and compare design of malaria-control processes.

    c. Describe and compare management and implementation of malaria-control processes.

3. Describe and compare internal customer (health worker/provider) and external customer (users of the health services) satisfaction.

4. Describe and compare "quality" of outcomes or products of malaria-control processes.

Estimating the malaria burden was beyond the scope of this study and not likely to show much difference in this brief an evaluation. Many cases are managed at the household level and reported cases, for which data is readily available, are no indicator of the actual burden. Community-based studies of incidence and prevalence of malaria involved costs well beyond the study budget.

DESCRIBING, ASSESSING, AND COMPARING MANAGEMENT SYSTEMS

The major questions here were: "What are the alternatives being compared?" and "What will be the indicators to use to assess and compare?" The alternatives being compared were defined as:

    a. Current management system for malaria control.

    b. Proposed management system (CQI) that would use teams trained to use the FOCUS-PDCA approach summarized in Figure 4–3.

What is the product or outcome that needs improvement?
e.g., use of insecticide-treated nets (ITN)

What are the processes that are used to arrive at or lead to the
product or outcome and who is involved in the processes?
(Process and team identification)

❑ Find a process to improve
❑ Organize a team that knows the process

(Process analysis)

❑ Clarify the current knowledge of the process and its variation
❑ Understand the causes of process variation

(Process improvement)

❑ Select the process improvement
❑ PDCA: Work on the process improvement cycle

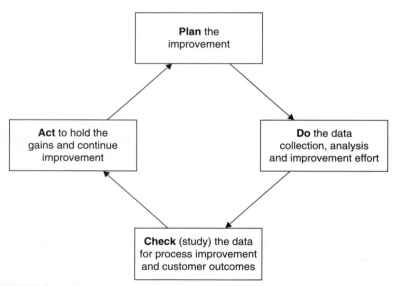

Figure 4–3 The CQI Planning and Implementation Cycle (based on the FOCUS-PDCA approach)

The selected indicators used for assessment and comparison of the different management systems were:

a. Clarity of definition and documentation of program objectives: Are malaria-control program objectives for the district/sub-district clearly described in measurable terms?

b. Deployment/Communication of program objectives: How aware is health staff of the malaria-control objectives for the district/sub-district?

c. Clarity of definition and documentation of strategies to achieve program objectives.

d. Deployment/Communication of program strategies: How aware is health staff of the malaria-control strategies for the district/sub-district?

e. Process identification: clarity of identification, definition, and documentation of processes that need to be undertaken to achieve the objectives.

f. Clarity of process analysis, i.e., steps that need to be taken to implement the process.

g. Are plans available?

h. Indicators of implementation of plans. How much of what was planned is being:

- Done?
- Done on time?
- Done the way it was planned?

Customer Satisfaction

The conceptual framework for assessing internal customer (provider) and external customer (patient/client) satisfaction was as shown in Figure 4–4. Each of the factors in this figure was framed as an indicator/variable for measurement.

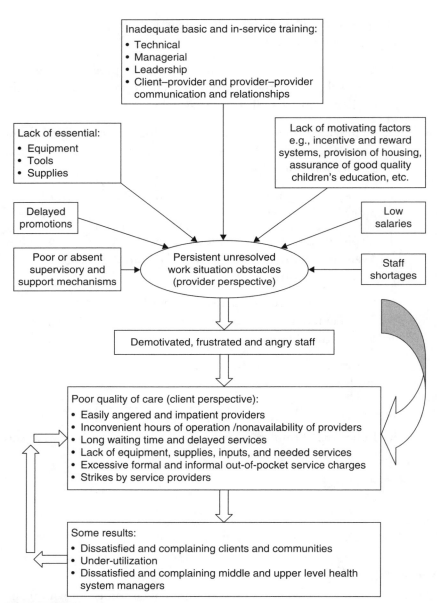

Figure 4–4 Factors Influencing Internal Customer Satisfaction and Performance in the Ghana Health Service

Data-Collection Methods and Tools

Both qualitative and quantitative methods of data collection were used. Quantitative data was collected pre- and post-intervention. Qualitative data was collected from district health-management teams and Accra Metropolitan sub-district teams using focus group discussions and also in the form of a few open-ended questions in the structured questionnaire administered to internal customers. The Focus Group Discussion Guide is included in Exhibit 4–2. In addition, non-participant observation was used during the training workshops and support process to observe the performance of trained teams. Finally, the flow charts, problem analysis diagrams, and plans developed by teams during training were compared with what was actually implemented.

EXHIBIT 4–2

Focus Group Discussion Guide

Evaluation of the impact of CQI on malaria control in the Greater Accra region in Ghana:

1. Would you say that malaria is a problem in this district/ sub-district? What is the reason for your opinion?
2. Who is in charge of malaria control for this district/ sub-district?
3. Design and management of processes for malaria control:
   a. Do you have a written vision; i.e., what you hope to achieve in the long term for malaria control in this district/sub-district? (Could be in district plans of action, an annual report, a stand-alone, etc.) If written, please have a look.
   b. What is your vision, written or not (i.e., what do you hope to achieve in the long term), in the area of malaria control in this district/sub-district?
   c. Do you have any short- and medium-term (next 1 to 5 years) objectives related to malaria control for this district/sub-district? If you do, what are they?

(continues)

EXHIBIT 4–2

   d. What are the processes or steps or activities you have planned or are planning to achieve these objectives?

   e. Moderator to look out and if necessary probe for:

- Clarity of definition and documentation of program objectives: Are malaria-control program objectives for the district/sub-district clearly described in measurable terms; e.g., 80% of children under 5 sleep under a treated net in district, etc.?
- Clarity of definition and documentation of strategies to achieve program objectives.
- Process identification: clarity of identification, definition, and documentation of processes that need to be undertaken to achieve the objectives. What processes are needed to attain the desired objectives (professional processes, managerial processes, etc.)?
- Clarity of process analysis; i.e., steps that need to be taken to implement the process.
- Plans available.

4. Implementation of processes for malaria control:

   a. If you mentioned any objectives in response to the previous question, have you started implementing them? Alternatively, are you undertaking any specific actions for malaria control in your area of coverage? Probe for the following areas:

     i. Prevention and promotional activities; e.g., use of bed nets, home management, etc.

     ii. Proper clinical-case management of fever/malaria.

     iii. Antimalarial prophylaxis for antenatal clients, etc.

   b. Can you tell us what you are doing and how you are managing it?

   c. When did you start, and how long do you plan to go on for?

(continues)

EXHIBIT 4–2

   d. Do you have any monitoring indicators and plans? If yes, please tell us about them.

   e. Moderator to look out for:

- Indicators of implementation of plans. How much of what was planned is being:
  - Done
  - Done on time
  - Done the way it was planned

5. For those who took part in the CQI training:

   a. If you were asked to objectively evaluate the usefulness of the CQI training and support for the implementation process you have been through, what would you say?

   b. How would you recommend that the training be improved? What was done poorly and needs to be changed? What was done well and needs to be maintained?

   c. Was the training helpful in any way to you in addressing the problem of malaria in your area of coverage?

   d. Was it helpful to you for any other reason?

   e. Do you think it is worth providing you with follow-up training and support for CQI implementation? For malaria control and for other programs?

   f. Would you recommend that we extend the program to the other sub-metros and districts in the region? Please explain your answer.

6. Interpreting results of pre- and post-test surveys. Share results of pre- and post-test surveys with participants and ask: why do you think you have improved or not improved?

   a. Multiple prevention?

   b. Clinical-case management?

   c. Internal customer satisfaction?

RESULTS

Knowledge and Understanding of Malaria-Control Objectives

In the preintervention study (January 2002), 83% of primary-care clinic staff interviewed in the region stated that they were aware of the objectives of malaria control in Ghana, or what we were trying to achieve. There was not much difference between the five districts (the six Accra sub-metros make up the Accra district) that make up the region apart from Dangme West, where there was noticeably higher awareness.

Responses to the open ended question, "If yes, what are they?" for staff who said they knew the objectives included some vague answers such as "to control malaria." Others were more specific such as "to prevent malaria and to reduce deaths due to malaria" and "to prevent malaria so that deaths due to malaria will reduce, productivity will be high, and save government spending." Still others were inaccurate such as "to eradicate malaria."

Staff who answered "yes" to the question "Do you know how we are trying to achieve malaria-control objectives/goals? i.e., What strategies are we using to try and control malaria in Ghana?" were even higher than those who said they knew the objectives; 91% of regional staff with a range of 82% to 100% across sub-districts and sub-metros. Most of the strategies mentioned were related to environmental sanitation, health education, and use of insecticide-treated nets as ways of preventing disease. Only a handful of people mentioned prompt and appropriate treatment of acute disease episodes as a strategy. The major reported sources of information for staff on malaria-control objectives and strategies were written materials, the mass media and workshops, and in-service training programs and seminars.

Postintervention data were similar. It appears that there was a problem with comprehensive and adequate communication of the objectives of malaria control and the strategies for malaria control to primary-care staff in the region. It is also possible that communication was not being made frequently enough for the information to be retained.

DESIGN, IMPLEMENTATION, AND MANAGEMENT OF PROCESSES FOR MALARIA CONTROL

The focus group discussions (FGDs) carried out with sub-metro and sub-district health teams in October 2003 suggested that health teams in the region were not really focused on design, implementation, and management of processes for malaria control. Even though the situation was somewhat better in the CQI intervention area, there appeared to be a lot that remained to be done in these areas, too.

All the Accra sub-metro and sub-district health-management team participants in the FGDs agreed that malaria was a problem locally and had been their major cause of morbidity for a long time. However, though all the teams who attended the CQI training now said they had a vision statement as to what they were trying to achieve in malaria control, they often could not remember what it was. These teams were similarly vague about who was in charge of or coordinating malaria control in the district or sub-metro. It appeared to be a case of everybody's business had become nobody's business. In one group, a control sub-metro, everyone was quiet and looked at their director's face, perhaps for inspiration, when the question was asked about their malaria-control objectives as a team, before talking vaguely about issues related to environmental sanitation, health education, and use of bed nets. In yet another control sub-metro, the response was "Auntie has a copy (of the sub-metro objectives) and an action plan. I cannot remember if malaria control is stated on it."

Not surprisingly, given the problems about lack of a clear sense of direction in terms of visions, objectives, plans, and strategies for malaria control, there was some vagueness in the findings related to actual implementation and management of malaria control, especially in the nonintervention districts and sub-metros. During the postintervention FGD, the teams in the nonintervention districts and sub-metros were asked for copies of any malaria-control plans and processes. None of the teams were able to produce them.

The situation was a little better in the districts that had gone through CQI training, though there was still a lot of room for improvement. It appeared that perhaps the members of the district or sub-metro health-management teams that were trained in Aburi and given a refresher in Legon had not deployed the vision and objectives to the other members of the team and had themselves forgotten some of it. Thus, in one intervention district, the answer to the question about the team's vision for malaria control was, "There is something, we carried something when we came from the workshop, from Aburi." Another participant tried to help by saying, "We were at Abokobi sometime ago, and the national objective was that malaria should be reduced by 50%."

Process Analysis

During the CQI training, each team analyzed the processes that led to the malaria-control process they were trying to improve, as well as the reasons why the resources were inadequate. The problem analysis was summarized in the form of a fishbone diagram and the process analysis in the form of a flow chart. Examples of these are presented in Figures 4–5 through 4–8. The teams then went on to design a course of action to improve their processes.

The two teams that chose to address the issue of the time clients spent in the clinic before completing care and going home decided to collect further data to help them understand where the 'time waste' bottlenecks were greatest. They requested and were provided with support from the trainers to design a simple process to record time spent by clients at the

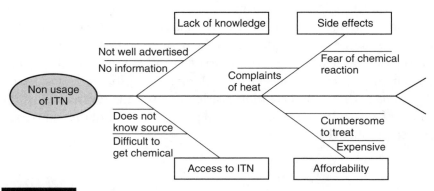

Figure 4–5 Ablekuma Sub-metro (Mamprobi polyclinic)

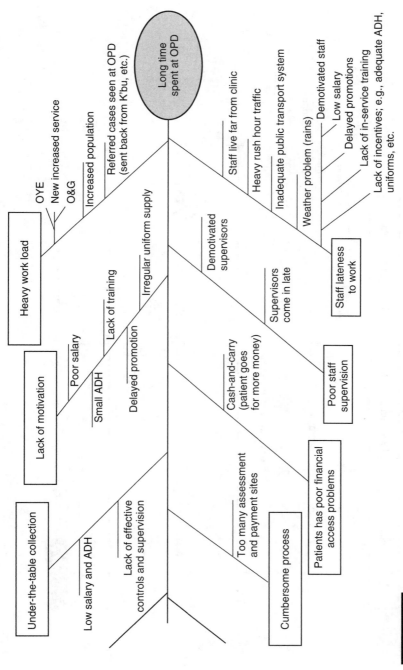

Figure 4-6 Problem Analysis (Fishbone diagram)—Kpeshie Sub-metro

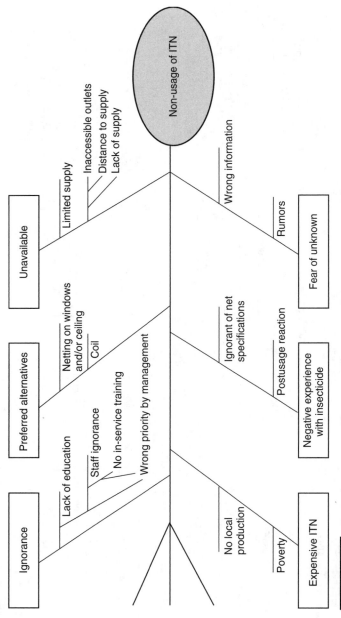

Figure 4–7 Problem Analysis (Fishbone diagram)—Ashiedu-Keteke

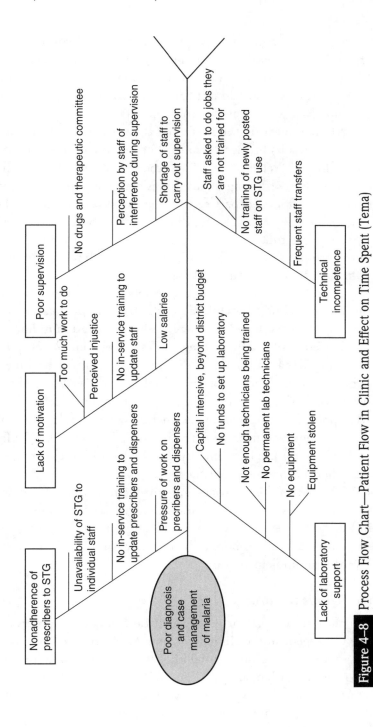

Figure 4–8 Process Flow Chart—Patient Flow in Clinic and Effect on Time Spent (Tema)

service locations in the clinic, such as the pharmacy, that contributed to the time spent by clients at the facility. They needed to understand which units were contributing most to the wait time and why. At the time of the postintervention survey, they had just completed collecting and analyzing this data themselves with support from members of the intervention team. They referred to this in the FGD, but they were still working on it and hoping to see results further down the line because time was needed. Comments included, "When we did CQI, the record and revenue offices have been going through changes and things are going on well. I know when we fully take off in all departments things would change for the better" and "After the (CQI) training we did a survey to find out our weaknesses; especially the time element. . . . It helped us to really educate clients on the waiting time. . . . It is not just getting lab results but waiting to get quality. It also helped us advise."

All districts and sub-metros across the region had received subsidized insecticide-treated bed nets for children under five and pregnant women and were selling the nets. However, there was some variation in how districts and sub-metros were approaching this task. For some it was purely an issue of selling nets at the clinics with some accompanying health education. Others, such as Kaneshie (a control sub-metro), were actively taking the health education on nets out into the community with a mobile van. In Mamprobi (an intervention sub-metro) staff was taking the nets out into the community during satellite clinics as part of their CQI effort. "Our health education has been intensified. We have been able to get in touch with other sub-metros about the use of ITN."

In the CQI intervention districts and sub-metros, some efforts were started to implement something based on the analysis carried out in the Aburi workshop. However, teams were still early on in the process and expressed a sense of needing more time and more on-the-job support to move forward with implementation.

Quality of Clinical Care

Review of data from outpatient department cards as well as observation of the total time spent in the clinics by clients was carried out in 20 primary clinics across the region. A total of 779 clinical consultations with clients was reviewed in January 2002 and 636 contacts in August 2003. Enrollment problems were experienced at three clinics, but the numbers were sufficient to retain in the sample at two of them.

Clinical Examination and Diagnosis

Despite the fact that all the reviewed clients presented with a complaint of fever, only 88% had a temperature recorded. When the data is disaggregated, most clinics were doing fairly well on temperature recording and the low regional average is accounted for mainly by two clinics.

Recording of weight was also consistently poor across the region, the exception being Dangme West, where 94% to 100% of clients were weighed and the weight recorded in all four clinics, both pre- and post-intervention. In all the other clinics, weighing and recording of weight varied from 0% to 12% of clients seen preintervention. This is even though children under 12 years formed about half (48%) of all clients with fever and drugs for children are supposed to be prescribed by weight. Postintervention the situation had improved somewhat though performance was still less than desirable. Weighing of clients and recording of the weight had increased substantially in most intervention clinics and somewhat less in the control clinics.

Examination results were recorded for 63% of clients preintervention and 58% postintervention. Performance clinic-by-clinic showed no apparent pattern. A diagnosis was recorded in approximately 98% of cases preintervention and 95% postintervention overall. Again, there did not appear to be any particular consistent pattern of change. Over 90% of diagnoses included malaria. Sometimes the diagnoses were a record of a symptom or cluster of symptoms rather than an actual diagnosis. Examples of such diagnoses included:

- Malaria and vomiting and fever
- Malaria and headache
- Frequent mucoid and watery stools
- Intermittent fever
- Malaria and painful leg
- Diarrhea and fever

Use of Laboratory Results for Diagnosis

Fifteen of the clinics had laboratories. Preintervention, blood film for malaria parasites was requested for only 13% of clients (n=101), and

95% of the blood film requests were from clinics with laboratories. Even in clinics with laboratories, only 17% of fever cases had a blood film requested. Given that over 90% of the diagnoses made included malaria, it seems the diagnosis of malaria in primary-care clinics in the region is mainly clinical regardless of the availability of a laboratory. The post-intervention data told a similar story.

Mean Time Spent at the Clinics

There was very little or no change in the mean time spent at the clinic by the client in most instances, or where there was a change it was upwards. However, there were some exceptions. Time spent at the Maamobi Poly-clinic, Ada-Foah Health Centre, Sege Health Centre, and Tema Polyclinic dropped by almost half or more. Ada-Foah and Tema were intervention clinics where the team decided to apply CQI to reduce the time spent. In all these clinics, the longest time spent by any particular client also dropped substantially. Sege Health Centre is under Ada-Foah and over-seen by the same team working in Ada-Foah to reduce the time spent. Maamobi, however, was a control clinic. La Polyclinic was an intervention clinic that tried to use CQI to reduce the time spent. However, paradox-ically the average and median time spent increased a little, even though the range narrowed.

Multiple Malaria Prevention Intervention

Knowledge Related to Malaria Prevention

Knowledge that the mosquito causes malaria was very high (almost 100%) all across the region in rural as well as urban districts. Some 96% of respondents said they got this information over a year before the sur-vey. Only 2% had only obtained this information within the last 12 months. Across the region only 2% of respondents were not aware that the mosquito causes any illness.

Knowledge about bed nets was near 100% across the region in the Jan-uary 2002 preintervention survey. Not surprisingly, there was no change to record in the August 2003 survey. Knowledge about insecticide-treated nets was lower in the preintervention survey with 66% of respondents across the region being aware of insecticide-treated nets. The levels of knowledge were lowest in the two rural districts and the Ashiedu-Keteke sub-metro, with 56% of respondents in Dangme East, 54% in Dangme

West, and 59% in Ashiedu-Keteke saying they knew about insecticide-treated nets. The highest level of knowledge was in the other sub-Metros, with between 70% and 74% of respondents saying they knew about insecticide-treated nets.

Postintervention knowledge about insecticide-treated nets increased, and the percentage of people who knew about insecticide-treated nets in the region as a whole rose from 66% to 83%. The increase in knowledge about insecticide-treated nets was statistically significant in all districts. The levels of knowledge in the rural districts and Ashiedu-Keteke, where knowledge was lower in the January 2002 survey, had more or less caught up with the levels in the urban districts.

Actual Use of Nets

Despite the uniformly high level of knowledge about mosquitoes causing diseases, mosquito nets, and insecticide-treated nets across the region, actual use of mosquito nets was very low, apart from in the two purely rural districts of Dangme East and West. The use of insecticide-treated nets was even lower with no exceptions. Practice in terms of use of bed nets treated and untreated did not appear to directly follow knowledge *per se.*

In the January 2002 (preintervention) survey only 5% to 10% of adults in the Accra sub-metros used bed nets. About half of the households in the urban districts had children under five compared to about three-fourths of rural district households, and the use of bed nets for children under five was slightly higher though still low and ranged between 9% and 21% depending on the sub-metro. On the other hand, in Dangme East 69% of adults and 77% of children under five, and in Dangme West 53% of adults and 58% of children under five were sleeping under bed nets. Use of insecticide-treated nets was uniformly low at about 2% all across the region. There was no difference between rural and urban or children and adults.

In the August 2003 survey (early postintervention), there was an overall increase in the use of bed nets by adults from 20% to 24% (Pr=0.000 for the difference) and an increase in the use of bed nets for children under five from 32% to 38% (Pr=0.000 for the difference). However, unlike the increase in knowledge, where the change was across the board in all the districts and sub-metros in the region, the overall increase in practice was due to selective increases in specific sub-metros. The Ablekuma sub-metro (Mamprobi) showed a statistically significant increase between the pre- and the postintervention survey among adults (6% to 15%) as well as in children under five (12% to 31%) using a bed net. The Ashiedu-Keteke sub-metro showed similar increases in the use of bed nets by adults increasing from 5% to 11% and use by children under 5 increasing from 9% to 22%. In both cases the differences between the pre- and postintervention data was significant. Both Ablekuma and Ashiedu-Keteke were in the CQI intervention category and chose to address the level of bed-net and insecticide-treated net use in the sub-metro as their product for improvement with CQI.

However, the Ayawaso sub-metro in the control group where there was no CQI intervention also showed significant increases in bed-net use by adults (7% to 18%) and by children under five (17% to 36%). In the control group, Okai-koi also showed significant increases in bed-net use by adults (8% to 14%) but none by children under 5. Kpeshie and Tema, in the CQI intervention group, which chose to improve the "time spent by fever clients at the OPD," also showed significant increases in the use of bed nets by children under 5.

Use of insecticide-treated nets showed increases in almost all the districts by adults and by children under 5. The numbers involved were so small that no attempt was made to use statistical tests to compare the results.

Use of bed nets by the few pregnant women in the sample was very low and remained low in both the pre- and the postintervention surveys. Antenatal clinic use was high all across the region. Use of anti-malaria prophylaxis was, however, much lower.

Internal Customer Satisfaction

Pareto analysis was used to determine which factors were making the most contribution to the problem at hand, in this case, staff dissatisfaction with the organization and the subsequent effects on staff motivation and quality of output. Pareto analysis can be useful in CQI as a way of assessing which factors, if changed, will make the most difference. Figure 4–9 summarizes the regional preintervention data in a Pareto chart. Apart from low salaries, which rank highest among work situation obstacles in all districts, there were some differences between districts in how high the factors rank. The differences are important to the extent that they reflect the diversity and socio-economic contrasts of Greater Accra that have already been discussed in the introduction. They may

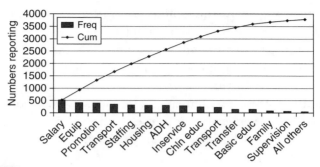

Figure 4–9 January 2002—Pareto Analysis of Internal Customer Problems: Greater Accra Region Totals

sometimes also be a reflection of local health administration for factors such as in-service training where most of the funds for training have been decentralized to the district.

Even though there was some reshuffling in ranking in the post-intervention data, the five to six most frequently mentioned obstacles did not change and the shifts were slight. The problems were essentially still the same.

Salaries

Low salaries ranked as the most frequently mentioned workplace obstacle, with over 95% of staff in all districts selecting it as a problem. Staff working in the Ghana Health Service could be described as permanent staff or temporary/casual staff. Permanent staff have their names on the payroll and are paid from the centre by Government of Ghana funds. They are paid amounts defined by law according to their rank in the organization and have social security and its accompanying benefits. Temporary/casual staff are employed locally by the institution. They are paid based on a process of negotiation with the institution based on what the institution can afford and what they are willing to accept. They have no social security and its accompanying benefits. When it becomes possible, temporary staff convert to permanent staff. However, it can take several years or never happen because there is a freeze on how many of a given category of staff can be employed. The pay of the casual staff tended to be slightly lower than, but fairly close to, what the equivalent permanent staff were paid. Both groups of employees, casual and permanent staff, were equally dissatisfied with their pay. Scheffler *et al.* (2010) have calculated that wage gaps throughout all sub-Saharan Africa, including Ghana, will continue to be a serious problem.

Within each category of staff there are slight variations in income related to rank. Staff are promoted to the next highest rank and its accompanying salary based on years of service in the organization. When asked, given their dissatisfaction with their current income, what would be a reasonable income given their needs and expenditure, most workers asked for about three times what they currently earned.

Personal Means of Transport

This was the second most important problem for staff in the Accra metropolis, but of much lower priority in rural Dangme East and Dangme West, and in between in priority in the Tema and Ga districts, which were a mix of rural and urban. In the Accra metropolis, most staff lived in rented accommodations all over the city. There was no truly public transport system *per se*. Public transport was actually private transport, a wide network of minibuses and taxi cabs in the city organized by the Ghana Private Road Transport Union of the Trades Union Congress. Though the networks were good, the service quality could be poor with long wait times and crowded buses, especially at commuting peak periods. Traffic in the city was also an increasing problem because of poor road networks. Depending on where staff lived in the city, they may have had to make several changes before getting to work. Transportation to and from work thus becomes an important problem or obstacle. In the more rural areas there tended to be clinic accommodation provided by government and located within walking distance of the rural health centre or hospital. In a rural area, the town may still be within walking distance of the clinic.

Inadequate Staffing

This ranked second as a concern of staff in Dangme East, the most remote of the two purely rural districts in Greater Accra and the least desired posting. Getting staff to accept postings there was extremely difficult. This was seen by the staff working there as a significant workplace obstacle. It is of fairly high concern for staff in Dangme West and Ga districts but of relatively low concern in the Accra metropolis and Tema municipality. Both of these urbanized settings are regarded as highly desired postings. Indeed, there is increasingly a problem both within the Greater Accra region and in the health sector as a whole of how to stop staff from requesting transfers to these areas given the already skewed staff distribution in their favor. The Ministry of Health has recently said that it will sanction medical officers who avoid assignment to rural areas.

Lack of Essential Equipment, Tools, and Supplies

In the other districts apart from the Accra metropolis and Dangme East, lack of essential equipment, tools, and supplies ranked as the second most pressing problem. Even in Accra and Dangme East it ranked third. The unavailable essential equipment, tools, and supplies were very basic in most instances: dustbins, brooms, disinfectant, soap, mops, bed sheets, pens, pencils, and rulers that institutions should be able to readily purchase themselves out of their internally generated funds, mostly from direct client payments at point of service. Observation suggested that part of the problem might be a lack of appreciation, the negative effect of these unmet needs, or indifference among institutional managers who directly control the spending. Among the relatively more sophisticated unmet needs in terms of tools and equipment to work with were things such as sphygmomanometers, thermometers, suturing sets, surgical instruments, and weighing scales all of which were relatively easy to obtain.

Promotions

Delayed promotions and perceived unfair promotion procedures featured among the five top ranking problems in all districts. Promotions were important not only because of the status of having a higher rank, but also because a higher rank is accompanied by a slightly higher income.

In-Service Training

Ninety two percent (92%) of staff who had had in-service training in the last five years considered that some of the in-service training they had received had made them better able to contribute to malaria control. Sixty-three percent (57 of 91) of those who felt their education to date had not adequately equipped them to cope with the work they were currently doing had not had any in-service training in the last year compared to 47% (216 of 458) of those who felt their education to date had adequately equipped them to cope with the work they were currently doing.

The difference was statistically significant. The data suggest that though a fair amount of in-service training is going on, it is perhaps not being properly targeted to areas of greatest need. There apparently was a need to put more effort into staff-training-needs assessment before arranging in-service training.

Other Factors

Additional duty payments were a motivator as well as a demotivator. They acted as a demotivator because, despite the effort to link them to extra hours worked, they are still seen by some staff as not really related to actual output. They acted as a motivator because they addressed to some extent the issue of low basic salary. They have been expanded considerably since 2003.

Other factors included availability of children's education and official means of transport to work. The factors discussed here cover over 90% of stated workplace obstacles. A minor factor mentioned in some clinics was the need for a workers' canteen of sorts.

LIMITATIONS OF THE STUDY

A major limitation of this study is that CQI is a long-term effort to change a system. An early evaluation such as this one (within 12 months of initiating the intervention) though useful cannot really be completely conclusive. Ideally, it should have been followed up with a medium-term evaluation (3 to 5 years) of the impact of continued intervention.

Another limitation of this study has been the financial and human resources needed to support the intervention. The original training for the intervention teams that was supposed to take about one and a half to two weeks had to be cut down to one week to fit into the available resources. Only four members could be trained from each district or sub-metro health-management team rather than the ideal situation where all members are trained together.

The few staff in Dangme West who already had training and some experience in CQI implementation and could facilitate the regional training by acting as trainers and also provide posttraining implementation support had to add this work on to their already full schedules. This was a limitation, but is also the reality of working in the Ghanaian health sector where the chronic loss of trained and skilled personnel was accelerated at the time of the study by the mass exodus of nursing personnel to the UK and elsewhere.

This limitation also affected the intervention teams since they also already were short staffed. During the training and the follow-up implementation support visits it was clear that they were struggling with how to prioritize amidst a multitude of responsibilities that sometimes seemed to overwhelm them.

It was also not possible to provide the needed follow-up support to the regional steering committee to increase their competence in CQI application and provision of support to the trained teams. This created a gap that needs to be addressed in any future intervention.

With hindsight, given these constraints, the study was probably too ambitious in trying to work with half the sub-metros and districts in the region, and in allowing teams to select what problems to tackle. It may have been simpler to select a product for all intervention teams to improve and focus on that single product to make the evaluation clearer and simpler. The disadvantage of this approach, though neater for evaluation purposes, is that it would not have been so supportive of the principles of decentralization and encouragement of local initiative that the Ghana health service is striving for.

It would have been very difficult to have a clear-cut neat experiment for this type of evaluation because one cannot control the many complex variables that influence health-system performance. All that could be controlled was who got the training and support visits for implementation and who did not. It was not possible to control transfer of key staff from one sub-metro or district to another. Neither was it possible to control the regular interactions and exchange of ideas that go on between sub-metros and districts in the region. Some teams in the control area wanted to know why they had been left out of the intervention and when they were going to get the chance to participate. Especially in the Accra metropolis where the sub-districts are physically very close to each other, staff meet and talk with each other regularly and units exchange ideas, staff, and programs, it is extremely difficult to control contamination of control sites by intervention sites.

Also related to contamination, though intervention districts and sub-metros selected different issues to address, they were trained together and listened to and discussed each other's analysis and plans during plenary sessions. Teams were encouraged to address only one product each with CQI because of the need to focus and prioritize given their staffing, time, and financial resource constraints. However, it was clear during the support visits and also from the FGDs that in some cases they had made some effort to apply CQI to malaria and other health problems.

IS CQI A VIABLE APPROACH IN MALARIA CONTROL?

To determine whether CQI is a viable approach in malaria control and is worth continuing, it is necessary to answer the question "Has the CQI intervention made any noticeable change?" Because this was an early evaluation of a complex management intervention that takes time to become institutionalized and produce marked effects, even small changes could imply that "big changes" are possible.

In the area of multiple prevention solutions for malaria control, specifically in getting people to move from knowledge about bed nets to the actual use of bed nets, the intervention even at this early phase does seem to have made a difference. There were statistically significant increases in bed-net use by adults and children under five in the two sub-metros that chose the use of bed nets, as their CQI focus. Despite the confusion introduced by the increase in use of bed nets by adults but not children under five in one control sub-metro, bed-net use did not increase in any of the remaining seven sites that did not choose this topic as a CQI project. The negative finding of no increase in practice in all other the nonintervention areas combined with the positive finding in the two intervention areas supports the probability that the positive change was important. Moreover, the one nonintervention sub-metro that showed an increase in bed-net use among adults borders an intervention sub-metro. Sub-metro borders are streets with related communities on each side. Contamination is very easy.

There was some confusion introduced by the increase in bed-net use by children under five in Tema, an intervention district, and La, an intervention sub-metro, that did not choose that product for improvement. However, since all the intervention sub-metros and districts were trained together, listened to presentations of each other's plans and analysis in plenary and commented and critiqued, the chances of contamination among the intervention areas in the different products they choose to address was very high. Moreover, even these intervention districts and sub-metros that did not choose this as their primary issue to address with CQI had copies of the resource materials (flip charts) about malaria and treated bed nets that Ablekuma developed to plan their intervention were available from the training process.

Finally, that CQI probably made a difference in increasing bed-net use in Ablekuma and Ashiedu-Keteke is further supported by the fact that though there was a uniform increase in knowledge about insecticide-treated nets all across the region, actual practice only selectively increased for both adults and children under five in these two sub-metros. In the bordering control sub-metros where there were increases, the increases were limited to adult use.

The uniform rise in knowledge of insecticide-treated nets across the region on the other hand suggested that CQI was not the change factor here. The most likely factor was the mass media adverts by the malaria-control program. Most adults mentioned the mass media as the source of their knowledge on insecticide-treated nets. For more than a year, the national malaria-control program had regularly been airing adverts about insecticide-treated nets on the mass media. The majority of sources of information on this subject cited by adults were radio and/or TV. Most people had also acquired the information within the 12 months preceding the interviews.

The gap between the increases in knowledge across the board in the region and the increase in practice only in specific districts indicate that it takes more than information provision to cause behavioral changes. A study of the approaches taken by the teams that chose bed-net use as the focus for improvement shows that in their analysis of the problem they tried to identify and address constraining factors. Specific actions were still needed to remove constraints and change practice.

In almost all the other areas monitored as part of the evaluation of the CQI intervention, there was no clear change in any direction. They were being managed under the normal system that operates in the region. Again, this "negative" finding probably further supported a proposal to continue the CQI intervention and further evaluate it in the medium term when CQI has had time to become more institutionalized.

A few comments need to be made about the issues related to provider or internal customer satisfaction and its effects on health-system performance in malaria control and other programs. Quality of care in public-sector facilities in Ghana has been a long-standing and continuing concern for users of the health services and civil society as well as health-sector policymakers, providers, administrators, and managers. User complaints and media reports of rude and impatient providers, inconvenient hours of operation, long wait times, lack of drugs, and other essential inputs have been common. In recent times, long-standing health-sector brain drain in the form of a steady exodus of trained professionals such as nurses, doctors, dentists, and pharmacists has accelerated to epidemic proportions.

Findings from the 2003 study confirmed earlier qualitative work and reviews of the literature that part of the reason for low quality of health-service delivery in the public sector was a labor force that faced a daily barrage of workplace obstacles that frustrated and demotivated them. In addition, some of the workplace obstacles such as lack of essential tools and equipment to work with and poorly targeted in-service training in and of themselves directly helped to lower the technical quality of care. Al Hussein *et al.* (1993), in a study in the central region of Ghana into factors leading to poor quality of nursing care, made similar observations about lack of basic equipment and supplies, ineffective supervision, and inadequate basic training as well as delayed promotions and inadequate allowances negatively influencing work performance. The daily unresolved frustrations of workers in health service reduced their willingness to exert and maintain efforts towards attaining the stated organizational goal of providing high-quality care. Moreover, sometimes their pent-up frustrations turned outwards onto clients in the form of rudeness, anger, unfriendly behavior, and resentment.

With a problem as complex as the quality of care and a health system as resource-constrained as the Ghana Health Service has been, it is necessary to prioritize to decide where to apply scarce resources. There are very hard choices to be made. The introduction of Additional Duty Hours (ADH) payments increased the proportion of the recurrent budget formed by salaries. In 2002, salaries including ADH payments formed almost 60% of the health recurrent budget—including external donor assistance. If external donor assistance is excluded, salaries formed closer to 90% of the recurrent budget.

Remunerating staff by salary alone did not provide an incentive to improve output and quality. The incentive for providers under a salary system of payment is to reduce the number of patients and number of services provided (Adams and Hicks, 2000). If an increase in income is to result in an increase in output, some part of staff remuneration should be linked to work output.

The problem of lack of essential tools, equipment, and supplies presented fewer tough choices than the salary problem. It was perhaps as much a problem of management and administration as of resources. In 1999, funds generated locally by institutions from client out-of-pocket charges at point-of-service use constituted as much as 14.2% of the health recurrent budget (Ministry of Health 2001). All this money was retained by the facilities that collect them with the understanding that they are to use it to improve quality of care. Most institutions had a balance in their bank accounts. How come institutional managers were not using some of this money to address the needs of staff for inexpensive tools and equipment to work with? Are they not aware of the needs or aware but do not consider them important? Observation suggests that in many instances, decisions about use of local funds were almost entirely in the hands of the facility head and there was little involvement or dialogue with the other staff. Apart from extra resources, more participatory management of resources and raising the awareness and training levels of facility, district and regional managers in equipment and supplies management and maintenance might have helped address this problem.

CONCLUSIONS AND RECOMMENDATIONS OF THE INITIAL STUDY

The CQI effort and its application to malaria control needed to be continued into the medium term (3 to 5 years) and further evaluation carried out to be able to make stronger conclusions. It was suggested, however, that instead of dividing the same region in two and comparing such closely related and interacting teams and geographic areas, the whole region undergo the CQI effort. Comparison could then be done with different regions to reduce the chances of contamination.

A regional team to carry out the training and provide the support for implementation needed to be specially selected and trained and given the time to devote to this effort, especially the very important task of providing follow-up support to the trained CQI teams without having to struggle to combine it with normal duties. The role of the regional steering committee also needed to be strengthened through further training and support provided to them to actually implement and follow through on their CQI plans and create an organizational culture and climate that supports continuous improvement.

Despite the limitations already described, the study was nevertheless useful. It provided baseline and early evaluation data that should make it easier to compare and carry out medium- and long-term evaluation should the CQI program continue in the region.

Longer Run Results

While no follow-up study was specifically conducted because the resources could not be obtained, the Greater Accra region has continued to encourage the use of continuous improvement efforts. Other parts of the national health sector seem to have expressed limited interest in the broader issues or quality improvement compared with the specific issue of clinical quality assurance. Thus, there is a national clinical quality-assurance program with manuals and a facilitator pool but no national quality-improvement program that goes beyond specific clinical problems within facilities and addresses managerial and system issues. The Greater Accra region's 2009 report listed a then-current set of objectives for the next year.

Manage and Improve Service Provision

This is related to the thematic areas of the Ghana health sector's third program of work labeled reproductive health and nutrition, aspects of health systems strengthening, and regenerative health and nutrition.

Specific objectives were:

1. Improve referral services organization, procedures, and staff attitudes:

   a. Hold at least one regional QA conference.

   b. Organize best QA awards.

   c. Make sure that all remaining district and sub-district level GHS institutions in the region (hospitals, polyclinics, health centres) that have not received QA training are trained in 2008 and all GHS institutions in the region have functional QA teams.

2. Strengthen selected priority interventions and programs:

    a. Malaria. Priorities included:

        i. Sustain current household insecticide-treated nets availability to children under five of 80% or more in all districts and sub-metros except Ashiedu-Keteke and Okai-koi.[1]

        ii. Devise and implement strategies to ensure Ashiedu-Keteke and Okai-koi also attain 80%.

        iii. Continue public education to ensure actual and sustained use of the nets for the children.

        iv. Start monitoring bed-net availability and use by pregnant women.

        v. Manage policy change from chloroquine as first line drug to artesunate-amodiaquine combination as first line drug including management of Adverse Drug Events and reporting.

        vi. Improve clinical-case management.

It is interesting to note that Ashiedu-Keteke, an intervention sub-metro that had focused on insecticide-treated nets, in the earlier study had fallen behind most of the other health districts in insecticide-treated nets availability and needed renewed attention.

In terms of malaria clinical-case management, the region reported in 2008 that

> There continues to be a problem of very low confirmation of malaria diagnoses. Most cases reported as malaria are best labeled "febrile illness presumed malaria." Only 5.7% of cases diagnosed as malaria were confirmed. Thus, even though overall there were more reported cases of malaria in 2008 than in previous years, it is uncertain how much of this was a real rise in cases and how much of it was a rise in diagnosis. Much work also still remains to be done to improve the quality and completeness of routine data reporting.

---

[1]This contrasts sharply with the 2006 reported use of insecticide-treated nets in the Greater Accra region of about 16% for under 5 children, the second lowest among the regions of Ghana (UNICEF, 2007).

Among the priorities in the Greater Accra region for 2008 were:

Manage and Improve Resource Generation
Specific objectives were:

1. Improve the availability, distribution, and management of human resources in the region.

2. Improve the availability, distribution, and management of essential equipment, tools, and supplies in the region and reduce the incidence of stock outs and non-availability of essential logistics, equipment and supplies.

3. Improve the availability, management, and use of transport in the region.

Despite overall personnel increases, the region still lacked adequate professional and technical staff to cope with the increasing ambulatory and inpatient clinical care workload especially with the introduction of the National Health Insurance Scheme. Most of increases in personnel were at the sub-professional and paraprofessional levels. Urbanization had also exacerbated the problems of mal-distribution of professionals within the region and the brain drain of professionals had continued. The 2009 regional report did not touch on the issues of pay levels, promotions, and media promotion priorities, which were not controlled at the regional level. However, some of these issues of overworked and undermotivated staff still seemed evident in various regional reports for 2007 and 2008.

CQI ELSEWHERE IN GHANA

Even though the study of malaria services reported here was not continued due to lack of funding and lack of interest within the health sector, external funding and support staff for CQI-oriented programs have been supplied by a number of international organizations. Dr. Agyepong's staff have recently received funding from The Netherlands to apply CQI as a managerial tool for human-resource management in the Greater Accra and Northern regions. IHI has had a project in Ghana, called Five Alive!, which includes CQI in collaboration with the Catholic Health Service in two northern provinces. In addition, a Management Science for Health and the USAID Leadership Development program focused on

HIV/AIDS and maternal health have had programs with CQI components, which were operating in Egypt and are now being implemented in Ghana. These use both expatriates and experienced implementers to supply the training and support that had been added to the duties of the Dangme West staff during the study reported earlier.

CASE ANALYSIS

This case reports on an extensive and experimental set of applications of improvement techniques to Ghana's malaria-control program. The experiment was ambitious, perhaps too ambitious, and many systemic problems were highlighted. Each local team was allowed to choose a part of the program to improve in their district or sub-metro. Facilitators were provided from a nearby district and a normal CQI process was followed. Measurement of impact was very difficult and institutionalization did not appear to occur. Dr. Agyepong is currently the regional health director and continues to support the use of CQI, but the strongest other support for the approach appears to be coming from outside the country. One way to dig into this case is to ask yourself the question, "If I were able to run such an experiment today, to make a business-case for quality improvement in Ghana, how would I realistically go about it?"

ASSIGNMENT QUESTIONS

1. In the report of the results of the initial study there were three recommendations:

   • That the study be continued for up to three to five years.

   • That the effort go region-wide with comparison being made to a region without the CQI program.

   • That a regional CQI training team be established so that the trainers did not have to neglect their duties in their own district.

   What do you think of these recommendations?

2. The tension between the senior authorities in health care and the provider cadre seems common in less-developed countries. What seems to be behind it? How might CQI contribute to its amelioration?

3. The earliest study reported here showed the negative effects of the "cash-and-carry" system. How has the introduction of the Ghana health-insurance program affected quality, both negatively and positively?

4. Over a ten-year period the use of CQI in Ghana's Greater Accra region has been a management strategy. What are its strengths and weaknesses in this environment?

5. The Five Alive! program began as an improvement effort in 2008 in rural northern Ghana, eventually partnering with IHI and the Ministry of Health and the Catholic health system, which provides about a third of the care in Ghana. What would you suggest they learn from these earlier experiences?

6. What do you consider to be the controllable variables at the regional level in Ghana that should be studied in support of an expanded quality-improvement effort?

CLASS EXERCISE

Research the current status of health care in Ghana in general and of malaria control specifically. Which of the issues of concern today seem amenable to a CQI approach? What inferences can you draw from the case and this exercise about the applicability of CQI in resource-restricted countries?

ACKNOWLEDGMENTS

The investigation reported here received support from the UNICEF/ World Bank/UNDP/WHO Special Programme for Research and Training in Tropical Diseases (TDR).

ORGANIZING FOR CONTINUOUS QUALITY IMPROVEMENT

Over the last 20 years in the evolution of CQI many ways of organizing for improvement have emerged. The variety of approaches has been accelerated by the blending of patient-safety concerns with continuous quality-improvement efforts. There are too many possibilities to cover here with a limited set of cases, but the four cases allocated to Part II illustrate a wide variety of organizational situations and structures, which, although limited to the United States, have implications globally as well.

Case 5, The Intermountain Way to Positively Impact Costs and Quality, represents the strategy of enlisting virtually the whole organization in the development of evidence-based, effective protocols for a substantial portion of its clinical activity. As an integrated delivery system (IDS) Intermountain focuses on costs as well as revenues and outcomes and involves both its salaried and fee-for-service clinicians in research into process improvement. It can also integrate financial data and its electronic medical record systems across a large and stable set of subscriber patients. It is often considered as a model for bending the U.S. cost curve.

Case 6, Planning a Transition, involves a physician taking over an existing position as health and safety officer at a university teaching hospital. Although salaried physicians are the core staff in both cases, the degree of organizational control and the attitudes toward organizational learning are probably quite different in the two institutions. In many university settings the emphasis tends to be on developing individual intellectual capital and professional service revenues are allocated more directly to the fiefdoms of departments and even subspecialty divisions.

At Dawn Meadow Hospital (Case 7) one observes the involvement of the Board of Directors in the continuous-improvement process. The primary issue is how to aggregate and present command and control data to the top management of a community hospital as effectively as possible. Management wants to be informed, but the demands on board time and attention are great.

Case 8 looks at the seldom-seen workings of a large national health-insurance company. The company had a great deal of claims data but relatively little incentive at that point in time to mine it for quality-improvement purposes. The initiative was left up to the local medical directors. Three subsets of medical directors worked at different organizational levels within the company. The local level was concerned primarily with local physician relationships including geographic coverage and pricing of contracts. Medical directors at the regional level were concerned with clinical utilization and its impact on quality, while a headquarters unit was assigned the overall quality mission. The latter would appear to be concerned primarily with legal challenges to the company based on service issues. The class participants need to understand how this industrial-type assignment of roles and responsibilities creates both opportunities and challenges for effective quality improvement.

The Intermountain Way to Positively Impact Costs and Quality

Lucy A. Savitz

INTRODUCTION

Intermountain Healthcare is often cited as a leader in high-quality, lower-cost care (Bohmer, 2009; Staines, 2009) and a model for others in the United States. It shares many of the characteristics of highly regarded systems, including many salaried physicians, strong information technology and accounting systems, and a consistent long-term corporate strategy for improving care. But Leonhardt (2009) has reported that some experts consider Intermountain Healthcare more advanced than most in terms of its use of evidence-based medicine and the extent of its deployment of quality concepts throughout the organization.

> "It's the best model in the country of how you can actually change health care," Wennberg told me. I heard nearly the same argument from Anthony Staines, a health scholar and hospital regulator in Switzerland who recently completed a study of some of the world's most-admired hospitals. "Intermountain was really the only system where there was evidence of improvement in a majority of departments," Staines said. (Leonhardt, 2009, p. 3)

Leonhardt drew on interviews with such famous names in healthcare quality as Dr. John Wennberg at Dartmouth and Dr. Lucien Leape at Harvard. This case examines that internal quality, safety, and education system as it impacts clinical care.

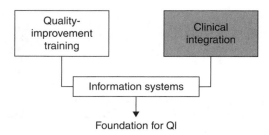

Figure 5–1   Mission Critical Support for Performance Excellence

It describes experiences of Intermountain Healthcare with evidence-based (EB) care process models (CPMs) that have reduced costs while maintaining and improving quality of care delivered to its patients. Figure 5–1 outlines the three major supports that underlie Intermountain's quality-improvement efforts:

- Clinical integration;

- Quality-improvement training; and

- Information systems.

Background

Intermountain Healthcare (IH) is a community-owned, integrated, non-profit healthcare system based in Salt Lake City, Utah. It was established in 1975 to own and operate 15 hospitals in Utah that had been established in local communities by The Church of Jesus Christ of Latter-day Saints, including LDS Hospital in Salt Lake City. The Church decided in 1975 that the operation of healthcare facilities was no longer critical to its religious mission. IH added an insurance arm, IHC Health Plans in 1983. In 2006, the insurance operations, which covered care to beneficiaries at both IH and other health organizations, were placed under separate management and renamed SelectHealth.

In early 2010, IH was the largest healthcare provider in the Intermountain West, with over 32,000 employees serving Utah and southeastern Idaho residents. Its resources included 24 hospitals, over 130 outpatient facilities, over 750 physicians and clinicians in the Intermountain Medical Group, a broad range of clinics and services, health-insurance plans from

SelectHealth, and the Intermountain Institute for Health Care Delivery Research (IHCDR). The IH corporate Web site defines its mission as one of providing "clinically excellent medical care at affordable rates in a healing environment that's as close to home as possible." It serves approximately 60% of Utah's population of approximately 2.8 million. Due to the low population density in the region, about half of its hospitals have less than 100 staffed beds. The system also includes Life Flight, a medevac unit with dispersed helicopters and fixed wing aircraft.

Quality-improvement History

Formal improvement efforts began in 1986 with the introduction of Quality, Utilization, and Efficiency (QUE) Studies involving health-services research looking at variations in clinical practice. Leading those QUE studies was Dr. Brent James, MD, MStat, a surgeon and biostatistician. He was a native of Blackfoot, Idaho with all three of his degrees from the University of Utah. After positions with the National Cancer Institute, the American College of Surgeons, and Harvard School of Public Health, he had returned to Salt Lake City in 1986 as IH's Director of Medical Research and Continuing Medical Education. One attraction for him was that IH had been a leader with electronic medical records (EMRs). Fortunately, it also had an activity-based accounting system, which had been implemented throughout the organization.

After attending a lecture by Dr. Deming who argued that higher quality could lower costs, Dr. James successfully tested that idea and began to add cost data on individual clinical conditions and their treatments to his studies. The organization responded to the Total Quality Management (TQM) movement in 1988 by establishing a Quality Council, approving a Quality Mission Statement, and placing responsibility for TQM with the Vice President for Professional Services. Quality educational efforts were expanded in 1990 with the establishment of the IHCDR, which began to offer internal education programs.

In 1992, the first Advanced Training Program in Health Care Delivery Improvement (ATP) was offered beginning with senior managers. It was followed two years later by "An Introduction to Clinical Quality Improvement" course for physicians. This 20-day course was followed by a 9-day mini-ATP course in 1999 and "A Culture of Patient Safety" course for physicians in 2005.

The mission of the ATP is:

- To recommend strategic priorities regarding health care delivery and outcomes research, based on community needs within a managed care environment.

- To provide data, statistical analyses, and coordination to internal and external health care delivery and outcomes research efforts that advance Intermountain's strategic objectives.

- To provide research, technical support, and education for Intermountain's Total Quality Management strategy.

- To seek external collaborations and funding to achieve the specified objectives, with the approval of the Institute's administrative leadership for specific projects.

The Institute currently offers half-, 2-, 9-, and 20-day courses to internal and external participants. Specialized frontline staff training offered in a series of 20-minute modules on DVD is also provided. The Institute is co-located with IH senior administration at a central office in a downtown Salt Lake City facility.

The Change to Clinical-Care Management and Integration

In 1991, IH formed a Core Quality Committee. Then-CEO Scott Parker requested that 40 senior IH executives, including himself, attend a special offering of the IH Facilitator Workshop Series (involving 4 sessions totaling 8 days). During that period, those managers reached consensus that clinical care (vs. facility management) was the core of their business and that protocols were central to improvement (Bohmer and Edmondson, 2003). Clinicians were involved further in 1992 through a special version of the Facilitator Workshop series. Since then, there has been widespread participation of professionals and administrators in the ATP workshops that require a clinical-improvement project. The set of administrators, physicians, and nurses who attended those early programs and completed their own projects spread commitment to clinical management throughout the organization between 1992 and 1995. Literally thousands of administrative and facilities-oriented improvement projects were undertaken and some 65 clinical protocols had been developed and implemented. By 2003, these early adopters had produced about $20 million in net annual savings in a clinical operating budget and significant gains in clinical quality (Bohmer and Edmondson, 2003).

In 1995, Executive Vice President (later CEO) Bill Nelson questioned the strategy of many independent improvement projects. Management then focused in on a developing a comprehensive clinical-management model.

Since the quality movement's inception, most care-delivery organizations have focused exclusively on improvement. Few systems have built a comprehensive quality infrastructure (see Figure 5–1) that integrates this improvement work with preplanning design and postdevelopment control. In 1996, Intermountain began to implement such an integrated program—clinical integration—across its many inpatient and outpatient practices. Clinical integration depends on effective communication between frontline (microsystems) units of care—where new ideas are generated and implemented based on the needs of patients and clinical staff—and system-wide quality management infrastructure (mesosystems)—where large-scale resources support and coordinate frontline efforts (James and Lazar, 2007).

A Corresponding Improvement Structure

Key process analysis conducted by Dr. James and Dr. Dave Burton led to a phased implementation of nine clinical programs with staffing and technology to support evidence-based care and accelerated improvement. They are:

- Cardiovascular
- Oncology
- Women and Newborns
- Intensive Medicine
- Primary Care Pediatric Specialties
- Surgical Services
- Behavioral Health

There is also a Patient Safety Initiative functioning as a clinical program. Clinical programs are staffed with a medical director, nurse administrator, statistician, and support team that includes information technology and finance personnel. Clinical program workgroups identify problems and work to develop, test, and implement EB-CPMs in a phased approach as warranted. Bohmer (2009) provides a more detailed description of clinical programs and the role of the Institute for Health Care Delivery.

Initial teams were established to develop CPMs for important segments of the Cardiovascular and Women and Newborns programs. Overall, there are some 60 or more teams at work on these clinical programs, each focused on a clinical service or work process.

Clinical programs were defined (by the templates used for Independent Contract Agreements for Physician Administrative Services) as interdisciplinary teams of providers of related specialties (e.g., cardiologists, cardiac surgeons, thoracic surgeons, and vascular surgeons), clinical operations personnel (e.g., nurses, EKG echo, cath lab technologists), and support staff (e.g., data manager, outcomes analyst, data architects, information technologists, education specialists, knowledge engineers) organized to develop and implement CPMs in order to set and achieve goals for improvement of outcomes.

There is a core team for each clinical program and work groups under each core team charged with studying specific processes. Figure 5–2 outlines this organizational structure.

Individual team members are charged with staying current on the evidence associated with a process or process component and with IH's current performance in order to signal which aspects to analyze and improve. While individual patients would have nearly unique process requirements, just as in a manufacturing job shop, studies have shown that 10% of the clinical processes account for 90% of the volume. James and Lazar refer to the result as mass customization (James and Lazar, 2007, p. 97).

These processes often occur and/or cut across traditional medical and professional departmental boundaries. For example, the mental health integration program is based in primary care and aimed at offering coordinated medical and mental health services in an integrated manner that best meets the needs of patients. The work of these teams involves not only protocol development and process analyses, but also identification of information needs and process quality and outcome measures, and the corresponding reports of patient satisfaction and resource utilization deemed

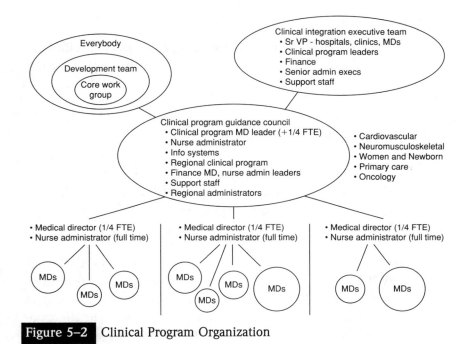

Figure 5-2 Clinical Program Organization

relevant to their efforts. In fact, the large spreadsheet used to track the status of the development teams has the following column heads:

- Name of team and CPM

- Date started

- Routinely reviewed metrics

  - **Clinical processes** encompass the volume of cases, tests, and procedures, length of stay, room utilization, and test results that do not directly measure the major clinical outcome.

  - **Process monitoring** refers to metrics for which there is no clinical guideline and therefore no judgment is being made about compliance (check yes or no).

  - **Process compliance** indicates whether the clinician followed the available clinical guideline (check yes or no).

- **Compliance rate** (actual)

- **Outcomes** encompass mortality, functional status, readmission rates, complication/infection rates, and test results that directly measure the major clinical outcome.

  - Cost

  - Satisfaction

- **External metrics**

  - CMS/Joint Commission measures (parties other than the clinical programs that receive regular reports on these metrics)

  - Board goal (check yes or no)

Clinicians in the relevant units are kept informed as the CPMs are refined and the evidence behind the recommendations is presented. After field testing, the CPMs are integrated into the information system to provide decision support and periodic prompts for the clinicians relating to high volume conditions, such as diabetes, asthma, and chronic heart failure. These prompts are designed to increase physician efficiency as well as quality of care, for example, by calculating recommended antibiotics and calculating dosages of drugs or initial clinical equipment settings based on current data in the patient's electronic medical record. The models are reviewed and updated approximately every six months.

The Compliance Problem

Intermountain's clinical investigators have long recognized the need to reduce variation in compliance with EB guidelines together with making these guidelines adequately explicit. A guideline is a systematic statement of policy rules or principles, representing state-of-the-art knowledge, which often directs a clinician where to go, but does not necessarily specify how to get there. Conversely, protocols or CPMs are precise and detailed plans for the study of a medical problem and/or for a regimen of therapy, indicating how to get there. An adequately explicit protocol or CPM provides enough detail to lead different clinicians to the same patient-specific decision via a reproducible clinical decision method. Clinical decision support (CDS) tools can then include all the ways in which healthcare knowledge is represented in health-information systems. The advantages of EB-CPMs are that they:

- Provide readily accessible references and allow access to knowledge in guidelines that have been selected for use in a specific clinical context;

- Often improve the clarity of a guideline;

- Can be tailored to a patient's clinical state; and

- Propose timely decision support that is specific for a patient.

Key steps of IH's strategy for developing such protocols or CPMs include:

- Identify the problem;

- Establish the evidence base; and

- Develop, test, and implement using quality-improvement tools (e.g., Six Sigma—define, measure, analyze, improve, control; or PDSA).

Evidence-Based Care Process Model: Examples

Five examples of Intermountain Healthcare EB-CPMs are provided in Table 5–1, with indication of clinical program, cost drivers impacted, observed cost savings, and scope. While many more CPMs have been implemented across IH clinical programs, this sample demonstrates that the common cost drivers targeted are reduced length of stay (LOS), readmissions, and emergency room visits. Unfortunately, given reimbursement perversities in the current dispersed U.S. delivery system, their implementation in nonintegrated systems will also require modified incentives to coordinate care and minimize financial penalties when achieving such cost savings, such as shifting care across the continuum from inpatient to outpatient service.

Dr. Carrie Byington's[1] work with the Care of the Febrile Infant EB-CPM provides a specific example. Dr. Byington practices at Intermountain's Primary Children's Medical Center (PCMC) and is a clinical leader

---

[1]Professor of Pediatrics and Infectious Disease at the University of Utah.

Table 5-1   Examples of Evidence-Based Care Process Models at
Intermountain

Evidence-Based Care Process Model	Clinical Program	Cost Driver(s) Impacted	Observed Cost Savings	Scope
Care of the Febrile Infant	Pediatrics	Avoided unnecessary admissions, reduced readmission, avoided adverse events	$3,000 per infant→$6 million per year to IH system; extrapolated to $2 billion per year for the U.S.*	4 hospitals
Multi-disciplinary Colon Surgery	Surgical Services	ALOS, readmission	$1,534 decreased hospital cost per admission; 1.7% reduction in 30-day readmission rate→$1.3 million estimated savings to IH system	System-wide
Management of Elective Labor Induction	Women & Newborns	ALOS	$100 per case cost savings & CPM non-compliance went from 28% to 2%→$600,000 per year savings to IH system	System-wide
Achieving Optimal Extubation Times for Patients Following Surgery	Cardiovascular	Reduction in ICU and hospital LOS	Median extubation time <7 hours for CABG→$20,000 per patient at IH	System-wide
Mental Health Integration (MHI)	Primary Care	Reduction in ER Visits & ALOS	$667 per patient with depression Dx if treated in MHI clinic vs. usual care at IH	69 clinics; clinics in 5 other states including FQHCs

Source: Adapted from data from Intermountain Healthcare

*670,000 infants × $3,000 = approximately $2 billion nationally.

in the Pediatric Clinical Program. Impetus for Dr. Byington's problem identification (Byington, 2004) in addressing care of the febrile infant is attributable to knowledge that:

- Expert (Rochester) guidelines that address the issues of diagnostic testing and hospitalization for febrile infants were published in 1993.

- Other existing guidelines, developed before 1990, provide no information regarding viral diagnostic testing or management of infants with confirmed viral illness who make up the majority of the group.

- The ability to rapidly diagnose viral illness has changed significantly.

- Physicians need guidance regarding the appropriateness of viral diagnostic tests and implications of positive/negative test results on risk for serious bacterial infection (SBI).

This University of Utah/Intermountain EB-CPM was developed using an EB-CPM derived from prospective research together with a Six Sigma process. Fever in infants 1–90 days of age is one of the most common reasons for medical encounters (i.e., 20% of physician visits and 58% of all Emergency Department (ED) visits at PCMC). Fever of $\geq 38°C$ is associated with SBIs—bacteremia, meningitis, and urinary tract infection (UTI)—and UTI is the most common SBI. Patient records showed that only 49% of febrile infants managed in hospital-based outpatient facilities had both a complete blood count (CBC) and a urinalysis (UA), as recommended by guidelines. This understanding of the problem led Dr. Byington's team to conduct the following analyses:

- Reanalysis of Rochester Criteria and risk for SBI;

- Analysis of age and risk for SBI;

- Analysis of viral diagnostic testing and risk for SBI;

- Analysis of CBC and UA as predictors for SBI; and

- Analysis of missed SBI.

Figures 5–3 and 5–4 show algorithms developed by the team for use with febrile infants presenting at the ED and in the inpatient setting.

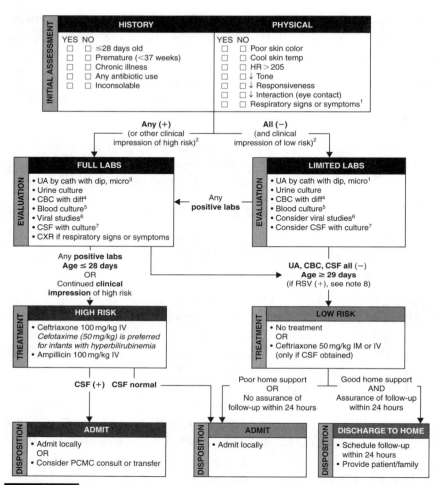

Figure 5-3 Algorithm: Emergency Care of Febrile Infants 1–90 Days Old

Sixteen peer-reviewed publications document this foundational work to develop and guide clinicians in an adequately explicit protocol that incorporates state-of-the-art medical knowledge and more newly developed laboratory testing capabilities. From this, the work in building the evidence base led to the development, testing, and spread of a CPM and standing orders involving CBC and urine analysis of febrile infants (approximately $60/patient tested), which seems minor relative to the estimated cost of $1 million for a missed case of meningitis. Key quality

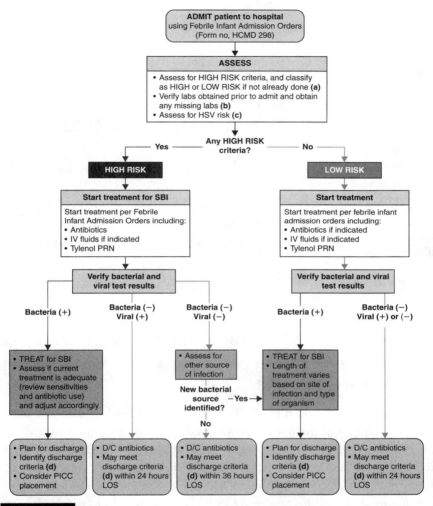

Figure 5–4 Algorithm: Inpatient Care of Febrile Infants 1–90 Days Old

measures used to monitor the process and clinical compliance with the CPM include:

- Receive core laboratory tests and viral testing as indicated;

- Admit patients at high risk for SBI as indicated by CPM threshold;

- Give appropriate antibiotics per CPM;

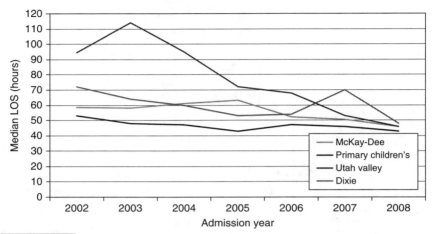

Figure 5–5   Median LOS for Febrile Infant with Negative Cultures by
Admission Year

Source: Intermountain Institute for Health Care Delivery Research, by Analyst K. Valentine, MS

- Stop antibiotics within 36 hours for febrile admission with bacterial
  negative cultures; and

- Length of stay (LOS) 42 hours or less.

Appropriate evaluation in 100% of infants is the goal. Figure 5–5 presents the changes in median LOS observed across four facilities over time,
documenting achieved decreases in LOS variation. These data warrant
replication in adult ED settings outside the children's hospital setting
where the EB-CPM was developed. Cost drivers targeted included: patient
volume, prolonged/unnecessary LOS, reduced repeat ED visits and readmissions, decreased morbidity/mortality, and minimized family burden.

The overall impact on costs of the Care of the Febrile Infant CPM
includes:

- Getting infants from a 3-day (mean 69-hour stay) to a 36-hour
  stay—this saves $3,000/infant (note that societal vs. payer savings
  would be much larger; however, this represents a loss in hospital revenues given reimbursement perversity);

- Ten percent of infants develop a fever in the first 90 days;

- Decreased readmission; and

- Less adverse events, including preventable bacterial infection.

The Care of the Febrile Infant EB-CPM has been tested at four Intermountain facilities with similar quality and cost results. Drs. Byington and the case author have been awarded a grant from the Agency for Healthcare Research and Quality to expand this EB-CPM, document the cost effectiveness across Intermountain facilities, and assess dissemination of an EB-CPM across IH and to external systems of care. Most notably, this EB-CPM was adopted by the American Board of Pediatrics for Maintenance of Certification requirements.

Caveats

EB healthcare does not spread automatically (Dopson and Fitzgerald, 2005); diffusion of such innovations will require national attention, training, and perhaps national priority setting. As described by Bohmer (2009) and Staines (2009), Intermountain Healthcare provides:

- Supportive infrastructure and culture for improvement;

- Commitment from leadership; and

- Necessary staff training, education, and feedback information.

The question at hand is how much of the Intermountain savings can be realized by adopting clinics, hospitals, and health systems. As shown by the Institute for Healthcare Improvement in its 100,000 Lives Campaign (Wachter and Pronovost, 2006), improvements can be realized across disparate systems of care when there is a focused effort; we have also seen others show improvements from adopted models with grant funding. Dr. Alan Morris has reported replicable results across disparate care settings for his eProtocol-insulin (another example)—LDS Hospital, National University Hospital in Singapore, University of Virginia, Baystate Medical Center (Morris *et al*, 2008). The real, unanswered question is how sustainable are these cost savings beyond the focused implementation initiative and/or grant award given the perversities of U.S. payment incentives.

Deeper Understanding of the Supporting System

Supportive Infrastructure and Culture for Improvement

In 1993, IH invited physicians to participate more fully in the operation and governance of the organization. As of April 1, 2010, 6 of the 22 member board of trustees were physicians as was the President and CEO, Charles W. Sorenson, with the remaining seats occupied by volunteer community leaders and IH senior management. In addition, many clinical staff and hundreds of community members served on the boards of local facilities.

Its quality efforts have been going forward for decades, especially through training programs of Institute for Healthcare Delivery Research, led personally by Dr. James. IH management has supported the quality effort through heavy investments in information systems, clinical studies, process and accountability measures, and aligned incentives and organizational structures. Well over 500 employees have completed the ATP course and have formed an enthusiastic core of implementers. All participants in the Guidance Councils and improvement teams are expected to have completed ATP training. Few doubt that this has worked well, although there are those who would question whether its protocol-based CPMs are warranted. Some have framed that debate as a battle between systems analysis and physician intuition (Leonhardt, 2009).

Nonemployed Physicians

Many observers have attributed the effectiveness of integrated delivery systems like Kaiser Permanente, Geisinger Clinic, and Mayo Clinic in improving quality and lowering cost to their use of employed physicians. Employed physicians at IH have seemed to be generally involved in improvement efforts as they interact with management and regularly receive feedback on their performance and modest incentive payments. Large numbers of them have been through the Institute's training programs. However, they provide only about half of the system's patient care. Involvement of the nonemployed physicians who make up some two-thirds of the physicians using IH facilities has been a concern. One component of the IH strategy relevant to their possible leadership and involvement has been contracting with them separately for participating in a series of improvement committees and incorporating both groups of physicians into those deliberations and their implementation.

The extent to which nonemployed physicians have engaged in strategy deployment also varies. Despite the flexibility built into the system and its bottom-up development, an ongoing challenge is the perception of physicians outside the IH medical group that the clinical integration strategy comes at the cost of local and professional autonomy and micromanagement from high-level decisionmakers. IH has assumed that achieving improvements among those physicians closely aligned with the system will help to win over the rest. But will IH again need to change its relationship options to attract more physicians as employees or articulate strategies to develop more clinical champions among the nonemployed group? (Baker *et al.*, 2008, p. 174)

For the nonemployed physicians two characteristics have had to be addressed: (1) geography and (2) compensation. One might also add that it is likely that the nonemployed physicians are a self-selected group less subject to and probably more resistant to corporate controls.

Geography

Intermountain's base of employed physicians has tended to be centered in the large population centers and the nonemployed physicians more towards the periphery. In those outlying areas, the time cost of travel and the other demands on physician time can loom large. IH has considered a physician aligned if s/he billed more than $100,000 annually to IH's insurance plan, SelectHealth. Those physicians have their time for their services in the clinical program activities contracted for and paid for.

Compensation

The employed physicians typically receive a base salary, plus a modest incentive withhold. The nonemployed, aligned physicians are paid on a fee-for-service basis. For certain activities, they may also be paid on an hourly basis. They provide about 40% of the system's care. Some physician groups also receive performance bonuses. Compensation of IH managers includes incentives for meeting clinical as well as financial objectives and the Board spends much of its time reviewing clinical measures as well.

The Organization Behind the Clinical Program

How nonemployed physicians have been incorporated into the quality-improvement infrastructure can be seen from the contract templates that provide job descriptions for the following six physician administrative roles:

- Clinical Program Medical Director
- Clinical Program Guidance Team Chair
- Clinical Service Medical Director
- Clinical Program Development Team Chair
- Clinical Program Work Group Physician Expert
- Clinical Program Clinical Research Coordinator

That contract template also provides the following definitions:

- *Clinical Service*: A division of a Clinical Program consisting of Providers of a single specialty (e.g., cardiology) or closely related specialties (e.g., maternal-fetal medicine, obstetricians, family practice obstetrics providers, and certified nurse midwives), clinical operations personnel and support staff organized to develop and implement Care Process Models for Clinical Work Processes and/or Conditions within the purview of their specialty or closely related specialties.

- *Clinical Operations Officer*: The clinical manager (nurse or technologist) designated by the Administrative Officer to supervise the clinical operations aspects of a Clinical Program or clinical service within a Facility.

- *Clinical Work Process*: A grouping of all-patient refined diagnosis related groups ("APR-DRG") which are integral elements of a Care Process Model (e.g., Percutaneous Intervention – Ischemic Heart Disease).

- *Condition*: A grouping of clinically related diagnostic ICD-9s (e.g., Ischemic Heart Disease).

For each clinical program actively being worked on, there is a clinical program team at each of the three IH Regional urban hubs with a one-fourth full-time-equivalent (FTE) Medical Director. All three clinical program regional medical directors belong to that clinical program's system-wide Clinical Program Guidance Council with one classified as the one-fourth FTE Clinical Program Medical Director (Leader) or Chair. This structure deals in part with the geographic dispersion issue. Each regional team also has a full-time clinical operations manager and each guidance council has an assigned full-time statistician and at least one full-time data manager and meets monthly (James and Lazar, 2007). IH documents frequently present this structure with the diagram in Figure 5–2.

Once the clinical program structure is operating, each guidance council oversees a key process analysis, which leads them to set priorities for condition-based work processes, each to be managed by a development team. Each development team has a physician leader and a geographically balanced set of members, mostly physicians and nurses with front-line hands-on clinical experience with that care process. The development team also includes "knowledge experts," usually specialists from each region. If these physicians are nonemployees, they are compensated by the hour according to their prearranged contract with the regional administration.

Definitions and Position Descriptions

The contract template provides job descriptions for the various physician roles. For example, the position of a Clinical Service Medical Director includes the following administrative roles and responsibilities:

- *Facility Clinical Service Management Team*: whose purpose is to coordinate the efforts of Clinical Service physicians, clinical operations and support personnel within the Facility Service so as to provide:

  a. Implementation leadership and Data Feedback for Clinical Program Care Process Models;

  b. Collaborative development and implementation support for accreditation, compliance and patient safety initiatives for those that are not already included in Care Process Models that have been implemented; and

  c. Support for clinical research and graduate medical education (as applicable).

- *Enterprise-wide Clinical Program Development Team*: which consists of Facility Clinical Service Management Teams (Clinical Service Medical Directors and clinical operations counterparts) from each Facility which provides the Clinical Service whose purpose is to coordinate enterprise-wide efforts of the specialty-specific subdivisions of the Clinical Program, including, but not limited to:

  a. Setting annual outcome and process goals (subject to approval of the Clinical Program Guidance Team);

  b. Approving priorities recommended by Clinical Program Work Groups and participating with them (as assigned reviewers) in the development of Care Process Models;

  c. Working collaboratively with enterprise-wide leaders to develop recommendations regarding clinical research and graduate medical education for the Clinical Service;

  d. Recommending infrastructure priorities for the Clinical Program Guidance Team (e.g., capital expenditures for facilities and equipment; electronic infrastructure pertaining to the Clinical Service); and

  e. Monitoring progress in implementation and accomplishment of Clinical Service goals (outcomes reports and work plan progress).

Data Feedback provided by:

1. Assisting in the development within the Clinical Program Guidance Team and Development Teams of standardized measurement systems and outcomes reports;

2. Presenting Clinical Program outcomes reports in Facility medical staff department, division/section or other meetings relevant to specialists who belong to the Clinical Service; and

3. Providing individual mentoring to members of the Clinical Service to assist them in improving outcomes. (IH, 2008, pp. A-S-3i-ii)

Intellectual Property

The contract templates also make it clear that, while there is the desire to share information through customary professional channels such as journals

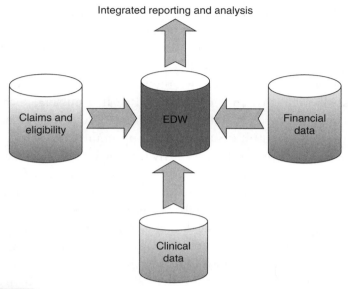

Integrated reporting and analysis

Figure 5–6 Data and Reporting

and meetings, the organization is a learning one that is engaged in developing and preserving its intellectual capital and deploying that capital to improve its services and enhance its reputation as a deliverer of services.

The concept of clinical integration clearly includes the notion that the implementation of evidence-based medicine is an institutional responsibility rather than the responsibility of the individual physician. That being said, the EB-CPM protocols and decision support tools all include the opportunity for the physician to deviate from the protocol, but require documentation of that decision. It facilitates learning by pointing out where protocols could be improved and to respond to the situation with the individual patient who is another source of variation through co-morbidity or through genomic or situational differentiation.

Information Feedback

IH has a highly developed electronic medical record (EMR) system. It is designed to allow effective feedback in a variety of formats. This is achieved by having the capability for an electronic data warehouse (EDW) allowing integration of EMR information with insurance claims data and with activity-based cost information. Figure 5–6 provides a schematic of this system.

The EDW provides the capacity to create registries that generate reports to support population-based management (Figure 5–7) with summary information about complex patients (Figure 5–8) and a worksheet with suggested responses (Table 5–2). For example, in the case of this patient presenting the increasing symptoms of depression, the worksheet indicates what information is available and what is missing, such as the patient's height. These are linked, electronic reports that provide clinicians with drill-down abilities that support optimum care.

The responsible work groups regularly (usually monthly) review population-based reports to look for outliers and opportunities for process improvements. For example, Leonhardt (2009) reports on how the labor-and-delivery committee responded to data that an obstetrician outside Salt Lake City had a number of deliveries that were taking longer than average and a relatively large number of Cesarean sections. The organization has been largely successful in reducing inductions done before 39 weeks from 30% in 2001 to less than 2% by 2010, thereby reducing C-sections and respiratory problems correspondingly. The committee chair wrote the doctor about the findings and he argued that the data was in error. The information system enabled the committee to respond with a complete list of his deliveries that were in question and also a comparison with other obstetricians in the system as well as a request that he identify which cases were classified in error. Physician acceptance of this information system has been high because it has taken productivity into account and allows physician override in almost all cases. The latter is a conscious component of the IH strategy as a continuously learning and improving organization.

CASE ANALYSIS

The EB-CPM approach has been successful at Intermountain Healthcare following more than two decades of effort. The interesting question will be its reproducibility throughout the U.S. healthcare system. Some observers will attribute its success in part to the geography, demography, and culture of the region and to self-selection by its providers. On the other hand, IH fits the description of the type of system that many management gurus have recommended for the U.S. health system. An

Intermountain Primary Care Clinical Programs: Patients with Depression
Reporting Period starting: 01-Apr-2007
Physician ID: -48xx

ID No	Sex	Age	Birth dt	PCP last non mh	PCP last mh	Last phq9	Severity	Symptom	phq9 count	Last mh visit	pvdr type	inpt dt	inpt ct	er dt	er ct	RX order dt	RX order	Order pvdr	RX fill dt	RX fill	Fill pvdr
	F	62		12/18/07	11/7/07	11/8/07	27	9	1	7/11/08	PSYCHOL					4/30/08	DIVALPROEX SODIUM, 500MG				
	M	62		10/5/07	11/15/07	11/16/07	25	9	1	11/28/07	Other								11/19/08	ALPRAZOLAM, 0.5MG	30×05
	F	33		4/2/08	2/28/08	2/29/08	23	8	2	3/27/08	PSYCHOL					9/17/08	BUSPIRONE HCL, 10MG CITALOPRAM	80×0 82×4	7/7/08	ALPRAZOLAM, 0.5MG CITALOPRAM	80×0 82×4
	M	50		8/18/08	8/18/08	7/8/08	22	8	2	9/25/08	PSYCHOL			6/26/08	1	11/15/07	HYDROBROMIDE, 20MG	82×4	11/15/07	HYDROBROMIDE, 20MG	82×4
	M	22		11/15/07	11/15/07	11/16/07	22	8	1												
	M	51		8/18/08	6/16/08	6/16/07	21	7	1							6/16/08	ALPRAZOLAM, 0.5MG	82×4	6/16/08	ALPRAZOLAM, 0.5MG	82×4
	F	46		9/8/08	9/8/08	9/8/08	21	7	1							9/8/08	TRAZODONE HCL, 50MG	82×4			
	M	31		8/27/08	8/27/08	8/28/08	21	7	1							4/2/08	BUPROPION HCL, 150MG CITALOPRAM	82×4 82×4	4/2/08	BUPROPION HCL, 150MG CITALOPRAM	82×4 82×4
	F	37		4/2/08	4/2/08	4/3/08	20	7	1							8/27/08	HYDROBROMIDE, 20MG	82×4	8/27/08	HYDROBROMIDE, 20MG	82×4
	F	17		8/27/08	8/27/08	8/28/08	20	8	1												
	M	36		8/20/08	5/28/08	5/29/07	19	7	1	9/15/08	LCSW					8/12/08	BUPROPION HCL, 300MG	29×56			
	M	19		7/2/08	12/31/07	1/1/08	18	6	2	2/28/08	LCSW					12/31/07	SERTRALINE HCL, 50MG	82×4			
	F	16		8/14/08	8/14/08	7/15/08	18	6	2	9/16/08	PSYCHOL					8/14/08	ALPRAZOLAM, 0.5MG	82×4			
	M	33		3/19/08	3/19/08	3/20/08	17	6	2							2/28/08	ALPRAZOLAM, 0.25MG	2×8	3/1/08	ALPRAZOLAM, 0.25MG	2×8
	F	23		4/24/08	4/24/08	4/25/08	17	6	1							4/24/08	SERTRALINE HCL, 50MG	82×4	4/24/08	SERTRALINE HCL, 50MG	82×4
	M	56		8/18/08	8/18/08	8/19/08	14	3	1							8/18/08	VENLAFAXINE HCL, 75MG	82×4	8/18/08	VENLAFAXINE HCL, 75MG	82×4
	M			5/30/08	5/30/08	5/31/08	14	7	2							5/30/08	CITALOPRAM HYDROBROMIDE, 20MG	82×4	5/30/08	LORAZEPAM, 0.5MG	82×4
	F	38		9/23/08	8/25/08	8/25/08	13	5	1							8/25/08	SERTRALINE HCL, 50MG	82×4 82×4	8/25/08	SERTRALINE HCL, 50MG	82×4
	M	22		1/18/08	1/18/08	1/19/08	12	5	1												
	F	28		7/10/08	4/8/08	4/8/08	12	3	1												
	F	59														4/7/08	CITALOPRAM HYDROBROMIDE, 20MG	82×4	4/7/08	CITALOPRAM HYDROBROMIDE, 20MG	82×4

For patient and provider privacy purposes some data has been masked or altered.

Figure 5-7   Selected Population from Registry

Intermountain Healthcare-MHI Patient Report

All Visits (1 year)

Pt ID	VISIT_DT	PRVDR_ID	CLINIC_NM	MED_DIR_REGION	LAST_NM	FIRST_NM	PRMRY_SPCLTY_CD	PRVDR_TYPE	PT_TYPE_CD
	2/7/08	82×4	IMG - Adamson	URBAN NORTH	Welbee	Mark	FP	PCP	Non-MH
	2/7/08	82×4			Welbee	Mark	FP	PCP	O
	2/28/08	82×4	IMG - Adamson	URBAN NORTH	Welbee	Mark	FP	PCP	Non-MH
	2/28/08	82×4			Welbee	Mark	FP	PCP	O
	2/28/08	28×16	IMG - Adamson	URBAN NORTH	Housa	Joe	FP	PCP	Non-MH
	3/8/08	28×16	IMG - Adamson	URBAN NORTH	Housa	Joe	FP	PCP	Non-MH
	3/11/08	69×4			Froid	Syd	PSY	PSYCHOL	O
	3/27/08	69×4			Froid	Syd	PSY	PSYCHOL	O
	4/2/08	82×4	IMG - Adamson	URBAN NORTH	Welbee	Mark	FP	PCP	Non-MH

PHQ9 History (2 years)

Pt ID	TEST_DT	TEST_NM	SEVERITY	SYMPTOM
	2/8/08	phq9	21	8
	2/29/08	phq9	23	8

All Rx Ordered and/or Filled (1 year)

Pt ID	Med dt	Order Name	Order Dt	Order Prvdr	Order Qty	Order Days Supply	Fill Name	Fill Dt	Fill Prvdr	Fill Days Supply
	10/28/07						ALBUTEROL, 90MCG	10/28/07	17	3
	2/7/08	CITALOPRAM HYDROBROMIDE, 20MG	2/7/08	82×4	30	30				
	2/28/08	SERTRALINE HCL, 50MG	2/28/08	82×4	30	30				
	3/8/08						CITALOPRAM HYDROBROMIDE, 20MG	3/8/08	30	30
	4/13/08						SERTRALINE HCL, 50MG	4/13/08	30	30
	5/27/08						ALBUTEROL, 90MCG	5/27/08	17	3
	6/28/08	ALBUTEROL, 90MCG	6/28/08	28×16	17	15				
	6/28/08	AMOXICILLIN TRIHYDRATE, 500MG	6/28/08	28×16	60	10				
	6/28/08	FEXOFENADINE HCL, 60MG	6/28/08	28×16	30	30				

For patient and provider privacy purposes some data has been masked or altered.

Figure 5-8 Drilling Down, Single Patient History

Table 5-2 Comprehensive Patient Detail

11/05/2008   *PATIENT WORKSHEET*   *Comprehensive*

Problems
Depression

Active Medications
1. 'Chantix 0.5mg and 1mg starter pack': No dose found: As Directed
2. Prozac (Fluoxetine Hcl), 20Mg. Capsule. Oral; 1 CAPSULE (HARD, SOFT, ETC.): QD (daily)

Allergies
No Known Environmental Allergies
No Known Food Allergies
No Known Drug Allergies

Disease Management

Dysthymia	*Functional Difficulty*	
01/22/2008	Yes	Very
12/05/2007	Yes	Extreme
10/17/2007	Yes	Not At All

PHQ-9 Symptom Count		*PHQ-9 Severity Score*	
01/22/2008	9	01/22/2008	23
12/05/2007	4	12/05/2007	11
10/17/2007	1	10/17/2007	3
04/24/2006	2	04/24/2006	6

Preventive Care
Tetanus Vacc
Yes

Clinical Laboratory Data

Lipid Profile	*LDL (<100)*	*Trig (<150)*	*HDL (>45)*	*CHOL (<200)*	*TC/HDL Ratio*	*hsCRP*
No Data	—	—	—	—	No Data	No Data —

Fasting Blood Glucose	*2-Hr GTT*
No Data	No Data

Homocysteine
No Data —

(Continued)

Table 5-2 Continued

11/05/2008   *PATIENT WORKSHEET*   *Comprehensive*

Clinic Data

Date	Weight	BMI (<25)	Weight Class	Blood Pressure (<130/80 mmHg)	
01/22/2008	160.8 kgs	Need Ht	—	01/22/2008	118/74
12/05/2007	73.03 kgs	Need Ht	—	12/05/2007	126/76
10/17/2007	71.67 kgs	Need Ht	—	11/13/2007	145/70
06/22/2006	68.31 kgs	Need Ht	—	10/17/2007	110/78
05/19/2006	67.59 kgs	19	Normal	06/22/2006	114/70

Waist Circumference   <u>*Depression Screening*</u>

No Data   No Data

Blood Pressure Legend: *(H) = Home Reading (A) = Average Home Reading (C) = "In Control" selected for blood pressure data*

Reminders

Procedures

[ ] Tetanus Immunization - Suggested every 10 years.

Preventive

Entering height of patient once in CW will allow for BMI to be calculated.

obvious topic for classroom discussion is how it can be replicated suffi-
ciently to influence overall quality and to bend the cost curve.

This is one of the most studied healthcare organizations in the country because it has a long and effective history of continuous improvement.
Your task is to figure out what is behind that success, what is or is not
transferable to other settings, and how one decides which of its
approaches to adopt. It has not tried to replicate itself elsewhere. Organizations that have been successful and then attempted to replicate their
approach elsewhere in the U.S. have had a mixed set of outcomes.

ASSIGNMENT QUESTIONS

1. Compare the process of "clinical integration" at IH with the
   improvement process in your local settings.

2. What would it take to replicate this successful program in your
   local institutions?

3. It has taken over two decades to develop and implement this program at IH. How quickly could it be replicated at the institution
   that you had in mind in answering the preceding two questions?

4. Estimate the investment that IH is making to support "clinical
   integration."

5. What are the pros and cons of organizational learning vs. professional learning as outlined in the case? How can the two be kept
   complementary?

6. Read up about the concept of mass customization. How does the
   concept as it is applied at IH fit with what you found?

CLASS EXERCISE

Continue to update your knowledge of Intermountain Health. What has
been their influence on others? What do they appear to be working on
currently?

ACKNOWLEDGMENTS

The author wishes to give special thanks to Institute for Health Care Delivery Research analysts Erick Henry, Craig Gale, Karen Valentine, Thomas French, and Pascal Briot for providing summary results of clinical program CPMs. The author would also like to thank Dr. Brent James, Director of the Institute and Chief Quality Officer at Intermountain Healthcare, for his vision and leadership in providing analytic infrastructure to clinical programs as well as guidance in placing Intermountain's quality-improvement work on the national agenda. Finally, thanks to Dr. Carrie Byington and Dr. Alan Morris for agreeing to share their work that exemplifies the impact of EB-CPMs.

Planning a Transition

Gwenn E. McLaughlin

INTRODUCTION

In 2008, Gwenn McLaughlin, MD, was asked to consider taking on the duties of Chief Quality and Safety Officer for the 254-bed Holtz Children's Hospital, associated with the University of Miami Miller School of Medicine Medical School and the Jackson Health System. A pediatric intensivist and Professor of Clinical Pediatrics, she had been on the medical school faculty and hospital staff for almost 20 years, since completing her residency and fellowship elsewhere. During that period, she had participated in the clinical governance of the hospital in a number of ways, including the Pharmacy & Therapeutics Committee, the Credentials Committee, the electronic medical record implementation team, and director of quality improvement in the Pediatric Intensive Care Unit. With her husband established in his private medical practice and her children in college, she had recently completed all the course work for an MPH degree locally and was considering her career alternatives.

Job Descriptions

While she negotiated other terms and conditions of the job to assure continued income and an appropriate balance between clinical and administrative duties, she began to look at the position itself. She was provided the job description shown in Exhibit 6–1. After considerable discussion with the Hospital Chief of Staff and Chief Medical Officer, the job description given in Exhibit 6–2 emerged. It was further refined in 2009 as shown in Exhibit 6–3.

EXHIBIT 6–1

Initial Job Description for Chief Quality and Safety Officer

The Holtz Children's Hospital Chief and Safety Quality Officer will report to the Hospital Chief of Staff and work in coordination with the Hospital Chief Medical Officer to provide leadership for the Hospital's Quality and Safety Program. Working in partnership with Hospital leadership and medical staff leadership, the Chief Quality and Safety Officer will provide leadership in the development and measurement of the Hospital's approach to quality/performance improvement and medical safety.

This individual will:

1. Initiate and oversee the development of a comprehensive quality/performance improvement program.
2. In conjunction with the medical staff and Children's Hospital (CH) leadership, the Chief Quality and Safety Officer will direct and coordinate quality/performance improvement initiatives for the Children's Hospital.
3. In collaboration with clinical staff and service chiefs, participate in the development, monitoring, reporting, and improvement of activities related to clinical pathways and guidelines.
4. Foster and maintain collaborative relationships with external agencies, purchasers, and stakeholders related to quality/performance initiatives.
5. Chair the CH Quality and Safety Council and work with the council to establish quality/performance improvement priorities.
6. Lead the development of CH policies and procedures related to quality improvement/medical safety and participate as a stakeholder in the crafting of CH policies.
7. Ensure the development of such policies and secure overall Medical Center approval.
8. Monitor activities for and ensure compliance with laws, government regulations, Joint Commission requirements, and CH policies.
9. As directed, implement external and internal audits of Quality and Safety within the Children's Hospital.

EXHIBIT 6–2

Revised Job Description for Chief Quality and Safety Officer

The Holtz Children's Hospital Chief Quality and Safety Officer reports to the Hospital Chief of Staff and works in coordination with the Hospital Chief Medical Officer to provide leadership for the Hospital quality and safety program. Working in partnership with the Hospital leadership and the medical staff leadership, the Chief Quality and Safety Officer will provide leadership in the development and measurement of the Hospital's approach to quality/performance improvement and medical safety.

This individual will:

1. Initiate and oversee the development of a comprehensive quality performance improvement program that tracks both established nationally accepted and innovative locally developed quality indicators for the Children's Hospital.

2. In conjunction with the medical staff and CH leadership, implement patient safety initiatives in accordance with best practices as established by national bodies.

3. Lead the development of CH policies and procedures related to quality improvement/medical safety.

4. In conjunction with the medical staff and CH leadership, create and lead project improvement/process redesign teams to facilitate patient care and flow within the system.

5. In collaboration with medical staff, participate in the development of clinical pathways and guidelines.

6. Supervise the physician and nursing clinical educators in their role to educate the staff regarding best practices, clinical pathways, policies, and procedures.

7. Create monitoring programs to document compliance with best practices, clinical pathways, and hospital policies.

8. Review all incident reports and attend all root cause analyses to determine where there are systems problems that can be addressed.

(continues)

EXHIBIT 6-2

9. Foster and maintain collaborative relationships with external agencies, purchasers, and stakeholders related to quality/performance initiatives.
10. Chair the CH Quality and Safety Council and work with the council to establish performance improvement priorities.
11. Provide advice and direction for individual quality improvement teams to identify goals and facilitate implementation of the recommendations to achieve those goals.

EXHIBIT 6-3

Further Revised Description for Chief Quality and Safety Officer

The Holtz Children's Hospital Chief Quality and Safety Officer reports to the Hospital Chief Medical Officer and the Service Chief for Pediatrics to provide leadership for the Children's Hospital quality and safety program. Working in partnership with the Hospital leadership and the medical staff leadership, the Chief Quality and Safety Officer will provide leadership in the development and measurement of the Hospital's approach to quality/performance improvement and medical safety.

This individual will:

1. Initiate and oversee the development of a comprehensive quality performance improvement program that tracks both established nationally accepted and innovative locally developed quality indicators for the Children's Hospital.
2. In conjunction with the medical staff and CH leadership, implement patient safety initiatives in accordance with best practices as established by national bodies.
3. Lead the development or revision of CH policies and procedures related to quality improvement/medical safety.

(continues)

EXHIBIT 6–3

4. In conjunction with the medical staff and CH leadership, create and lead project improvement/process redesign teams to facilitate patient care and flow within the system.
5. In collaboration with medical staff, participate in the development of clinical pathways and guidelines.
6. Supervise the Quality Manager(s) in review of incidents, monitoring of quality indicators, performing quality audits and implementation of action plans derived from these data sources and their analysis.
7. Supervise the physician and nursing clinical educators in their role to educate the staff regarding best practices, clinical pathways, policies, and procedures.
8. Create monitoring programs to document compliance with best practices, clinical pathways, and hospital policies.
9. Assess the impact of CPOE on the care of children and work to maximize the potential for safe implementation.
10. Review all incident reports.
11. Conduct all root cause analyses to determine where there are systems problems that can be addressed.
12. Foster and maintain collaborative relationships with external agencies, purchasers, and stakeholders related to quality/ performance initiatives.
13. Chair the CH Quality and Safety Council and work with the council to establish performance improvement priorities.
14. Provide advice and direction for individual quality improvement teams to identify goals and facilitate implementation of the recommendations to achieve those goals.

CASE ANALYSIS

The role of safety and quality officer is a relatively new one for hospitals. There has long been the need to relate to The Joint Commission and other organizations demanding conformance quality. However, the quality movement in health care did not start out with such a position in mind. It has evolved in part because the regulators have asked institutions to show evidence of their involvement with improvement efforts. This case focuses on job description development while "taking over" this role. What are some other elements of taking over as the designated professional staff leader for quality in an institution?

ASSIGNMENT QUESTIONS

1. Review the job description in Exhibit 6–1. What definition of quality and safety does it represent? How would you want to change it, if you were thinking of taking the job?

2. Now consider the job description in Exhibit 6–2. What are the significant changes in the job that it suggests? Would it make it more attractive to you?

3. Now consider the job description in Exhibit 6–3. What are the significant changes in this iteration of the job description? Assuming that they were requested by Dr. McLaughlin, what do you think that she was trying to accomplish with those changes?

4. Which of the duties in that final job description would you personally like to handle or not handle? Why?

CLASS EXERCISE

Obtain the job descriptions for this or similar jobs from local institutions and circulate them in the class. Come to class prepared to contrast and compare them with the job descriptions in this case. What explicit or implicit criteria are you using to evaluate them? What would you recommend as a job description, if you were being considered for that job? Are you thinking about an ideal or about the process of "taking charge?"

Dawn Valley Hospital: Selecting Quality Measures for the Hospital Board

Joseph G. Van Matre, Karen E. Koch,
and Curtis P. McLaughlin

INTRODUCTION

Dr. Eli Harrington, Chair of the Board at Dawn Valley Hospital, requested that the management staff provide a monthly report for the Board as part of a dashboard presentation of a Balanced Scorecard for the Hospital. This was to include a representation of quality and safety at each major facility—the inpatient hospital and two off-site primary care clinics. The Board and the CEO, Mr. Donald Farrington, had been receiving a number of quarterly spreadsheets showing costs, operating efficiency, utilization, outcomes, process variables, customer satisfaction, and other numbers by facility. Some of this data was clearly related to quality, but Dr. Harrington believed that the information was not in its most useful form. He wanted the quality-related measures grouped together for focus and in a form that allowed comparisons to be made both within Dawn Valley and with other institutions. He also was concerned that the number of measures be "manageable." The task of developing the new quality and safety dashboard was assigned to Ms. Harriet Kleindorfer, RN, MPH, Director of Quality Improvement. She was aware that there were numerous aspects to the issue and that selection would be an arduous task. There was agreement in the literature that active hospital board reviews of quality and safety using dashboards were associated with better performance, but not on the best designs or measures (Denham, 2006; Kroch *et al.*, 2006; Jha and Epstein, 2010). She also knew of the relatively new composite indicators that might prove helpful in reducing the candidate set. The Joint Commission Glossary defines a composite measure as "a measure that combines the results of all process measures within a set into a composite rating." Most U.S. rating systems do not apply composite ratings to outcomes, although the Quality Adjusted Life Year (QALY) standard used around the world for comparative effectiveness studies is such a measure.

Mr. Farrington's instructions had been brief:

1. Present a clear and honest picture.

2. Don't overwhelm us with detail.

3. Try to use data and indicator sets that "we are likely to end up preparing for outsiders anyway."

4. We need indicators that "don't hop around a lot" so that trends will be visible.

The Emergency Department was not to be included for now because it was contracted out to a separate provider group. Still, she suspected that the Board might request data on the Emergency Department whenever there were complaints or their contract was up for renegotiation.

Ms. Kleindorfer also knew that the medical staff, including Dr. Harrington, would push back if physicians were required to enter new variables into the recently purchased electronic medical records (EMR) system. While the EMR system was now functioning pretty reliably, there were still some hard feelings about its negative impact on physician productivity during its first six months of implementation.

Possible Methods

Ms. Kleindorfer found a number of demonstrations and proposals out there for aggregate measures that could be used for pay-for-performance (P4P) and for guiding the selection of providers by third parties and consumers. Those that seemed most likely candidates for implementation in the future (with revisions of course) were:

1. National Hospital Quality Measures, which are reported on The Joint Commission "Quality Check" and the CMS "Hospital Compare" Web sites. Dawn Valley Hospital was already participating in this system, which pertained to in-hospital patients only.

2. The Joint Commission's ORYX Core Measures System, which allowed the hospital to report the data required by CMS and The Joint Commission, but allowed each hospital to select core measures and use them in combination with other optional measures. This might be a way around the fact that Dawn Valley might not have sufficient cases for some conditions to allow reliable and stable reporting.

Premier Hospital Quality Incentive Demonstration (HQID) is a demonstration program, which has gone on for a number of years. It uses composite measures for heart-attack care, heart-failure care, and pneumonia care. The indicators for this are listed in Exhibit 7–1. The APU (501B) column shows the original requirements under the Medicare Modernization Act of 2003, which closely parallel those of The Joint Commission as noted in the adjacent (JCAHO) column. The indicators for HQID and the HQID extension are noted in the remaining two columns.

Still, a fourth system was available called QUEST (Premier's Quality, Efficiency, and Safety with Transparency), which also used five sets of indicators:

- Mortality Ratio (risk adjusted)

- Appropriate Care—Evidence Based

- Cost of Care

- Harm Avoidance

- Patient Experience based on the standard Hospital Consumer Assessment of Healthcare Provider and Systems (HCAHPS) results

This would require agreement of all the major divisions of the hospital, which would have to be decided at the CEO or Board level. QUEST

EXHIBIT 7-1

Clinical Conditions and Measures for Reporting and Incentives—Year 4

Measure	APU (501 b) JCAHO	HQID Current	HQID Extension
Acute Myocardial Infarction (AMI)			
Aspirin at Arrival	✓	✓	✓
Aspirin Prescribed at Discharge	✓	✓	✓
ACEI/ARB for LVSD	✓	✓	✓
Beta Blocker at Arrival	✓	✓	✓
Beta Blocker Prescribed at Discharge	✓	✓	✓
Primary PCI Received within 90 minutes of Hospital Arrival	✓	✓	✓
Smoking Cessation Advice/Counseling	✓	✓	✓
Fibrinolytic received within 30 minutes of Hospital Arrival	✓	✓	✓
Inpatient Mortality Rate (JCAHO Risk Adjustment)[T,1]	✓	✓	✓
30 Day Mortality Rate[T]			T
Readmission within 30 Days Rate[T]			T
AHRQ Patient Safety Indicators (combined to a complication index)[T,2]			T
Isolated Coronary Artery Bypass Graft			
Aspirin Prescribed at Discharge		✓	✓
CABG Using Internal Mammary Artery		✓	✓
Prophylactic Antibiotic Received within 1 hour Prior to Surgical Incision	✓	✓	✓
Prophylactic Antibiotic Selection for Surgical Patients	✓	✓	✓
Prophylactic Antibiotic Discontinued within 48 hours of Surgery End Time	✓	✓	✓
Inpatient Mortality Rate (3M APR-DRG™ Risk Adjustment)			

(continues)

EXHIBIT 7–1

Continued

Measure	APU (501 b)	JCAHO	HQID Current	HQID Extension
Postoperative Hemorrhage or Hematoma				✓
Postoperative Physiologic and Metabolic Derangement			✓	✓
30 Day Mortality Rate[T]				T
Readmission within 30 Days Rate[T]				T
AHRQ Patient Safety Indicators (combined to a complication index)[T,2]				T
Heart Failure				
Evaluation of LVS Function	✓	✓	✓	✓
ACEI/ARB for LVSD	✓	✓	✓	✓
Detailed Discharge Instructions	✓	✓	✓	✓
Smoking Cessation Advice/Counseling	✓	✓	✓	T
30 Day Mortality Rate[T]				T
Readmission within 30 Days Rate[T]				T
AHRQ Patient Safety Indicators (combined to a complication index)[T,2]				T
Inpatient Mortality Rate[T] (AHRQ IQI)				
Hip and Knee Replacement[3]				
Prophylactic Antibiotic Received within 1 hour Prior to Surgical Incision	✓	✓	✓	✓
Prophylactic Antibiotic Selection for Surgical Patients	✓	✓	✓	✓
Prophylactic Antibiotic Discontinued within 24 hours of Surgery End Time	✓	✓	✓	✓
Recommended Venous Thromboembolism Prophylaxis Ordered	(Jan 07)	(Jan 07)		
(Required for APU and JCAHO effective Jan 2007 discharges)	✓	✓		
Appropriate Venous Thromboembolism Prophylaxis within 24 hours	(Jan 07)	(Jan 07)		

(continues)

EXHIBIT 7–1

Continued

Measure	APU (501 b)	JCAHO	HQID Current	HQID Extension
Pre- and Postoperative Period (Required for APU and JCAHO effective Jan 2007 discharges)				
Postoperative Hemorrhage or Hematoma			✓	✓
Postoperative Physiologic and Metabolic Derangement			✓	✓
Readmission within 30 days to Acute Care Inpatient Rate[4]			✓	✓
AHRQ Patient Safety Indicators (combined to a complication index)[T,1]				T
Pneumonia				
Appropriate Initial Antibiotic Selection	✓	✓	✓	✓
Influenza Vaccination	✓	✓	✓	✓
Oxygenation Assessment	✓	✓	✓	✓
Pneumococcal Vaccination	✓	✓	✓	✓
Smoking Cessation Advice/Counseling	✓	✓	✓	✓
30 Day Mortality Rate[T]				T
Readmission within 30 Days Rate[T]				T
AHRQ Patient Safety Indicators (combined to a complication index)[T,1]				T
Inpatient Mortality Rate[T] (AHRQ IQI)				T

[T] Measure is important to evaluate for future use and will be used for test purposes only. Measure will not be used in the Composite Quality Score calculation for incentive payment.

[1] 30 day Mortality rate—uses CMS hierarchical model based on administrative data
[2] All applicable AHRQ Patient Safety Indicators will be applied to each appropriate clinical area (AMI, Isolated CABG, HF, PN, and H/K). See PSI list.

(continues)

EXHIBIT 7–1

Continued

[3]Hip and Knee population is expanded to all payers effective with October 1, 2006 discharges.

430 day Readmission rate—uses Premier data risk-adjusted with 3M APR-DRG[TM] methodology

Agency for Healthcare Research and Quality (AHRQ) Patient Safety Indicators (PSIs)

PSIs applicable to the HQID populations:

1. Complications of Anesthesia
2. Death in Low Mortality DRGs
3. Decubitus Ulcer
4. Failure to Rescue
5. Foreign Body Left during Procedure
6. Iatrogenic Pneumothorax
7. Selected Infections due to Medical Care
8. Postoperative (postop) Hemorrhage of Hematoma
9. Postop Hip Fracture
10. Postop Physiologic and Metabolic Derangement
11. Postop Pulmonary Embolism (PE) or Deep Vein Thrombosis (DVT)
12. Postop Respiratory Failure
13. Postop Sepsis
14. Technical Difficulty with Procedure
15. Transfusion Reaction
16. Postop Wound Dehiscence

The PSIs will be used to create a complication index which will be a risk-adjusted composite of all of the applicable PSIs for each specific clinical area at the hospital level.

Centers for Medicare and Medicaid Services (CMS)/Premier Hospital Quality Incentive Demonstration Project has been reporting a separate risk-adjusted mortality ratio for all hospital deaths together with a separate Core Measures composite score, which describes "appropriate care."

CMS Hospital Compare

This system allows professionals and consumers to compare hospitals on the Web. It does not attempt to provide composite ratings. It provides reporting of measures of process of care, outcome of care, patients' surveys, and Medicare payment and volume. As of 2010 its process of care measures includes:

- Seven measures related to heart-attack care;

- Four measures related to heart-failure care;

- Six measures related to pneumonia care;

- Eight measures related to their surgical-care improvement project; and

- Three measures related to asthma care for children only (added in 2009).

The outcomes of the care measures were 30-day risk-standardized readmission rates and mortality rates for heart attack, heart failure, or pneumonia. The patient survey results were based on the HCAHPS survey. The cost and volume data were for Medicare patients only, whereas the other data was based on all relevant patients or a sampling of records at large institutions. While these measures were already collected for The Joint Commission, CMS, and others, they were not aggregated into a single or a few numbers.

Joint Commission ORYX Core Measures

The Joint Commission has allowed hospitals the opportunity to mix and match sets of indicators, both core and noncore, to better align with their offerings. In addition to the indicators required under Compare, The Joint Commission also had core standards for stroke, venous thrombosis, pregnancy and perinatal care, hospital-based inpatient psychiatric services, and hospital outpatient departments. The outpatient standards pertained to both the management of chronic disease and disease prevention, so they could be applied to the primary care activities of the off-site outpatient clinics. The Joint Commission only required the reporting of four core measure sets and allowed the substitution of noncore indicators, about three noncore indicators for each core indicator set less than four. However, CMS requirements made it increasingly hard to avoid not reporting the five sets of indicators cited in preceding section. Still, there was no attempt by The Joint Commission to aggregate the core measures into composite measures.

Health Quality Incentive Demonstration

This P4P demonstration program started in 2003 and provided incentive payments based on an aggregate measure. For each condition a composite score was computed using an additive model for process variables and zero to three risk-adjusted outcome indices depending on the condition. Initially, five composite measures were used, associated with the following conditions:

- Acute myocardial infarction (8 process variables plus survival index)

- Coronary artery bypass surgery (5 process variables plus 3 outcome indices)

- Heart failure (4 process variables)

- Community-acquired pneumonia (7 process variables)

- Hip and knee replacement (3 process variables plus 3 outcome indices)

The Composite Quality Index for each condition was a weighted sum of the Composite Process Rate and the Risk-Adjusted Outcomes Index. Risk-adjusted survival rates were applied to acute myocardial infarction and coronary artery bypass grafts cases. One hip and knee replacement outcome measure was risk-adjusted readmissions 30-day post discharge. For coronary artery bypass and hip and knee replacement cases, two additional outcome measures were calculated: postoperative hemorrhage or hematoma and postoperative physiologic and metabolic derangement. Because low values of outcome measures are better and high values of process measures are better, the outcome variables were rescaled. The actual rates are subtracted from one to give the survival and avoidance indexes used in the composite measure. These five quality scores were averaged to get the institutional score used for reimbursement. Exhibit 7–2 illustrates the weighting process for hip and knee replacement at that time.

Sensitivity Concerns

One interesting aspect of the QUEST approach was that it used all-or-none measures in some process areas to aggregate data into composite measures rather than the additive approach in line with its objective of achieving "perfect care." This meant that one either met the full set of process objec-

---

EXHIBIT 7-2

Sample HQI Composite Quality Score Calculation for Premier Memorial Hospital

Hip and Knee (HNK) Replacement Composite Quality Score:

Patient Level

Hip/Knee	Process Component		
Patient 1:	**Process Measures**	**Eligible**	**Actual**
	Prophylactic antibiotic received < 1 hour prior to surgical incision	Yes	Yes
	Prophylactic antibiotic selection for isolated CABG patients	Yes	Yes
	Discontinued < 24 hours after surgery and time	Yes	Yes
	Total for patient 1	3	3

Opportunities for intervention and actual interventions for all individual measures are aggregated to the patient level.

(continues)

tives for a patient associated with a diagnosis for full credit or got none. Nolan and Berwick (2006) have argued that this type of measure:

1. Better represents the interests of the patient;

2. Fosters a systems perspective on care; and

3. Offers a more sensitive scale for measuring improvements.

The all-or-none approach is also referred to as the multiplicative method for making a composite measure (Van Matre, 2006).

EXHIBIT 7–2

	Hospital Level	
Process Component	*Eligible*	*Actual*
HNK Patient 1	3	3
HNK Patient 2	3	2
.		
.		
.		
.		
HNK Patient n	3	3
Total	312	291

Patient level values are aggregated to the facility level.

Actual and expected 30-day readmission rates calculated.

Actual and expected postoperative hemorrhage/hematoma rates calculated (Actual postop H/H rate) and (Expected postop H/H rate).

Actual and expected postoperative physiologic end metabolic derangement rates calculated (Actual postop PMD rate) and (Expected postop PMD rate)

(continues)

EXHIBIT 7–2

Composite Quality Score

Composite Process component:

Eligible	Actual	Facility Rate	Component Weight	Composite Process Score
				(Facility rate × Weight × 100)
312	291	0.9327	0.50	46.63

Composite Outcome component:

	Facility Rate	Component Weight	Composite Outcome Score
Actual postop H/H avoidance rate (1–Actual postop H/H rate)	0.9700		
Expected postop H/H avoidance rate (1–Expected postop H/H rate)	0.9600		
Postop H/H avoidance index	1.0104	0.167	16.87
Actual postop PMD avoidance rate (1–Actual postop PMD rate)	0.9890		
Expected postop PMD avoidance rate (1–Expected postop PMD rate)	0.9800		
Postop PMD avoidance index	1.0092	0.167	16.85
Actual 30-day readmission avoidance rate (1–actual 30-day readmit rate)	0.9400		
Expected 30-day readmission avoidance rate (1–Expected 30-day readmit rate)	0.9570		
30-day readmission avoidance index	0.9822	0.167	16.87
HQI Composite HNK Quality Score			**96.73**

Centers for Medicare and Medicaid Services (CMS)/Premier Hospital Quality Incentive Demonstration Project

Scaling

Ms. Kleindorfer was concerned about sensitivity in scaling. In general, additive P4P scales tended to cap out rapidly near their maximums creating a problem in motivating further improvement. (For example, The Joint Commission had reported that in 2008 97.5% of hospitals were performing at-or-above a 90% level in providing aspirin on arrival for AMI patients.) However, Dawn Valley was a relatively small hospital and was likely to have small numbers of patients in some categories, so a few patients might easily destabilize the overall scores, if all-or-none scales were used.

Another sensitivity issue was whether to use weighted or unweighted measures in the aggregation of the indicators. As Exhibit 7–2 indicates, the HQID methodology used equal weightings. If there were five process indicators and three outcome measures, then each was essentially weighted 12.5%. For example, for the acute myocardial infarction condition where there was one outcome indicator (mortality avoidance) and eight process measures, then the outcome measure was weighted one-ninth. It was possible that in the small sample sizes reported monthly at Dawn Valley, a couple of missed smoking cessation opportunities would have the same impact on the score as a death not avoided. A similar concern had been published concerning the knee and hip replacement condition. When all three outcome indications were expressed as an avoidance rate rather than a complication rate, the composite scores were almost completely determined by the processes scores. This was attributed to lack of variability in the current set of outcome measures (Bhattacharyya, *et al.*, 2009). Therefore, it seemed likely that most U.S. measurement systems would move away from process measures toward outcome measures as reliable outcome measures were developed, similar to how the U.K. Quality and Outcomes Framework has evolved.

The question of how to weight low probability events also needed to be addressed. So far the HQID system had only done so by subtracting their rate from one, but that meant a high value of the resulting index. Some observers were concerned that there was diminished motivation from improvement as the percentage values centered in the high 90s.

Sample Sizes

Because Dawn Valley was only a 200-bed hospital, it had relatively small sample sizes for some conditions during specific periods. There was also considerable seasonal variation in sample size and in patient mix due to the nearby winter tourist attractions. Most comparative reporting systems dropped the reporting of a condition's quality indicators when quarterly volume was less than 30 cases. Since the Board wanted monthly data, month-to-month variability was likely to be a major problem at Dawn Valley. Ms. Kleindorfer would have to make it clear to the Board what the policy was missing or what the underrepresented values were in the aggregate measures or how to compensate for that problem in displaying trends in the data.

CASE ANALYSIS

Senior management has asked for a set of indicators to monitor the state of healthcare quality and patient safety within the institution. These can be only a subset or an aggregation of the many possible measures that could be followed. That is how the issue of aggregation comes up. How will we know whether we are doing better or worse overall? When and how is it appropriate to convert individual indicators into a composite score? People often work hardest to improve what is measured, so these decisions are nontrivial. What messages do we want to send and to whom?

ASSIGNMENT QUESTIONS

1. Discuss the wisdom of the Board's request for an aggregated quality score monthly.

2. How do the information needs of a managing Board and a potential patient differ and why?

3. Discuss the pros and cons of the various quality-measurement systems for an institution like Dawn Valley Hospital.

4. When the quality measures have been selected, how will they be displayed and in what context to help the Board interpret the results?

5. The literature notes that all these measures show current quality levels at the institution, but do not indicate where improvement can and should be made. What additional information, if any,

should the Board request to help it guide future improvement? Which method of aggregation, if any, should Ms. Kleindorfer recommend to Mr. Farrington for the quality and safety data that he will present to the Board?

CLASS EXERCISE

Learn more about quality and safety dashboards. One might ask whether these represent a command-and-control mentality, whereas CQI seemed to have started out with a participatory management philosophy. So how can these two philosophies be part of the same effort? Try to explain the apparent shift over time from one philosophy to the other.

Dr. Charles Bethe, DO, Network Medical Director

William Q. Judge and Curtis P. McLaughlin

INTRODUCTION

Charles A. Bethe, DO, MBA, reviewed his six months of experience as a network medical director for the Southeast region of Vigilant–Xtra Mile HealthCare (Vigilant–XMHC) located in Atlanta, Georgia. He was one of two physicians responsible for developing and managing the professional medical network of providers and hospitals serving this market, which included the states of Alabama, Georgia, and Mississippi. His duties involved recruiting providers, negotiating contracts, promoting the company's disease-management approaches, credentialing physicians, maintaining National Committee for Quality Assurance (NCQA) accreditation, reviewing cost and quality data as well as provider report cards, arranging education efforts for outliers, and controlling the unit cost side of the firm's medical loss ratio in that market.

Dr. Bethe had a full plate of responsibilities that were new to him and his organization. Furthermore, he had limited staff to delegate duties to, and there were overlapping responsibilities with two other medical directors in his office, which needed to be coordinated carefully. Despite these challenges, he felt fortunate to have a supportive and powerful boss and he was convinced that Vigilant–XMHC was the wave of the future. His immediate challenge was fundamentally a matter of time management.

Although Dr. Bethe was highly organized, he felt he was constantly "putting out unexpected fires," and these urgent projects tended to push out longer-term strategic issues. For example, in the last month, his schedule had been consumed by several unexpected activities including: (1) supervising a database cleanup; (2) addressing open enrollment administrative glitches in January; (3) being available for audits of the Medicare program by HCFA and the state of Georgia; (4) preparing for a mock NCQA audit; and (5) dealing with supervisory and human relations issues within his unit. These issues tended to get in the way of refining his network of providers and overseeing quality, but they had to be addressed. Dr. Bethe hoped that with time things would settle down.

Background

When Charles Bethe graduated in 1970 from Baldwin-Wallace College in Berea, OH with a BS in Zoology and Philosophy, he went to work as a pharmaceutical salesman in Ohio and Western Pennsylvania. He was successful there, but he wanted direct patient contact, so he decided to pursue a medical degree. In 1973, he entered the Midwestern University–Chicago College of Osteopathic Medicine. Graduating in 1977, he interned at Hospital Corporation of America (HCA) Northlake Hospital in Tucker, Georgia. In 1979, he founded the East Cobb Family Practice in Marietta, Georgia and joined the staff of the Archway Hospital. He became Board Certified by the American Board of Osteopathic Family Practitioners and a fellow of the American Academy of Family Practice in 1986 and a diplomat of the American Board of Medical Management in 1997. In the late 1980s, Dr. Bethe and his partner differed markedly over the importance of managed care. His partner did not want to participate, while he was convinced it was the wave of the future. When he witnessed the loss of 20% of his patients after Lockheed Marietta moved all of its employees to managed care, he was convinced that he needed to change his practice. He had been participating in management workshops provided by the American College of Physician Executives (ACPE) and decided to enter Emory University's weekend executive MBA program. He found this to be a valuable learning experience, particularly his thesis project, which involved a study of methods of valuation for small medical practices. When he graduated in June 1991, he installed a total quality management effort in his family practice and asked his partner to leave within 90 days. After his partner left, Dr. Bethe increased the volume of the practice by 83% within 12 months, while accepting managed-care patients and adding a new partner, two physician assistants, and a nurse practitioner.

Dr. Bethe tried to start a group practice without walls in conjunction with other providers, but it "failed within six months due to lack of capital and physician management skills and involvement." Then in late 1994, he received four offers to sell his practice. One of the offers came from an organization that was connected to the hospital where he practiced. Ultimately, he decided to harvest his practice to this organization and become involved in the management of the resulting organization. Thus, he became one of the founding members and chief of family medicine for Dominion Northwest Physician's Group, a group with 180 physicians, 60 locations, and affiliations with 13 hospitals in the greater Atlanta region. There he spent half of his time in management and the other half in patient-care delivery.

The job with Dominion Northwest was a useful transition for him. He negotiated contracts for the physicians and was involved in developing methods for equitably dividing capitated payments among the specialists and primary-care physicians. He was on the contracting committee of the Dominion physician-hospital organization (PHO) and the Physician's Group, and on the strategic planning and the informatics committees as well as the physicians' advisory board. He learned more about working in large organizations with hours spent in committee meetings and dealing with larger bureaucracies. With time, however, he became convinced that this organization did not have sufficient physician involvement in decision-making to satisfy him in the long run, but he kept on learning about medical management and leadership.

Then one day an executive recruiter called him about the job at Vigilant–XMHC. Dr. Bethe felt he had nothing to lose in looking at it, especially since it was in Atlanta. He concluded that it was the type of job that would allow him to make a difference at a higher level. Vigilant–XMHC was looking for a physician with management skills, with a good reputation and credentials and well connected to the local network. Dr. Bethe had been very active in the Georgia Academy of Family Practice, was on the board of directors of Blue Ridge Area Health Education Center (AHEC) and of a couple of managed-care plans in addition to his involvement with administrative duties within Dominion.

In 1994, Governor Zell Miller appointed Dr. Bethe to the nine-member Georgia Joint Board of General Practice, which oversaw the allocation of $50,000,000 in state residency and training funds. Dr. Bethe worked with the other members to formulate state policy on funding of graduate medical education and to redesign all state funding mechanisms for medical education. He was currently secretary–treasurer of the board. He has also served as a preceptor for Emory University and the West Virginia College of Osteopathic Medicine and on the 6th District (Newt Gingrich's former district) Medicare Advisory Board Task Force on Alternative Plans for Medicare. In short, his connections and experience were ideal for the job.

The job carried with it a salary comparable to a good primary-care practitioner income with major upside potential in the long run. There were very good benefits, and he was part of the regional management team. Fortunately, Dominion–Northwest allowed Dr. Bethe to opt out of the remaining two years of his employment contract and he joined Vigilant–XMHC in August 1997.

His counterpart, Chris Donovan, MD, was a native of the West Indies who had previous experience as a medical director with Domina in Charlotte, NC. He was also new to the organization as he joined Vigilant–XMHC about the same time as Charley Bethe did. Dr. Bethe and Dr. Donovan had a good working relationship. Their responsibilities were basically the same, except for different parts of the market.

Corporate Background

Vigilant and Xtra Mile Healthcare merged in April 1996, bringing together two quite different firms. Vigilant was a traditional full-line insurance company founded in 1899 with 48 highly decentralized HMO operations and a rather conservative business outlook. It was headquartered in Boston. In contrast, Xtra Mile Healthcare was founded in Wheeling, West Virginia in 1978. It was a highly centralized and entrepreneurial company developed and managed by physicians. For example, Vigilant had 50 different claims processing centers, while XMHC had only one. In addition to structural differences, their growth strategies were also quite different. Vigilant had been buying primary-care practices, while Xtra Mile HealthCare did not buy any practices.

The resulting merger was a giant company with revenues in excess of $17 billion, more than half of which was in healthcare products. It divided the nation into six regions, which are depicted in Figure 8–1. In 1998, Vigilant–XMHC provided healthcare services to 23 million Americans in 50 states through networks involving 300,000 physicians and 3,000 hospitals. Roughly one insured American in 12 was covered for health care by the resulting organization.

The merged company developed a number of strategies aimed at capitalizing on its extensive asset base and unique array of competencies. First and foremost, it would offer a full line of healthcare insurance products (e.g., indemnity, preferred provider organization (PPO), point-of-service (POS), HMO, senior HMO) on a national basis to offer "one-stop shopping" to nationally-based organizations. The firm would not purchase medical practices or facilities, but would maintain an open panel of physicians and nonexclusive contracts with hospitals and ancillary providers. Its basic HMO contracting model called for primary-care physicians (PCPs) to serve as gatekeepers on quality-based capitation, with specialists paid on a discounted fee-for-service or capitated basis and hospitals paid at a negotiated rate by the case or per diem.

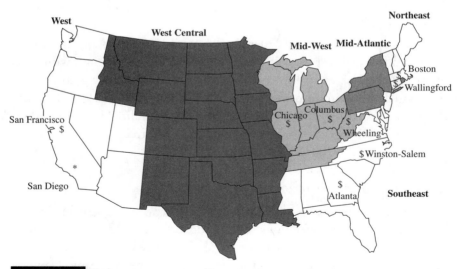

Figure 8–1 Six Regions of Vigilant—Xtra Mile HealthCare

By 1997, Vigilant–XMHC had an approved HMO in 23 states and the District of Columbia covering 73% of the population and had applications pending in the rest. Each physician recruited to the network was expected to service all Vigilant–XMHC healthcare products under one contract. This consistent national presence and full range of healthcare products allowed the company to approach large national employers on a highly competitive basis. The fact that they could also supply disability insurance, group life, retirement plans, 401Ks, dental insurance, and variety of other products to the same benefits managers nationwide was considered a strong competitive advantage. The company is a leading provider of Medicare managed-care services and could also service the company's retirees.

The two companies had been highly profitable in 1995 and 1996. However, profit margins narrowed and medical loss ratios rose sharply in 1997. The stock had dropped sharply from 1996 levels. The economies in operations and from scale that had been expected took much longer to achieve. Dr. Bethe talked about the loss of human capital during the reorganization that cost it dearly. According to Dr. Bethe, "In our efforts to re-engineer the organization, a lot of administrative help was eliminated. In so doing, we let go of a lot of Ms. Smiths. You know, Ms. Smith was the one in the local office who knew that Dr. Jones never checked box 30 on the HCFA 1500 form, but checked it for him rather than sending it back to his office."

The resulting delays and other glitches with new offices and employees slowed down claims processing and overstated initial earnings, with costs catching up later. However, the new organization was now getting more integrated and claims processing was functioning better in 1998. The new Vigilant–XMHC organization was partially decentralized into six regions. The Southeast region consisted of four markets stretching from Mississippi to Florida to Maryland.

Organizational Structure

The overall corporate headquarters was located with Vigilant in Boston, while the healthcare operations were headquartered at XMHC in Wheeling. The six regional offices reported to the Wheeling corporate offices. There were three medical director hierarchies in the company. Network medical directors, of which Dr. Bethe was one, reported to the general manager for each market who reported in turn to the regional manager. Patient management medical directors were involved with utilization management, preauthorizations, length-of-stay reviews, case-management development, retrospective reviews, and disease-management enrollment. They came under the regional medical director who reported directly to the core team at Wheeling. Finally, there was also a regional quality medical director who reported to quality-management staff in Boston. A detailed comparison of these three types of medical directors is listed in Table 8–1.

Dr. Bethe supervised a team of eight individuals—two provider relations managers who in turn led five professional service coordinators, and

Table 8–1 Excerpts from the Job Descriptions of Medical Directors at Vigilant–Xtra Mile HealthCare

Job Characteristics	Patient Management Director & Quality Management Director	Network Medical Director
Fundamental Role	Develop and manage a health services organization focused on reducing medical cost and improving clinical outcomes, member satisfaction, and provider satisfaction	Develop and manage a health services organization focused on reducing medical cost and improving clinical outcomes, member satisfaction, and provider satisfaction
Central Activities	Implement utilization and quality management programs through timely policy interpretation and local application	Provide strategic and operational direction for the delivery of performance-based medical management
	Manage budget	Manage budget and risk drivers
	Provide marketing support through sales presentations, site visits, and support for requests for proposals	Analyze and report business performance data to customers and colleagues
	Render medical necessity determinations	Handle Vigilant funds as if they were his/her own
	Chair committees in accordance with market and contractual needs	Participate in internal and external health industry development efforts
	Participate in national, regional, and local work groups as required	Participate in management of local profit and loss

(continues)

Table 8–1 Continued

Job Characteristics	Patient Management Director & Quality Management Director	Network Medical Director
	Serve as liaison between field organization, home office, and governmental agencies	Serve as liaison with regulatory and accrediting agencies and other business units within the company
	Develop local medical review and coverage policies	Develop and maintain strong provider relationships
Leadership	Maintains a customer driven passion for excellence and commitment to action and change	Maintains a customer driven passion for excellence and commitment to action and change
Direction Setting	Ability to make timely and high quality decisions as well as implement them	Ability to make timely and high quality decisions as well as implement them
Selection	Hire, develop, and reward staff to effectively support the company's strategy	Hire, develop, and reward staff to effectively support the company's strategy
Communication	Excellent verbal and written skills as well as negotiation and conflict resolution skills	Excellent verbal and written skills as well as negotiation and conflict resolution skills
Business Knowledge	In-depth knowledge of managed care, financial, business processes, and strategies and objectives	In-depth knowledge of managed care, financial, business processes, and strategies and objectives
	Job specific technical knowledge	Job specific technical knowledge
Other Requirements	Board certification is highly desired; State License must be active and unencumbered	Board certification is optional
	Demonstrated commitment to professional development (e.g., CME, conferences)	Demonstrated commitment to professional development (e.g., seminars)

an administrative assistant shared with Dr. Donovan. The professional service coordinators were the ones out on the firing line with the providers. There were numerous dotted line relationships among the various medical directors. In fact, when he was hired, Dr. Bethe had only dotted line relationships and no direct reports, so he recommended a reorganization in which he took on budgetary and supervisory responsibility for a portion of the provider services staff. He also made a determined effort to be seen as a contributor to the management team of the market and the region. For example, he hosted a weekend strategic planning session for regional management team at his summer home at Lake Lanier.

This meant considerable added workload due to supervision, performance review, objective setting, and process improvement. He typically worked from 7:00 AM to 6:00 PM two days a week, and 9:00 AM to 6:00 PM the other three and then usually had a couple of dinner meetings each week. Weekend activities such as a strategic planning retreat or a mock NCQA site visit exercise might tie up one weekend a month. Typically, he responded to about 60 internal e-mail messages a day and a large number of telephone calls. A two-month review of his calendar showed that he spent on average four hours a day in meetings, about 60% in the office and 40% outside. When he took the job, he was told to expect to be traveling four days a week. However, this market's business was very heavily concentrated in Georgia and in Atlanta in particular.

Management of Quality

In 1990, XM Data Driven, Inc. (XMDD) was established as a Vigilant–XMHC quality measurement subsidiary. With over 280 employees, it had access to a data warehouse of claims information from hospitalization, outpatient visits, pharmacy claims, and laboratory reports of 15 million enrollees. It was a pioneering and innovative unit with Vigilant–XMHC, developing clinical algorithms, identifying and risk-stratifying seriously ill members for disease-management interventions, providing risk-adjusted performance reporting systems, maintaining a disease registry for members with any of more than 65 chronic illnesses, and working with participating academic medical centers to conduct applied research. A more detailed description of XMDD is provided in Exhibit 8–1. An example of the type of report cards that they provide to management and to providers is shown in Exhibit 8–2.

EXHIBIT 8–1

XMDD Description

The XMDD health services research program is the dedicated research and development unit of Vigilant–Xtra Mile HealthCare. Physicians, PhD-level researchers, methodologists, nurses, statisticians, programmers, medical coders, and other experienced professionals make up this unit. Staff conduct applied research and develop methodologies that measure and improve the quality and efficiency of health care services for Vigilant–XMHC's membership. One of the main goals of the Health Services Research Program is to evaluate the outcomes and cost-effectiveness of managed-care programs.

The XMDD Health Services Research Program has access to an abundance of health-related data on more than 14 million insured members throughout the United States, and routinely analyzes both primary and secondary data for hundreds of practical applications. Research conducted by this unit is designed to benefit four primary customers which include: (1) individual members, (2) providers, (3) plan sponsors, and (4) the Vigilant–Xtra Mile HealthCare system.

When working with external organizations on collaborative research, XMDD staff provide methodological, data acquisition, and technical support, and assist with the grant application process as well.

Examples of XMDD Health Services Research:

- Health Profiling—Using a number of different data sets, clinical logic has been created to identify individuals with any of 65 chronic diseases. Each individual's disease-specific health status can be categorized and used in a number of applications. For instance, an individual's health profile is used as a predictor in risk-stratification models to determine who should be entered into disease-management programs. Health status is also used as a risk adjuster in physician performance compensation models. Furthermore, these profiles are used to calculate employer group disease-specific preva-

(continues)

EXHIBIT 8–1

lence rates, which help employers determine the best benefits package to purchase from Vigilant–XMHC.

- Risk-Stratification Modeling—XMDD has created empirically driven risk-stratification models designed to identify individuals who are at high risk for certain types of disease-specific acute exacerbations. These multivariate predictive models use previous utilization patterns to assign chronically ill individuals into one of five risk strata. After extensive cross-validation, these models are used to determine appropriate disease-management resources that are consistent with the health needs of each category of individuals.

- Clinical Outcomes Studies and Program Evaluation—Both pilot and long-standing managed-care programs are evaluated to determine their impact on members' health status. A number of different econometric, epidemiological, and statistical quasi-experimental models have been employed to evaluate these programs while controlling for important confounding variables.

- Severity-Adjusted Performance Measurement—Severity-adjusted performance measurement models have been developed for hospitals, specialists, and primary-care providers. These multivariate statistical models are used to provide feedback to providers and institutions about their performance relative to others in their field. Additionally, performance measurement information is used to determine a portion of each provider's reimbursement. By accounting for differences in patient mix by factoring in characteristics such as age, gender, and comorbidities, the playing field is leveled between providers, and performance results are more valid.

- Health System Research—A number of research projects are under way to further investigate the health system overall. Cost-effectiveness and practice pattern variation studies, for example, have been undertaken to more fully understand costs and utilization of the country's health system. Additionally, the impact of different insurance arrangements on utilization and health status are being studied. Results from these studies will help Vigilant–XMHC better understand how to resource high-quality health services.

EXHIBIT 8-2

Sample XMDD Report Card for Asthma

Practice Type: Family Practice
Office Number: XX   Region: XX
Office Address: 1 Street, Anytown, PA 19074
Reporting Period: 10/1/94–9/30/95
Number of our current insureds identified with asthma: 232

Prevalence Measures	Office	XMHC Average
1. Estimated overall prevalence of asthma	4.5%	4.0%
2. Estimated overall prevalence of asthma age 0–9	9.0%	7.9%
3. Estimated overall prevalence of asthma age 10–19	7.2%	6.8%
4. Estimated overall prevalence of asthma age 20–39	5.7%	4.0%
5. Estimated overall prevalence of asthma age 40+	2.5%	2.8%

Asthma Treatment Patterns		
6. Asthmatics on prescription drugs for asthma	65.8%	66.4%
7. Asthmatics receiving sympathomimetics	58.3%	58.3%
8. Asthmatics receiving theophylline	6.4%	11.0%
9. Asthmatics receiving only theophylline	0.0%	0.7%
10. Asthmatics receiving cromolyn	8.0%	8.7%
11. Asthmatics receiving inhaled steroids	21.4%	18.8%
12. Average annual number of beta agonist prescriptions for asthmatics receiving any beta agonist	4.29	3.72
13. Asthmatics on beta agonists receiving 2 or more prescriptions in one month	18.3%	17.9%
14. Asthmatics receiving one or more course of oral steroids	17.1%	18.3%

(continues)

EXHIBIT 8–2

Access Measures	Office	XMHC Average
15. Asthmatics seeing the PCP at least once	92.5%	86.9%
16. Average number of annual PCP visits per asthmatic	5.74	4.69
17. Asthmatics seeing a pulmonologist	8.8%	7.0%
18. Asthmatics seeing an allergist	14.5%	11.7%

Process Measures

19. Asthmatics with an outpatient chest x-ray	8.4%	8.9%
20. Asthmatics age 8+ receiving pulmonary function tests	8.3%	10.1%
21. Asthmatics receiving allergy testing	3.1%	4.8%
22. Asthmatics receiving allergy immunotherapy	7.5%	8.0%
23. Asthmatics using a home nebulizer	2.2%	2.4%
24. Asthmatics with at least one antibiotic prescription	63.1%	71.3%
25. Asthmatics on theophylline who have at least one theophylline level drawn	10.0%	18.9%
26. Average annual number of theophylline levels in asthmatics on theophylline	0.10	0.29
27. Asthmatics receiving at least one home care visit	3.5%	3.4%

Outcome Measures

Asthma-Related Conditions

28. Emergency room visits specifically for asthma/1000 asthmatics per year	57	86
29. Total admissions (acute) specifically for asthma/1000 asthmatics per year	44	40
30. Total inpatient days (acute) specifically for asthma/1000 asthmatics per year	273	177

(continues)

EXHIBIT 8–2

All Conditions for Asthmatic Members	Office	XMHC Average
31. Total emergency room visits for all conditions/1000 asthmatics per year	154	242
32. Total admissions (acute) for all conditions/1000 asthmatics per year	128	149
33. Total inpatient days (acute) for all conditions/1000 asthmatics per year	493	572
*Satisfaction Measures**		
34. Overall satisfaction with medical care at the PCP office of asthmatic members	100.0%	95.9%
35. Satisfaction with the ability to make appointments for illnesses	95.4%	92.1%
36. Satisfaction with the response to an emergency call within 30 minutes	98.6%	93.0%

*Percentage of respondents with Good, Very Good, or Excellent

Vigilant–XMHC believed that ultimately the market would be defined by quality. This was so important to Vigilant–XMHC that the company had established a unique quality-driven compensation system for primary-care physicians. The incentives in this system are balanced to attempt to avoid both over- and underutilization. Each practice receives a capitation payment, which is adjusted for the age and gender of the covered population. This payment is further adjusted by a quality factor that is revised every six months. The example in Exhibit 8–3 illustrates how the quality factor had been is determined.

Offices that failed to make a score of at least 2% received a 10% reduction in capitation payments during the subsequent six months. Those that maintained a score of at least 2% received an increase in their semi-monthly capitation payments equal to the percentage score. Thus, the ABC Practice would have received a 14.55% increment in its capitation payments.

EXHIBIT 8-3

Sample Quality Factor Calculation

Based on the quality of care, comprehensive service, and utilization, the ABC Practice earned the following quality factor, which is multiplied by their sex- and age-adjusted base capitation payment for the previous two weeks:

Quality Review Components:
a. Member Surveys (compared to others in HMO, range: 0.75 to +3.0)	2.00%
b. Focused Medical Chart Reviews (2/year, comparative, −0.75 to +3.0)	0.75%
c. Member Transfer Rates (comparative, −0.75 to +1.5)	0.50%
d. Philosophy of Managed Care (cooperation and participation with XMHC quality programs (subjective, −0.75 to +3.0)	<u>1.00%</u>
Quality Review Subtotal	4.25%

Comprehensive Care Components:
a. Membership Size (members/doctor or practice, e.g., range = 0, 1% at 100/doctor, 1.5% at 200/doctor, 2% at 300/doctor)	1.00%
b. Schedule Office Hours (range = 0, 0.5% for 50–59, 1.0% for 60–69, and 1.5% for >70 hours/week)	0.50%
c. Available Office Procedures (e.g., flexible sigmoidoscopy = 1.0%) max. = 3%)	1.00%
d. Program Education (completing XMHC educational courses (e.g., Current Concepts in Cancer = 0.5%,) max. sum = 2%)	0.50%
e. Internal Practice Coverage (1% if coverage is by practice for continuity)	1.00%
f. Catastrophic Care (practice has greater than the HMO type average total costs for catastrophic cases (e.g., > $20,000 = 1.5%)	1.50%
g. Patient Management (1% if practice supports and participates in XMHC patient management and directs hospital care of own patients)	1.00%
h. Practice Growth (XMHC membership growth (e.g., > 10% = 1.0%)	1.00%

(continues)

EXHIBIT 8–3

I. Computer Links to XMHC (transmits encounter and referral data electronically = 1.0%)	<u>1.00%</u>
Comprehensive Care Subtotal	8.50%

Utilization Components:

a. Hospital Utilization at the average bracket (range = −0.8 to +1.8%)	0.80%
b. Specialist Utilization one bracket greater than average (−0.8 to +1.8%)	0.40%
c. Emergency Room Utilization one bracket less than average (−0.8 to +1.4%)	<u>0.60%</u>
Utilization Subtotal	<u>1.8%</u>
TOTAL QUALITY FACTOR =	14.55%

Each practice also received a six-month Quality-Factored Distribution based on its three utilization components (hospital, specialist, and ER) year-to-date, which was adjusted by the Quality Review and Comprehensive Care Components (in the given example, 4.25% + 8.50% = 12.75%). If the practice had achieved a combined Quality Review and Utilization Component Score of at least 4% (4.25% + 1.80% = 6.05%), it was eligible for an Office Status Payment of 5%, if it had remained open for Vigilant–XMHC enrollment throughout the period or if it had accepted current patients as Vigilant–XMHC members throughout that period.

The large employers that the company sought out tended to insist on NCQA certification. Therefore, one of Dr. Bethe's main performance objectives was to have the network meet the NCQA requirement of meeting its own written quality standards. He spent much time and effort making sure that the network conformed to NCQA requirements such as having a certain percentage of members within 15 minutes travel time of a primary-care provider in the network and working with practices to help them achieve NCQA's Health Plan Employer Data and Information Set (HEDIS) standards for their patients. Another standard was that of keeping provider turnover below 5% per year.

The costs of achieving these standards can be substantial. In six months, the region had gone through an NCQA audit exercise, a Georgia exercise for Medicare, and a federal exercise for Medicare. Then there were the operational costs of maintaining standards. For example, NCQA standards required recredentialing each network physician every two years. With over 7,000 physicians in their network in Georgia, that was a substantial workload, the cost of which made Dr. Bethe consider strategies for narrowing the network where possible. HMOs in Georgia were licensed county by county by the state. As geographic coverage was expanded, the number of physicians to be credentialed expanded. He found himself having to trade off greater choice for his patients with the costs of providing the larger provider network in the served areas as well as allocating scarce resources between served areas and new target market areas.

One decision that Dr. Bethe had to make was how much time to spend requesting and reviewing report cards on the physicians in the network. XMDD could generate an almost infinite number of reports like the one in Exhibit 8–2. They could also generate statistical reports identifying outlier individuals and practices. Much of the data on over- or underutilization was of more concern to the regional medical director responsible for patient management, but that medical loss ratio was also part of his performance evaluation.

Dr. Bethe's Observations About the Job

Dr. Bethe had been in the job only six months when this case was written. So far, he was quite happy with the job and with its potential. He observed that the Dominion–Northwest had been a useful transition for him to enable him to see the comparative advantages of various types of healthcare organizations and to get used to working in a large organization. He was no longer seeing patients, but he was comfortable with that fact. He had already "seen enough patients to fill Fulton County Stadium three times" and no longer found practice much of a challenge. He often compared the practice of medicine to flying an airplane: "When you need a skilled pilot, that individual is important and one's skills are critical during the unique takeoff and landing periods. However, in between takeoffs and landings, most of the system is on autopilot and that gets old over time. The same is true of medicine."

There were always the fires to fight and there were always special projects related to process improvement. For example, the company had just gone through a major database cleanup of its provider records. Many physicians had changed their affiliations due to mergers and acquisitions and thus their tax ID numbers, but had not informed their payers. A wrong provider ID number on a claim could hold up payment and distort the company's data on activities and costs. That had been a major effort for his group.

He observed that most physicians would not be comfortable with the length of time that it took to get things done in a large organization. They, like he, were used to dealing with and reaching closure on a presenting problem every 15 minutes. Recruiting a substantial group practice into the network might take as much as a year with a meeting every month to establish a trusting relationship and to work out the details of the contract.

Medical directors also had to be comfortable working as part of a management team, to influence others where possible, but take orders when necessary. They would have to know when to keep quiet and when to speak up. For example, in the disease-management arena, the core management at Wheeling would often decide which disease-management programs were "Network Impactable" and he would have to make them work. He noted that he still had more to learn about the politics of large organizations and about the insurance industry in general, about group selection, underwriting, claims management, contracting, and marketing. He certainly felt that he had a better idea of what groups such as independent practice associations (IPAs) could or could not do effectively. Having seen the information system investment that Vigilant–XMHC had to support membership enrollment, claims processing, disease-management, and utilization review, he saw no way that much smaller, physician-led organizations could compete. On the other hand, he felt that insurance organizations knew relatively little about managing practices or running hospitals and were better off not trying to integrate them.

Dr. Bethe was aware of the high turnover rate among medical directors in the industry. In his own words: "The health care environment is in turmoil and one needs a mentor, someone looking out for them, if one is to survive. One has to be careful to avoid the lose-lose situations that many medical directors have gotten into." By way of example, he cited medical directors of Medicaid managed-care organizations when the Georgia state legislature decreed a 20% cut in funding, or those whose jobs were eliminated during mergers. He knew a local medical director working for MedPartners who was let go when the merger with Phycor was announced. Since the merger did not go through, they were recruiting a replacement.

He noted that most physicians are not at all prepared for the practices of large organizations. He had heard them speak quite heatedly about the experience of a terminated medical director at another HMO who was given 20 minutes under observation to clean out her desk, escorted to the door with security person on each side, and asked to hand over her keys at the door. After a few months in a data-driven organization, he fully understood why. Why give anyone a chance to download proprietary information onto a computer disk or destroy a data set? However, no practicing physician would ever expect to be mortified that way.

Dr. Bethe also felt that most physicians would have difficulty with having to clear so many decisions with the legal department or with public relations. Yet, while there were policies and procedures governing most everything, he did not feel that they would constrain his team from setting aggressive goals, developing plans to compete in the markets that they chose, and implementing them quickly and efficiently. However, most physicians would have trouble at first being resource constrained in what could be accomplished. When he was in practice, if he felt the practice would benefit from a piece of equipment, he bought it. It meant a loss in the profits distributed at the end of the month, but there was still enough. But when he wanted an additional employee to serve as a practice management coordinator, a highly skilled professional services consultant to go into network practices and help them solve billing or cost problems, he had to work hard to justify that position and show how it would contribute to meeting financial targets.

The Future

Dr. Bethe saw the provider community consolidating, which would give them more power in the negotiations with payer networks. He felt that payers would have to learn how to do a better job of partnering with the providers so that in sharing the risks they would both succeed. Thus far, providers had had a very poor track record in profiting by taking on risk, and he felt that one of his jobs in the future would be in helping them succeed.

He also saw many opportunities for expanding the network. There were many areas of Georgia, Mississippi, and Alabama that did not have rationalized provider networks. He recognized a need to tell the managed-care story more effectively given the current hostility in the profession and in the media, which was being echoed politically in Georgia and Washington, D.C. He also saw the need to become more effective in negotiating good contracts, closely observing quality and utilization, and moving population to the good providers. There were many opportunities, many issues, and many unknowns to be faced.

CASE ANALYSIS

This case is about the roles of medical directors in the quality efforts of large HMO companies and insurers. In this case, the primary focus is on gatekeeper contracts rather than PPO contracts. Dr. Bethe is just one of three types of medical directors in the firm, each reporting to a different level of the organization. The reader can use case data to review the apparent criteria used by the company in recruiting its market medical directors individually and as a team. There is also considerable information about the company's databases and their methods of motivating quality performance among participating primary-care physicians.

ASSIGNMENT QUESTIONS

1. Review Dr. Bethe's job history. What experiences contributed to his becoming a job applicant that was attractive to Vigilant–XMHC? How relevant are these to his current position and to his future career?

2. Review the set of job descriptions. What seem to be the salient differences between the three types of medical directors at this firm? What does that tell you about what Vigilant–XMHC really expects out of each medical director? Is that consistent with their other quality measurement and control systems evident in the case?

3. What do you believe Dr. Bethe's career depends on? If you were in charge, what practical and operational evaluative measures would you use?

4. Dr. Bethe observes that he expects to make a bigger difference at Vigilant–XMHC than he could have at the local integrating hospital system? Why do you think he believes that? How realistic do you think he was being about this? Why?

5. What does this case tell you about the advantages of scale that a large provider can bring to bear on the measurement of healthcare processes and outcomes? Can a small IPA ever overcome that?

6. What do you think of the "quality" incentive system outlined in the final exhibit of the case? What behaviors does it seem designed to motivate? How much do you think that it will actually impact on the PCP practices? How would you go about motivating them?

7. What advice can you offer Dr. Bethe about doing his job better in the future? Are you satisfied with his time allocation, or do you recommend some changes of strategy or tactics?

8. Would you be interested in this job? What is attractive about it? What is not attractive about it? What have you learned from it that you want to take with you in your attitudes toward any potential job search?

9. Another payer-oriented case is Case 3. Compare and contrast the governmental approach there with the activities undertaken by Vigilant-XMHC within its network. How and why are these two approaches so different?

CLASS EXERCISE

Find out what a specific healthcare insurer is doing to improve quality. Is that organization making use of the data that it has in house? Is it using other consortia or available databases to enhance clinical performance? What is behind the selection of that specific approach? How likely are other payers to use their accumulated data to enhance clinical quality?

EDUCATIONAL AND SOCIAL-MARKETING APPLICATIONS IN CONTINUOUS QUALITY IMPROVEMENT

Improvement can occur through education of consumers and providers. In the cases in Part III, we observe four situations where there is a strong educational component. In Case 9, we observe an implementation of the Safe Surgery Saves Lives (SSSL) checklist heavily publicized under the auspices of the World Health Organization. This effort has been studied and used at many prestigious medical centers and peer reviewed in medical journals but also widely reported on in the popular press, including television, newspapers, and magazines. Why wouldn't everyone immediately adopt it? The case suggests some possible reasons.

Prince Court Hospital, a private Malaysian provider catering to local demand and medical tourism (Case 10), finds itself responding to fear and lack of good information during the H1N1 influenza pandemic. This case shows how the hospital went about upgrading its responses internally and externally with an eye toward improving its quality culture in the long run.

In Case 11, a county health department in the United States sent one person for training especially designed to improve its financial management practices, often a problem area for freestanding government and nongovernmental agencies. That lone participant in a workshop offered by a professional association returned home and applied what he learned using financial ratio analysis in a manner that seems to be calling for major policy and procedural changes. How does top management respond to this analysis, one which seems to reflect negatively on its own performance?

Historically, quality has been attributed to the knowledge and skills of the individual professionals delivering the services. CQI focuses on making changes that involve the surrounding systems as well as the individual. Case 12 presents the activities of an established postgraduate medical education and credentialing professional organization aimed at involving its members in CQI. This approach has been adopted by many such organizations and takes place in parallel with the efforts of delivery institutions to improve performance. How organizations dealing with education, accreditation, and credentialing can best maintain a continuous rate of improvement is a major issue worthy of attention. It has been an elephant in the room ever since CQI concepts were introduced widely into the healthcare environment.

Forthright Medical Center: Social Marketing and the Surgical Checklist

Carol E. Breland

INTRODUCTION

The staff of the Forthright Medical Center decided to apply a social marketing approach after they met resistance to the surgical checklist, a successful intervention to reduce medical errors (Haynes *et al.*, 2009). The Turning Point Social Marketing National Excellence Collaborative, funded by the Robert Wood Johnson Foundation, had created a series of social marketing resources for applying social marketing principles to public health initiatives. While designed with health behavior interventions in mind, the concept seemed adaptable to healthcare processes such as changing operating-room procedures to decrease surgical errors.

The Application Environment

Monday morning started like many others, with Sarah Santiago, RN, groaning as she slammed the alarm off, pulling on her scrubs in the dark while her family was still sleeping. Her sister, Maria, would get the baby up and off to daycare before leaving for her own job. But today was going to be different. She was headed off to her new position as circulating nurse for the cardiac surgery unit. Having been a nurse at Forthright

Medical Center for the past 10 years, working in preop, postop, and critical care, she was excited to move into the more interesting area of surgery. As she clocked in, she could see the operating room was bustling with the usual activities for the first operation of the day, a cardiac bypass. The schedule was full, and it was her job to keep everything running smoothly.

"So Sarah, glad you could join us," said Bill Boston, the scrub nurse, with a yawn. Bill and Sarah had worked together in the ER a few years before. Sarah smiled in return, and as she pulled out the paperwork for the first patient, she reviewed the attached surgical safety checklist (identical to the WHO checklist, WHO, 2008, pp. 3–4) that was now to be implemented as part of a continuous quality improvement initiative. She wished her supervisor had had more time to provide training for the surgical team other than five minutes to briefly introduce it at the last staff meeting. Sarah had observed the surgeon, Dr. Robert O'Reilly, and the anesthesiologist, Dr. Barbara Yu, exchanging withering glances during the meeting that promised an uphill battle for its acceptance.

Over in the staff lounge, Dr. Yu was complaining to Grady Parti, the perfusionist, about the announcement that cardiac services would be taking the lead in improving the hospital's profitability. "I understand that the hospital needs more money," Dr. Yu fumed, "but why put the burden on us to increase our patient load and do more procedures in less time?" She stomped her foot, emphasizing her frustration. Grady responded, "Well, it's not like we have a choice. Nobody ever asks for my opinion." The nurse anesthetist, Tricia Hopewell, nodded but added, "I'm sure we will find a way. We are the best!" Grady laughed lightly as he and Tricia put down their coffee mugs and went to the OR to set up. Along the way, Tricia described the conversation she had heard last month over a hip replacement between two young orthopedists who were discussing whether or not to start their own surgicenter, if Forthright could not give them more OR time. "They even asked me if I would go over with them, but I thought they were joking. It would take an MD anesthesiologist to manage it."

Having finished her paperwork, Sarah hurried to the surgical suite. Tricia and Jane Mills, the OR tech, were standing next to an old IV pump, involved in a heated debate. "What seems to be the problem, Jane?" Sarah inquired. "Trisha says the new IV pump isn't working," explained Jane.

"All we have left are the old ones." "Which doesn't calculate the drip rates precisely," Trisha said, "and I don't have my sheet with me to adjust for it, since these new pumps were supposed to do that automatically!" "Jane, do you have the manual? Maybe Trisha can look it up," Sarah suggested. Jane shrugged, "I don't know where it might be. I've just been trained on the new ones." Bill walked in and overheard the argument. "See what you get to deal with, Sarah? Sure you want this job?" Jane, with a hurt look, left the room. Sarah started to get a queasy feeling in her stomach. "Hope I don't get a migraine," she thought to herself.

Finally, though, the operating room was ready and the patient was rolled in. "OK," announced Sarah, "it's time to start using the new surgical checklist that will help us improve patient safety. Remember, Janet Morelli talked about it during the last staff meeting. I'll be the coordinator. We'll be taking three scheduled pauses during this surgery to do safety checks and be sure we are all on the same page. It's been tested by the World Health Organization, so we know if we use it, it will save lives." "Look," Dr. Yu interrupted, "I know you are just trying to do your job, but we don't have time for more hospital bureaucracy. They want us to do more surgeries, so we can't also add time to each surgery by stopping three times." Grady piped in, "I agree. Let's get this show on the road. Need to start anesthesia if we're going to stay on schedule." "Can we just confirm we have the correct patient for this procedure?" Sarah insisted. "Sure, this is Father John from St. Michael's and he is having a triple CABG," said Tricia, "I talked to him about it last week after Mass." The rest of the team stared angrily at Sarah, who sighed and said, "OK, let's begin."

Things went smoothly for a while until the time came for Sarah to initiate the second pause, just prior to the surgical incision. "Everyone, let's take a time-out to make sure we are all on the same page. The checklist . . ." "Sarah," whispered Bill, "Dr. O'Reilly is ready to begin. He doesn't like to get interrupted." Sarah glanced over at the surgeon, who was holding the scalpel in a frozen position just above the patient's chest. The checklist had some questions he needed to answer, such as were there any possible risks that the team might need to know about, or any plans to adjust for longer than expected duration of the surgery, blood loss, or ensuring that radiology had sent over all the films he needed. Bill was supposed to verify instrument sterility, confirm that antibiotics had been properly administered, and all equipment was in order. These steps all seemed important to Sarah, but given the mood of the team, all she said was, "If Dr. O'Reilly is ready and no one has a comment or concern, let's begin."

All seemed well until Grady announced it was time to begin winding down. "No, it's not, I'm not ready to close," said Dr. O'Reilly. "I had difficulty extracting the mammary artery, that's why we started the bypass later than usual," he said to Trisha. "You should have said something earlier," said Trisha, who had replaced Dr. Yu to do the extubation. "You know as well as I do that older patients like Father John take longer," replied Dr. O'Reilly. "Well, I don't think you should assume the rest of the team knows that type of surgical detail," said Dr. Yu, who had come back into the OR in time to hear the exchange. Dr. O'Reilly sighed. "They know now, and we need to keep the patient on bypass for a while longer." "Hey everyone," said Grady, "instead of discussing lunch or whatever you're doing there, can you get this patient closed up? We are running out of time." "No, he can't. He says you should have known to plan for a longer operation," retorted Dr. Yu.

Suddenly, the patient's blood pressure began to drop. "Trisha, can you check your pressor drip?" Dr. Yu exclaimed. Trisha looked over at the drip. "For some reason, it seems to be . . . oh, yeah, it's this stupid pump! I did the calculation to adjust the drip rate, but maybe I made a mis . . . calculation." "Well, it's a fine time to tell us now," Bill said, looking with concern at the patient. "Well, you saw how Jane drug in this old equipment at the last minute. I don't even know where she got it from. I thought we had gotten rid of these dinosaurs. " Bill knew how much turn over in staff there had been in the OR tech group and began to wonder if the pump had even been cleaned properly. Dr. O'Reilly made a grimace and said, "Ok folks, I'm closing. Let's get this patient out of here before we run into any more issues." The team began scurrying to finish up their tasks, and the patient was sent off to postop.

Sarah stood still for a minute, checklist in hand, debating on whether to announce the final step—the sign out. This was where everyone on the team met together to make sure all the instruments were accounted for, the specimens were properly labeled, and any issues that had come up during the surgery were discussed. While she stood there, Bill came over pulling his gloves off, and said, "Sarah, I hope we didn't scare you off today. Really, we're a good bunch. We just like to do things the way we have always done them, and you see, everything usually works out ok. Can you do us a favor and get the suits upstairs to let us do our job? Get rid of the checklist. We'd all appreciate it." He patted her on the shoulder and walked off. Sarah was thankful it was time for a break. She walked over to her desk and punched in the number for Nursing Administration. She asked to speak with Janet Morelli, MSN, MPH, her manager, who was heading up the Surgical Quality and Safety Taskforce.

Janet's Challenge

Over sandwiches and coffee, Sarah related the events of the morning. Janet listened with dismay, realizing she was going to have to look for a new approach if she had any hope of implementing the checklist. She pondered her options. The Taskforce would be expecting a report on improvement in surgical outcomes in six months. Every meeting she had attended in the last month was focused on quality improvement, and this checklist had been recommended by the North Carolina Center for Hospital Quality and Patient Safety as a simple way to improve surgical safety. It had even been research tested by the World Health Organization, and she had followed their suggestion that the circulating nurse coordinate the effort.

> In order to implement the Checklist during surgery, a single person must be made responsible for checking the boxes on the list. This designated Checklist coordinator will often be a circulating nurse, but it can be any clinician or healthcare professional participating in the operation (WHO, 2008, p. 7).

Obviously, that hadn't worked, but she wasn't sure why. She was sure the team wanted to have better outcomes, but somehow she wasn't reaching them. What would convince them to use the checklist? What real reasons could they have for blocking it?

The Social Marketing Alternative

As her eyes moved from the window to her desk, she noticed that her alumni calendar from UNC at Chapel Hill, where she had completed her MPH the previous year, needed to be changed from January to February. "That's it!" she exclaimed to herself. "I'll try a social marketing approach like the one I learned about in my leadership classes. My surgical team needs to change their behavior to improve patient safety, and I'll use a social marketing approach to make that change happen."

That evening, Janet pulled out her notes from the class. She remembered that the key was to focus on your target audience. Thinking over the members of the surgical team, she decided that Sarah seemed to be the right person to be her primary target audience. Sarah was the most motivated to change, since her job was to make sure the operation was as successful as possible, and patient safety was definitely included in that success. However, Janet realized she needed some additional information about the role of the circulating nurse and what the risks and benefits might be for the person in this role. Also, she needed to consider what other influences might provide additional opportunities or even threats to the intervention. She recalled that "The Manager's Guide to Social Marketing," could be found on the Web site, http://www.turningpoint program.org. She accessed that site in order to create a plan using the six basic steps:

1. Describe the problem,

2. Conduct a market survey,

3. Create a marketing strategy,

4. Plan the intervention,

5. Plan what to monitor and evaluate, and then

6. Implement the intervention and evaluate the results.

As for describing the problem, Janet felt she had a clear enough picture of the issues. Now, for conducting the market survey, she would need to arrange for a focus group of circulating nurses to participate in one or more group sessions. She had a friend over in Public Relations who had interviewed her last month when the new Children's Day Hospital had opened. She would contact him, and also ask about what kinds of marketing he might suggest. She knew that The Four Ps were all important:

- Product—the behavioral change you want with its benefits, costs, and supporting services;

- Price including time, opportunity costs, overcoming barriers, and emotional factors;

- Place including equipment and managerial support; and

- Promotion including communication messages, materials, media channels, and activities that will effectively reach the target audience.

Next, Janet considered what she would monitor and evaluate. Her goal of reduction in surgical errors was supposed to be achieved in six months. Looking over her plan, she realized she did not know how she would even determine if she had achieved that outcome. In addition, that outcome timeframe was unrealistic. A 12-month plan was needed. Her team was struggling with constant change already. Real permanent change that improved outcomes would require careful monitoring and a clear method for evaluation. Her goals needed to be SMART: Simple, Measureable, Achievable, Realistic, and Timely.

She considered a number of goals she thought were important for the first three months before she settled on three of them:

1. Have all staff trained on the importance of the checklist at the regular staff meeting.

2. Identify one type of operation and operating team to pilot test the safety checklist.

3. Ask each pilot team member to submit at least one modification of the checklist that would help make it more useful.

In the meantime, Janet would oversee the focus groups and review the research results and help plan a marketing strategy with the assistance of the public relations department.

Janet then created three more goals for the second three months:

1. At the quarterly Taskforce meeting, report on her decision to use a social marketing approach and her progress to date and advise that additional time would be needed for implementation and evaluation.

2. Plan a launch date and events for the safety initiative, perhaps with a TV spot on the evening news with staff and team interviews.

3. Create an online survey linked to the local news channel Web site to gauge public interest and knowledge of the safety initiative at Forthright Medical Center.

During the next three months, the surgical team would pilot test the modified checklist. They would provide weekly feedback in a structured question format that also provided a free text area for comments. Sarah would compile the survey data weekly and give a report back to the team members. Outcomes data would be collected on infections, complications, and readmissions. At the end of the three months, Janet would review the data and meet with the team to discuss recommendations for improvement.

The intervention would continue for three additional months. At the end of the final three months, the outcomes data would again be reviewed and compared with outcomes data from the previous time periods. Feeling satisfied that she had a plan in place, Janet e-mailed Sarah to let her know that she had some ideas on how to make the checklist work, and that they would discuss it the next day. Turning out her light, Janet fell asleep before her head hit the pillow.

CASE ANALYSIS

This case introduces the concepts of social marketing and relates it to the issues around the Safe Surgery Saves Lives checklist. It illustrates the checklist's reception into the working environment peopled by very busy and resource-constrained healthcare professionals. It also introduces the fact that there are broad and powerful movements aimed at improving quality as well as local teams, but it raises some questions about whether knowledge and societal encouragement are sufficient to generate procedural and behavioral changes.

ASSIGNMENT QUESTIONS

1. Identify and define each team member as a separate target audience. How could a social marketing approach help target the intervention to improve the chances of success?

2. Medical culture has been traditionally hierarchical. The surgical safety checklist encourages breakdown of these traditional roles and evolution of a more collaborative approach. Discuss the impact of this flatter structure on the roles of each team member.

3. Think of the surgical safety checklist as a behavioral intervention for improving surgical safety. How are CQI and social marketing synergistic?

4. Discuss the benefits and barriers to implementation of the surgical safety checklist that each team member might voice at the weekly team member meeting. Who is most likely to be open to change?

5. Think about "selling" the product of the "surgical safety checklist." Consider the four Ps: Product, Price, Place, and Promotion. Help Janet create some marketing strategies for her campaign.

6. Review Janet's monitoring and evaluation plan for the second half of the year. Are the objectives "SMART"?

7. What are some health behavior models that might help Janet create an effective social marketing intervention?

CLASS EXERCISE

Review the literature on the surgical checklist. What have been its benefits and what are some of the reasons some providers have resisted it? What alternatives were tried to stimulate its acceptance? Did they seem more likely to be effective than Janet's social marketing idea? Why?

Prince Court Medical Centre: A Private Malaysian Healthcare Institution Prepares for a Pandemic of Influenza A (H1N1)

Roswitha M. Wolfram

INTRODUCTION

The staff of Prince Court Medical Centre (PCMC) moved in April 2009 to prepare their institution in Kuala Lumpur (KL), Malaysia for an outbreak of a pandemic of Influenza A (H1N1). Infection-control and patient-management measures were improved by applying sound clinical evidence, based on guidelines from previous experiences with pandemic outbreaks. They applied an integrated working model so that all involved parties had clearly-defined roles within the medical centre system. The aim was to reduce the number of patients developing complications from H1N1 infections requiring admission to an Intensive Care Unit (ICU) through early detection and appropriate treatment and to limit adverse drug reactions due to inappropriate utilization of antiviral medication.

Furthermore, effective personal protective equipment (PPE) measures were to be instituted to prevent hospital-acquired H1N1 infection of staff.

Background

The Prince Court Medical Centre (PCMC) is a 300-bed facility situated within the so-called "Golden Triangle" of KL, close to the major embassies and the twin towers. Owned by Petronas, the Malaysian state oil company, this futuristic facility was officially opened to the public in July 2008. Petronas employed an international consortium consisting of VAMED, an Austria-based company with a vast national and international experience with hospitals and hospital management and the Medical University of Vienna, Austria to manage the hospital. PCMC's Chief Executive Officer was originally from Australia where he had successfully managed hospitals for over 30 years and together with the Medical Director, who was from the Medical University of Vienna, blended their international knowledge with local experiences and needs to create this unique facility and hospital culture. The senior management of PCMC introduced a fairly new concept, for Malaysia, of hospital management focused primarily on providing the best medical services and care as well as thriving on continuous quality improvement and patient safety. This project would not have been possible without them and both the CEO and the Medical Director actively participated in and supported this project.

The healthcare workforce in November 2009 consisted of 600 nursing staff plus 80 consultants and 7 Medical Officers (MOs) in the Emergency Room (ER). The total medical centre personnel were 850 people including a number of contractors for outsourced services such as housekeeping. The patient population served was approximately 60% locals and expatriates and 40% medical tourists. While patients from all over the world were seeking medical care at PCMC, the majority of the medical tourists originated from Islamic countries. These customers are used to high international standards, usually undergoing treatment in the United States or Europe, and appreciate the comparatively low prices offered in Malaysia, while having the security that their religious and cultural needs are catered for in the same manner as their medical requirements. PCMC adheres to strict Halal food preparations and offers, besides a Surau or prayer room, pastoral care for all major religions and dedicated personnel proficient in several languages including Arabic. The other major group of medical tourists was from Australia as PCMC is providing an international high standard of care while being comparatively affordable. The decision for the

60/40% ratio and hence not to overly depend on "external" resources for revenue was made by the senior management of PCMC based on previous experiences during the Severe Adult Respiratory Syndrome (SARS) outbreak when a 50% decrease in tourism, including medical tourism, occurred in Malaysia and Singapore. The medical centre was accredited by Joint Commission International in 2008. By April 2009, 150 beds were open as the medical centre used a gradual rollout plan for introducing its services in order to maintain the high quality of care it aimed to deliver.

The need to cater to a multi-ethnic and multi-religious community also had to be taken into consideration. PCMC's customers are from different ethnic backgrounds, ranging from Malay, Chinese, and Indian, to expatriates and tourists from all over the world. In times of flu or other infectious disease pandemics the most important thing is ready and affordable access to care for everyone in the community. With the provision of both inpatient and much less expensive outpatient H1N1 treatment modalities, PCMC attempted to enable all patients to get the health care they require while minimizing costs. Follow up questionnaires and instructions for H1N1 patients treated on an outpatient's basis were developed along with brochures on when to seek urgent medical attention.

PCMC is a private medical centre, primarily catering to patients that have private insurance, are covered under respective corporate agreements with the medical centre, or are self-pay. PCMC, along with all other private hospitals in the Klang Valley, is not the primary choice of the average Malaysian seeking medical care as it is not on the panel of the government's Medicare equivalent. Patients without private healthcare insurance are usually cared for in governmental institutions where costs are borne by "public" insurance. However, emergency care and treatment has been provided to all patients at PCMC irrespective of their ability to pay. Therefore, every patient seeking medical care at PCMC's ER, including potential H1N1 patients, is treated. The sole difference is, if such patients should require admission for their condition after a visit to PCMC's ER, they are informed about their payment liability and offered and provided, if necessary, transfer to a governmental hospital. This practice also continued during H1N1 outbreak and necessitated that the ER, as the primary entry point, be prepared and ready.

Background from a Malaysian Perspective

The Ministry of Health (MOH) in Malaysia had failed to provide solid guidance during the early stages of H1N1 outbreak. Although there had been substantial previous experience in the region during the SARS outbreak in 2003, the MOH neglected to issue clear instructions on where and how to treat patients with suspected or confirmed H1N1 infection. Their initial directives were to treat patients only in dedicated governmental hospitals. At the same time there was an influx of patients to the ER with suspected H1N1 infections demanding screening and treatment. Although the MOH strictly declared that at that stage private hospitals were not to treat or admit patients with H1N1, there were no directives on how to screen or transfer patients to the dedicated facilities. Furthermore, there was a lack of supplies such as throat swabs, and the designated laboratory was unable to cope with the demand.

There was only one laboratory processing all throat swabs within the Klang Valley, which comprises the area of KL and its suburbs with approximately 3 million inhabitants, and the two governmental hospitals dedicated to treat and admit H1N1 cases were soon unable to cope with the increasing number of suspected and confirmed cases, plus the increasing concerns of the community demanding information and screening. The medical centre management realized that there was a substantial lack in communication and integration between the MOH, the dedicated healthcare providers, and the private hospitals in KL. In addition, the hospital's ER team was not prepared to deal with this influx of patients, and the facility was not set up to deal with many potentially infectious patients. Furthermore, availability of the antiviral Tamiflu was restricted. In early July 2009, the MOH declared that all hospitals had to screen, treat, and admit H1N1 patients, resulting in near panic throughout the private healthcare sector. There was a complete lack of public health service in the context of H1N1, and health education from governmental side had been practically nonexistent.

The Pandemic

During its first wave across the globe, experts believed that the H1N1 virus would be as deadly as the SARS outbreak in 2003 and that hospitals, especially ERs as the first point of contact with the patient, would likely see an increase of up to 20% more patients in the months ahead. Few healthcare institutions were equipped to deal adequately with such an increase without compromising patient care and exposing staff to the risk of infection. With limited existing resources available, it became important to define the needs of the institution, the healthcare workforce and the community, and to establish appropriate processes to be able to deal efficiently with this challenge.

The transmission of the H1N1 virus and rates of Influenza-like illness (ILI) continued to increase in some regions of the northern hemisphere such as North America. In Europe and Central and Western Asia, although overall influenza activity had remained low, an increase in transmission had been noted in a number of countries. While in some regions of the southern hemisphere influenza transmission had either returned to baseline or had declined dramatically (Australia), some countries in South East Asia were still reporting an increasing trend in respiratory diseases. Although the situation was seemingly under control in some countries, the experts anticipated that a second wave of the H1N1 pandemic had already commenced. In the United States and Mexico increasing numbers of patients presenting with H1N1 flu symptoms had been reported. The CDC stated "higher than expected" influenza hospitalization rates across the United States in September and October 2009, noting that the number of states reporting widespread influenza activity increased from 27 to 37 states within the previous week.

Studies from the CDC reported the number of deaths to be highest among people 25 to 49 years of age (39%), followed by people 50 to 64 years of age (25%) and people 5 to 24 years of age (16%), which is a different pattern from what is seen in seasonal influenza, where an estimated 90% of influenza-related deaths occur in people 65 years of age and older. Although a vaccine for H1N1 was under development and was supposedly coming on the market by mid-October, the quantity would not be sufficient to vaccinate the entire population and certain medical conditions were a contraindication for receiving the H1N1 vaccine. Furthermore, Malaysia was not one of the priority countries to receive the vaccine. As of October 14, the MOH Malaysia had been unable to provide the hospital with the information about when the vaccine would be available and had not specified the population to receive it first.

One essential observation was that this first wave of the H1N1 Pandemic could serve as a disaster drill to prepare everyone worldwide for the "real thing," the second and maybe third wave of the pandemic.

Start of the Project

Prior to kicking off this project, the situation in the medical centre was as follows: There were no directions on where to receive and screen patients with ILI. According to the MOH, PCMC and other private hospitals were not to take throat swabs, but were supposed to rely merely on clinical examination to diagnose ILI, and there were no other means of diagnosis available, such as questionnaires to investigate the travel history of patients presenting at the ER. Later on, PCMC was asked to use throat swabs but turnaround time of results was more than two days and not all samples were processed by the governmental labs, leaving the medical centre management to figure out what to do with the patients in the meantime. PCMC's ER was not set up to isolate potentially infectious patients. The medical centre had one isolation room per ward, each comprised of 12 single rooms. At the time of the outbreak a total of five wards and the ICU were open. Despite being fully operational since July 2008, the medical centre had only opened half of its wards to maintain and improve quality of care by gradually introducing its services resulting in capacity issues for admitting H1N1 patients. The ICU had 12 ventilator-equipped beds with two isolation rooms (negative pressure). Initially, there were no clear instructions on how to transfer patients, and PCMC doctors were faced with patients who did not want to be transferred to a public hospital. Based on the international situation, the medical centre's senior management anticipated that the designated governmental hospitals would soon reach their capacity to admit H1N1 patients, which happened in early July, but as an organization operational for a only one year, PCMC had no previous experience admitting this kind of infectious patient. There were no policies developed, and there was no process in place to guide patient flow from screening to potential admission and provision of continuity of care. The medical centre staff in the ER and on the wards was not prepared to deal with the situation. Most of them were concerned about themselves and their families being exposed to infectious patients.

Planning for the Project

Management perceived that with a new threat such as a pandemic it was crucial to develop an effective improvement process—to move the medical centre from an inadequate situation toward the goal of optimal patient care and the creation of a safe environment for staff, patients, and visitors.

The first step was to identify the available clinical evidence and guidelines; then to guide quality improvement via recording of baseline conditions and measuring the outcomes/effectiveness of the implemented new strategies. These included data collection as well as benchmarking these performance indicators with other private hospitals in KL and international data available from the WHO and CDC. Management sought to ensure that the outcomes were clearly defined and measurable. The outcomes measured during this project were admission of H1N1 patients to ICU due to complications, adverse drug reactions to antiviral medication, which were captured via PCMC's "Riskman" system, and medical centre-acquired H1N1 infections among the staff.

The most important step after identifying the goals was to establish a team, in this particular case, the Influenza Task Force. The Task Force was comprised of a Team Leader (Internal Medicine Specialist with vast experience in ICU and ER settings), an Infection Control (IC) Specialist, the medical centre's IC nursing team, Head of ER and Occupational Health/Primary Care Services and ER Head Nurse, the Director of Nursing or a representative, head nurses from the wards and ICU, the Medical Director, the Facility Manager, the Manager of Security and Housekeeping, Chief Engineer, Lab Manager, Chief Pharmacist, and the Head of the Purchasing Department, or their respective representatives. This core team consisted of 16 members, which may appear large, but was deemed necessary to "cover" all areas. Because teamwork was crucial, team members were selected based on interviews with regards to the requirements of the organization according to their knowledge, skills, and attitudes and their ability to effectively work together. The average number of team members present at each meeting was eight. Meeting minutes were distributed to all team members within two days of meetings via e-mail.

The Influenza Task Force Team Leader assessed the current situation by applying the eight characteristics of a microsystem or team described by Mohr and Batalden (2002). Due to the importance and complexity of the project, regular meetings were considered crucial for the outcome, to ensure integration of information. Strong leadership and full support by the senior management were considered necessary to ensure persistent pursuit of the set aim, consistency of the team, and anticipation of success.

During the first meetings of the Task Force, held weekly or as needed in between, the team analyzed available evidence from the CDC and WHO and identified the needs of the organization and community. The Influenza Task Force identified the essential requirements for this project, which are depicted in Table 10–1.

Potential issues that could hinder this project were identified utilizing an "Ishikawa Diagram" drawn on a white board during Task Force meetings, illustrating the steps and processes involved and allowing team

Table 10–1	Influenza Pandemic Preparedness Checklist		
To Do	**Fully Met**	**Partly Met**	**Planned**
Pandemic Coordinator/Pandemic Task Force?			
Contact numbers updated?			
Internal Influenza–Pandemic Plan available?			
Source of daily updated status report identified?			
Contacts at Ministry of Health identified?			
Communication with media via one person?			
Internal communication network implemented?			
Communication to stakeholders and suppliers?			
Information from staff on:			
Current status and possible risks			
Current case definition			
Personal hygiene measures			
Behavior during Pandemic (WHO Level 6)			
Planned organization's action for Level 6			
Organization's key personnel identified?			
Staff cross-trained in case of 30% staff dropout?			
Indicators identified when hospital needs to be closed?			
Projection on Business Continuity at Level 5 and Level 6?			
Minimum staff identified to continue medical services?			
Teleworking possible for certain staff?			

(continues)

Table 10-1 Continued			
To Do	**Fully Met**	**Partly Met**	**Planned**
Surgical masks available for staff?			
Surgical masks available for patients?			
Surgical masks available for visitors?			
N95 masks available for staff?			
N95 masks available for patients?			
Staff trained on when to use which mask?			
Mask distribution within hospital organized?			
Chemoprophylaxis/Therapy available?			
Start and indication for chemoprophylaxis regulated?			
Start for chemoprophylaxis of key personnel regulated?			
Pain medication/NSAR/Antibiotics available?			
Distribution and accessibility of drugs organized?			
Virucidal hand disinfectant available?			
Current stocks sufficient for minimum 3 weeks?			
Supplier can provide hand disinfectant within 2 weeks?			
Hand disinfectant accessible for everybody?			
Staff knows when and how to use hand disinfectant?			
Disposable gloves available?			
Current stocks sufficient for minimum 3 weeks?			
Supplier can provide gloves within 1 week?			

(continues)

Table 10-1 Continued			
To Do	*Fully Met*	*Partly Met*	*Planned*
If specific vaccine is available:			
Supply for hospital secured?			
Plan for vaccination of key staff implemented?			
Vaccination costs budgeted?			
Supply and storage of vaccine organized?			
Indicators and definitions for end of pandemic defined?			
Postpandemic briefing conducted?			

members to actively contribute. The following action items were identified as crucial:

1. Establish an Influenza Task Force Team to address all relevant issues.

2. Establish a comprehensive plan and measures to be taken in the medical centre according to level of pandemic internationally and in Malaysia.

3. Identify a location in the ER for screening patients for H1N1 and rectify facility requirements to ensure adherence to Infection Control measures.

4. Develop questionnaires for patients to facilitate the identification of suspected cases.

5. Develop a clinical assessment tool (Exhibit 10–1).

6. Develop checklists and follow up on items identified in the checklist.

7. Create information brochures for patients and visitors.

8. Identify strategy on how to perform temperature screening for everybody entering medical centre premises (including contractors, vendors, and all staff) and how access to the medical centre could be restricted if needed.

EXHIBIT 10–1

Clinical Assessment Tool

Patients with ILI and any of the following parameters should be considered for admission to the nearest hospital:
   Respiratory impairment: any of the following
   • Tachypnoea, respiratory rate > 24/min
   • Inability to complete sentence in one breath
   • Use of accessory muscles of respiration, supraclavicular recession
   • Oxygen saturation ≤ 92% on pulse oximetry
• Decreased effort tolerance since onset of ILI
• Respiratory exhaustion
• Chest pains
Evidence of clinical dehydration or clinical shock:
• Systolic BP < 90mmHg and/or diastolic BP < 60mmHg
• Capillary refill time > 2 seconds, reduced skin turgor
Altered conscious level (esp. in extremes of age):
• New confusion, striking agitation or seizures
Other clinical concerns:
• Rapidly progressive (esp. high fever > 3 days)

9. Mount hand disinfectants in strategic areas throughout the medical centre including all entrances with relevant instructions to disinfect hands prior to entering and leaving the medical centre.

10. Create and place information signage regarding flu symptoms and what to do at all entrance points of the medical centre.

11. Develop policies, work flows and guidelines on how to either transfer suspected/confirmed cases to other dedicated hospitals or on how to admit and treat patients at our institution.

12. Identify dedicated isolation wards (negative pressure) for admitted patients.

13. Identify the admission capacity of the medical centre for H1N1 patients with respect to availability of ICU beds with ventilator support and identify where to transfer patients once the medical centre reached admitting capacity.

14. Identify the need for antiviral medication and PPE, such as N95 masks, surgical masks, alcohol based hand disinfectant, throat swabs for all staff and patients and arrange for supply.

15. Arrange collaboration with local laboratory to test throat swabs.

16. Identify additional staff needed; establish comprehensive roster and education program for staff on H1N1, PPE, and treatment of Influenza patients. Staff education and competence was identified as essential to foster understanding about H1N1 and to ensure adherence to specified implementations.

17. Prepare medical education presentations on important information about H1N1 for staff and public, such as embassies, companies, and general practitioners.

18. Create weekly updates on new developments to be sent to all staff via e-mail.

Process mapping was identified as a powerful tool to gain more profound insight into the underlying requirements for the design and implementation of the new process. The key steps necessary to provide optimal patient care were identified, process flows drafted, and other supportive documents developed to help optimize care, while protecting staff from risk of infection. Mock runs identified whether the applied methods were comprehensible and feasible. Benchmarking was planned to help determine whether newly adopted processes were successful or whether they needed modification.

During the first weeks of the project, the Task Force realized that there was some resistance from staff, particularly the medical consultants, to adhere to certain measures implemented, such as informing the nursing staff when admitting a patient about his or her potential infectious status so that the staff could adhere to appropriate PPE. In one particular case, a medical consultant admitted a H1N1 patient to the ICU, failing to inform the ICU staff, resulting in the necessity to treat the exposed staff with Tamiflu as a postexposure prophylaxis. As personal intervention and education of the consultants by the Task Force Team Leader did not result in compliance by all consultants, the Medical Director sent out a staff memorandum informing all consultants that their admitting privileges would be withdrawn should they not adhere to implemented measures.

This finally led to a general acceptance and compliance to process guidelines issued by the Task Force.

Hand-Hygiene Compliance

Another issue was adherence to hand hygiene. The Task Force had hand disinfectants and information signs mounted in all strategic areas throughout the medical centre including all entrances, and everyone was informed to disinfect hands when entering and leaving the medical centre. The IC head nurse, who was doing hospital rounds on a regular basis, observed that some staff simply bypassed the hand disinfectants when entering hospital premises. The Task Force decided that more education was necessary to emphasize the importance of this simple measure and explain its background to all staff. After this was done, the medical centre experienced a substantially higher compliance rate.

The biggest challenge during the initial phase of the project was that medical consultants did not adhere to the guidelines with respect to admission of patients and prescription of antiviral medication. As there was considerable panic among patients with suspected or confirmed H1N1 infections, the demand for antiviral medication was high and consultants would prescribe the drugs to everyone irrespective of whether antiviral therapy was indicated according to international guidelines. The Medical Director had no choice but to restrict the sale of antivirals by the medical centre's pharmacy. This was necessary not only to avoid the development of potential drug resistance, but also to guarantee availability of Tamiflu for staff and severely ill patients. For approximately one month the Task Force Team Leader and the Medical Director reviewed every single prescription for Tamiflu and the respective patient's health status and decided on a case-by-case basis whether the pharmacy could release the medication for that particular patient. After these initial difficulties, consultants developed a more sensible approach to prescribing antiviral medication realizing that the duration of disease was not significantly abbreviated by Tamiflu and based on reported side effects.

Similar difficulties were encountered with admitting patients to the medical centre. During the "hot phase" of the pandemic in Malaysia, governmental institutions quickly reached their admitting capacity and soon the same thing happened to the private hospitals in the area. PCMC had to open additional wards and develop staffing rosters to complement the situation. As some of the medical centre's consultants did not adhere to the issued guidelines on whom to admit and whom to treat on an outpatient basis according to severity of disease and underlying comorbidities, PCMC soon reached its admitting capacity and had to refer some severely ill patients to other institutions. Hence, the Medical Director made the decision that admission of patients with suspected or confirmed H1N1 was also to be monitored and controlled by the Influenza Task Force Team Leader and in difficult cases by the Medical Director himself. Over the course of several weeks these somewhat drastic measures showed the expected results, and consultants accepted the implemented strategies and guidelines.

The utilization of flow charts, as described previously, based on sound scientific evidence, supported the improvement activities. Patients with underlying conditions such as asthma or heart disease had been described as more prone to develop severe complications from H1N1 infections. Therefore, care for these patients needed to be guided appropriately and systematically. An example of an algorithm the Task Force introduced into the ER to facilitate patient management is depicted in Figure 10–1.

The Task Force identified two major components that needed thorough measurement:

1. Whether staff, patients, and visitors complied with the implemented processes, and the analysis and benchmark of outcomes. The assessment of compliance was continuously monitored and reported back to the Task Force by the IC nurse, and the Team Leader included, for example, checks on compliance for hand disinfection and wearing appropriate PPE when caring for H1N1 patients. The Medical Director sent reminders to all staff to adhere to the implemented procedures during his weekly updates. The Task Force had chosen three defined outcomes, and data have been collected since the beginning of the project in April 2009. That decision was made based on the then-current literature and PCMC's mission to provide a safe environment for patients, visitors, and staff. It had been estimated that a quarter of patients with H1N1 infection would require ICU treatment and that antiviral medication such as Tamiflu could cause severe side effects and adverse drug reactions. The three quality indicators identified for this project were:

    *   Number of patients who require ICU admission;

    *   Number of staff with medical centre-acquired H1N1 infection; and

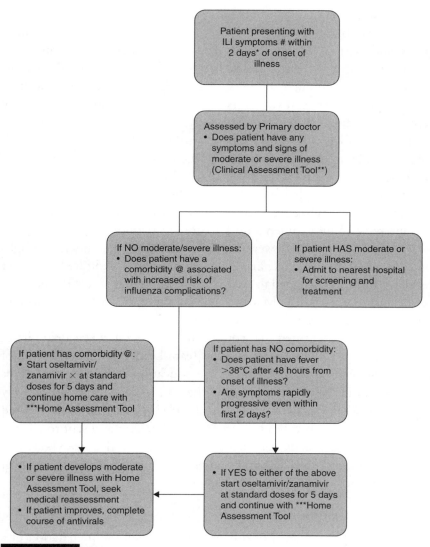

Figure 10–1 Algorithm for Treatment of ILI in Adult Patients with Comorbidities in an Outpatient Setting

- Number of adverse drug reactions or side effects of Tamiflu, captured by PCMC's "Riskman" System.

A preliminary analysis revealed that three patients had required temporary ICU admission without the need of ventilator support, and no casualties from H1N1 had been observed in the medical centre. Patient numbers were counted from April until August. After that, counting was stopped in accordance with CDC recommendations. A total of 102 inpatients and over 2000 outpatients had been treated during this time period, starting with 19 encounters in April and going up to 560 encounters in August. Although several staff members were home-quarantined after suspected exposure to H1N1 patients, there had not been any reports of medical centre-acquired infections. Two PCMC staff members were actually diagnosed with H1N1, but they had not had contact with infected patients. After benchmarking these preliminary outcomes with the reports from the CDC and WHO, the Task Force was able to assume that the measures implemented had so far been successful. The collection of data with regards to adverse drug reactions to Tamiflu was ongoing and was intended to be analyzed after a six-month period.

Patient feedback sheets were readily available at all counters throughout the medical centre and in patient rooms, and a dedicated customer feedback team was assigned to analyze these forms and report the findings to the Task Force and the Management on a monthly basis. Patients and families were encouraged to share their opinions.

Management identified staff education on H1N1 as a key action item, and consequently, the IC team and the Team Leader developed a series of continuing medical (CME) and nurse education (CNE) presentations with relevant H1N1 information, and the staff was encouraged to actively participate. Weekly updates on the current H1N1 situation were prepared by the Task Force Team Leader and Medical Director and sent to all staff via e-mail. These e-mails were identified as crucial so that everybody had access to relevant knowledge and understanding and to foster team spirit and compliance to implemented strategies.

Serving the Community

Although the primary goal of this project had been the preparation of a private medical centre in times of an H1N1 pandemic, to enable the provision of optimal care to patients while protecting the healthcare staff, other patients, and visitors from medical centre-acquired H1N1 infection, there was also a need to extend knowledge transfer and care beyond medical centre boundaries. As mentioned earlier, collaboration with the local healthcare authorities had been problematic as the issued directives were imprecise, unreliable, and sometimes even contradictory. When

PCMC started the project, the Influenza Task Force realized that general practitioners (GPs) in the surrounding area of the medical centre did not know how to treat or where to refer suspected H1N1 patients. Furthermore, there was an urgent need in the community, especially at companies and embassies, for information on H1N1. As the pandemic level was raised to Stage 6, the insecurity of the community increased. There was a total lack of public information on what to do, for example, when feeling sick, how to recognize the symptoms of H1N1, whether to avoid crowded places, what to do with children (whether to keep them at home or send them to school), whether the seasonal influenza vaccine would protect you from contracting H1N1, and the list continued on and on. PCMC's senior management realized the importance of information and also its obligation as a healthcare provider to educate the community based on the scientific evidence provided by international authorities such as the WHO and CDC. Therefore, the Task Force Team Leader, with the support of the IC team and the Medical Director, started to prepare regular newsletters on important H1N1 information for embassies, informing them about the importance of simple measures such as hand disinfection for personnel and visitors entering the premises and the availability of their services. Health education talks were given to companies and European Community delegations by the Influenza Task Force Team Leader and CME sessions initiated (free of charge) for GPs. In the absence of support from local health authorities, these simple measures may have contributed to an increased sense of security of the community and to risk reduction for contracting the H1N1 infection, and may have improved the delivery of patient care outside the medical centre.

Before August 2009, the MOH had not issued structured guidelines on how to treat patients with H1N1, and there was neither financial support nor the provision of medication and other supplies to private hospitals in Malaysia. Furthermore, the provision of antiviral medication and throat swabs had been restricted by local healthcare authorities to governmental institutions, and access to care had not been consistently provided to the entire community. Although there had been substantial previous experience with an infectious disease outbreak during the 2003 SARS epidemic, no national policy had been developed to support the community during a pandemic. PCMC's senior management realized that there was a need to develop proper strategies on how to provide care in the private sector and on how to educate the public in order to prevent further spread of disease. As a private medical centre wholly-owned by Petronas, the state oil and gas company, PCMC is not only a first class facility but also has solid financial backing. Financial issues, experienced in other institutions, did not apply to a similar extent, other than remaining competitive with other private healthcare providers. With regard to staying competitive and providing access to care to all patients, the market was thoroughly analyzed and vendor evaluations performed to identify cost-effective provisions and adequate supply of antiviral medication, hand disinfectants, PPE, and throat swabs. A substantial part of PCMC's patients, primarily from the local community in KL, was either not covered by insurance or not financially privileged enough to afford services in a private hospital. In response to the medical centre's obligation as a healthcare provider to ensure access to care for everyone and to reduce costs, if possible, the medical centre's management developed the following strategies: 1) Screening programs at the ER department, establishment of contact with a governmental hospital to transfer patients to, and development of transfer process flows; 2) development of strict admission criteria to avoid unnecessary and costly inpatient treatment; and 3) outpatient-based treatment plans where patients, after assessment and diagnosis was performed in the ER, would be prescribed appropriate medication and remain at home until recovered. Telephone follow-up by the hospital MOs was performed free of charge and ensured continuity of care. Furthermore, all patients were provided with relevant H1N1 information brochures.

Staff Development

Management sought to educate and motivate Task Force Team members during regular meetings where information was shared and discussed, and project progress and related strategies were regularly reassessed for their efficiency. Open communication facilitated the identification of potential problems and barriers. The understanding of being a part of a team within a system with clearly defined roles and responsibilities was intended to motivate staff to develop new skills and enhance their understanding of how changes in process flows are interrelated. Task Force members had been educated about the importance of personal improvement projects to gain the necessary insight and reflective capacity needed to drive a system-wide improvement project. Educating Task Force members and staff about the principles of quality improvement by applying Plan-Study-Do-Act cycles throughout this project and providing quality care and safety during a pandemic would yield experience that could be utilized for future improvement.

CASE ANALYSIS

The plan to "prepare" the medical centre to be able to cope should a pandemic arise turned into a real project over the period of several weeks. Once the goals were clearly defined the project started. Many techniques chosen by either the Influenza Task Force Team Leader, or the Team, were initially based on "common sense," such as the necessity to work as a team, to identify potential barriers, and to look through all steps in a process, to name a few.

The experience gained from this project by the time this case was prepared showed that simple measures like regular hand disinfection and education of people about cough etiquette and social responsibility in times of a flu outbreak had helped the community to stay healthy and to prevent further spread of disease. Even in the absence of clear instructions and guidelines from the local health authorities, it was possible to develop and implement a comprehensive strategy to prepare an organization for a pandemic, with the help of an Influenza Task Force and international resources from the Internet and to extend this knowledge beyond hospital boundaries to support the community in dealing with the current situation.

In this case we see an attempt to use the CQI approach in a mixed culture of both local and expatriate managers and care deliverers. The effort appears to be one of introducing concepts of continuous change to the staff. Although the owner of the medical centre is a government entity, the medical centre management finds itself in conflict with the demands of the Ministry and the demands of the community. One driving factor is the strategy of serving the international market, which has been very sensitive in the past to problems related to disease pandemics. Therefore, unusual measures are called for during the threat period.

ASSIGNMENT QUESTIONS

1. How did the situation at Prince Court Medical Centre in Malaysia differ from the situation experienced at a typical American hospital during the same time period?

2. How did its situation differ from that of most hospitals in Kuala Lampur during the same time period?

3. How much of the work done by the Task Force would have normally fallen to Ministry of Health authorities and how much was inevitably an institutional requirement?

4. What do you think of the structure of the Task Force?

5. What does Management need to do next to capitalize on the continuous quality improvement experience gained during the H1N1 epidemic?

6. How can the medical centre capitalize further on this effort in its work within the community?

CLASS EXERCISE

Research the Malaysian healthcare system. How is it that a state-owned oil company would have a large, modern medical centre? What is the public–private mix of healthcare providers in the country?

Financial Analysis and Quality Management in Patriot County, Ohio

Cheryll D. Lesneski

INTRODUCTION

Dr. Robert Chernow, MD, DrPH, Director of the Patriot County (Ohio) Health Department, was trying to decide what to do with the financial analysis that he had received from his fiscal officer, Thadeus Brewski, MBA. Thad had let Dr. Chernow know how much he appreciated the seminar that he had attended on using financial ratios for quality improvement in public health departments. Thad reported that the public health professionals at the seminar spoke about how local public health departments (LPHDs) have been experiencing a reduction in funding, following a brief surge of increased funding for surveillance and preparedness after the tragic terrorist events of 9/11/2001. In addition to competing with other governmental services for funding, LPHDs have difficulty demonstrating the effective and efficient use of public resources. This limitation is due in part to a lack of transparency and accountability about how public health revenues are spent. LPHDs have not employed standard financial ratios, commonly found in local government and other healthcare organizations, such as hospitals, to report on their financial condition (Honoré, Clarke, Meade, and Menditto, 2007). Thad presented Dr. Chernow with information about how financial ratio analysis provides a common language for understanding the financial condition of

LPHDs. Thad also learned that a number of LPHDs around the United States have had to drastically cut services because of poor financial management attributed in great part to the absence of financial analytical tools and their use by public health departments. Thad left the seminar confident that the use of financial ratios to assess and report on the LPHD's capacity to provide services, today and in the future, was a vital quality improvement strategy for his organization.

Thad's Analysis

Thad had received the form given in Table 11–1 at the seminar and had applied it to Patriot's current financial position.

Table 11–1 LPHA Financial Data for Ratio Analysis

Item Number	Local Public Health Agency (LPHA) Financial Data
	Revenues:
1	Federal Revenues (exclude Medicaid/Medicare reimbursements)
2	State Revenues
3	County Government Revenues
4	Medicaid Revenues
5	Medicare Revenues
6	Total Fees from Medical Services
7	Total Fees from Environmental Health Services
8	Total Fees from Vital Stats
9	Total Fees, Other
10	Total Other Revenues
11	**TOTAL OF REVENUES FROM ALL SOURCES**
	Expenditures:
12	Salaries
13	Fringe Benefits
14	Expenses
15	Other
16	Fixed Capital Outlay (Construction/Renovation)
17	**TOTAL EXPENDITURES**
	Specific Revenue and Expenditure Breakouts *(The amounts in this section are different breakdowns of the amounts above, not in addition to the above dollar amounts.)*
	Revenues:
18	Total Restricted (categorical) Revenues

Table 11–1 Continued

Item
Number   *Local Public Health Agency (LPHA) Financial Data*

19	One-Time Revenues
20	A. County Special Tax Revenue
	B. Millage Rate
21	Other Agency Venture Generated Revenues (provide description in Column T. Ex. wellness programs, mini-course grant writing, trainings, etc.)
22	Total Home Health Revenues
23	Total Grant Revenues
24	Total Environmental Health Revenues
25	Total Dental Revenues
26	Total Immunization Revenues
27	Total Medical Services Revenues (exclude Immunizations, Dental, STD, TB, Epi, HIV/AIDS, and Outreach activities)
28	Total Revenues in Annual Operating Budget
29	Actual Budgeted Revenues Received
	Expenditures:
30	Total Administrative Expenditures (defined in Column T)
31	Total Program Expenditures (all Agency Expenditures less Administration)
32	Total Laboratory Expenditures
33	Total Public Health Preparedness Expenditures
34	Total Chronic Diseases Expenditures
35	Total Home Health Expenditures
36	Total Medical Services Expenditures (exclude Immunizations, Dental, STD, TB, Epi, HIV/AIDS, and Outreach activities)
37	Total Pharmacy Expenditures
38	Total Environmental Health Expenditures
39	Total Dental Expenditures
40	Total Immunization Expenditures

Fund Balances

41	General Fund Balance

Other Financial

42	Accounts Receivable All Payers
43	Total Amount of Accounts Receivables That Are "Written-Off"
44	# of Programs with Expenditures That Exceed Dedicated plus Self-Generated Revenues
45	# of Programs w/ a Completed Cost Analysis

(continues)

Table 11-1	Continued

Item
Number **Local Public Health Agency (LPHA) Financial Data**

Demographics

46	Total Population
47	Median Population age
48	Number in Population under 18
49	Number in Population over 65
50	% of Population below poverty
51	# of residential building permits issued current FY
52	Number of people in county that are covered by Medicaid
53	Number of people in county that are uninsured

Workforce

54	Total FTE (Full-Time Equivalents)
55	Total Liability Days for Unused Vacation and Sick Leave (Include Comp Time)
56	# of Financial Management Employees with Discipline Specific Training/Education
57	# of Employees with Financial Management Responsibilities

Mission Critical (Other Financial and Related Indicators)

58	# of Priority Programs* in Annual Operating Budget (*Identified through Strategic Planning or Community Health Assessment Process)
59	# of Priority Programs Identified in Strategic Plan or Community Health Assessment
60	# of Community Health Outcomes Showing Improvement During a 3-Year Period
61	# of Community Health Outcomes Monitored Yearly
62	Total Expenditures Targeted to Health Disparity Programs
63	Total Number of Agency Programs

RATIOS

Revenue Ratios

1	Revenues per capita
2	Federal Revenues as % of Total Revenues
3	State Revenues as % of Total Revenues
4	County Revenues as % of Total Revenues

Table 11–1	Continued

Item Number	Local Public Health Agency (LPHA) Financial Data
5	Medicaid Revenues as % of Total Revenues
6	Medicare Revenues as % of Total Revenues
7	Total Grant revenues as a % of Total Revenues
8	Total Fees Collected as a % of Total Revenues
9	Total Home Health Revenue as % of Total Revenues
10	Other Revenue as % of Total Revenues
11	Restricted Revenues as % of Total Revenues
12	Total Margin (Total Revenues – Total Expenditures)/Total Revenues
13	Operating Surplus/Deficit (Total Revenues-Total Expenses)
14	One Time Revenues as a % of Total Revenues
15	Budgeted Revenues Received as % of Budgeted Revenues in Annual Operating Budget
16	Days of Revenue in Accounts Receivable
17	Accounts Receivables Written Off as a % of Total Fees Collected
18	General Fund Balance as a % of Total Revenue
19	Total Environmental Health Revenues as a % of Total Revenue
20	Total Dental Revenues as a % of Total Revenue
21	Total Immunization Revenues as a % of Total Revenue
22	Total Medical Revenues as a % of Total Revenue
	Expenditure Ratios
23	Expenditures per Capita
24	Full Time Employees per 1,000 Population
25	Fringe Benefits as a % of Salary and Wages
26	Salaries & Wages as a % of Total Expenditures
27	Administrative Expenditures as % of Total Expenditures
28	Average Accumulated Employee Leave Liability
29	Laboratory Expenditures as % of Total Expenditures
30	Public Health Preparedness Expenditures as % of Total Expenditures
31	Chronic Diseases Expenditures as % of Total Expenditures
32	Home Health Expenditures as a % to Home Health Revenue
33	Medical Services Expenditures as a % of Total Expenditures
34	Pharmacy Expenditures as a % of Total Expenditures
35	Environmental Health Expenditures as a % of Total Expenditures
36	Dental Expenditures as a % of Total Expenditures
37	Immunization Expenditures as a % of Total Expenditures

(continues)

Table 11-1	Continued

Item Number	Local Public Health Agency (LPHA) Financial Data
	Mission Critical Ratios (Other Financial and Related Indicators)
38	% of Monitored Community Health Outcomes w/ Improvement During 3-Year Period
39	% of Community Priority PH Issues in the Annual Operating Budget
40	County Special Tax Revenue as % of Total Revenues
41	LPHA Venture-Generated Revenues as % of Total Revenues
42	% of Financial Staff w/ 100% of Public Health Financial Competencies
43	% of Programs w/ Expenditures that Exceed Dedicated plus Self-Generated Revenues
44	% Programs w/ Completed Cost Analysis
45	% of Total Expenditures Targeted to Health Disparities Programs
	Community Statistics
46	Population Trend
47	Median Population Age
48	% of Population under 18
49	% of Population over 65
50	% Population Below Poverty Level
51	% Population Insured by Medicaid
52	% Uninsured Population
53	Residential Building Permits/1,000 Population

Source: Honoré and Lesneski, 2009

Dr. Chernow was considering whether to refer Thad's analysis to the agency's continuous quality improvement council or to take some other action or just make a mental note of the issues identified as another input to his thought processes in running the agency.

Thad's note had indicated that he had first conducted the analysis using the form shown in Table 11–2, and then he used the template that he had received to draw up the analysis reproduced in Table 11–3. The comments in the left-hand column are provided with the form, while the comments in the right-hand column are his conclusions.

Table 11-2 Patriot County Financial Analysis

Financial and Other Related Indicators

Patriot County Health Department
Enter "City"
Enter "State" and "Zip Code"
Enter "Area Code and Phone Number" (XXX) XXX-XXXX
Enter "Contact Person"

Fiscal Year: _____ to _____

County Public Health Department
City
State, Zip
Phone Number
Contact
Fiscal Year (12 month period only)

Item Number	Local Public Health Agency (LPHA) Financial Data	Actual 2008	% Change in Actuals from 2007	Actual 2007
	FINANCIAL			
	Revenues:			
1	Federal Revenues (Exclude Medicaid/Medicare Reimbursements)	$ 1,359,573	-3.0%	$ 1,401,600
2	State Revenues	1,724,741	-0.4%	1,730,944
3	County Government Revenues	4,343,985	-2.5%	4,457,000
4	Medicaid Revenues	2,139,615	0.4%	2,131,500
5	Medicare Revenues	500,366	0.6%	497,599
6	Total Fees from Medical Services	868,551	-7.1%	935,400
7	Total Fees from Environmental Health Services	925,600	-3.9%	962,900
8	Total Fees from Vital Stats	166,780	0.8%	165,500
9	Total Fees, Other	61,000	4.5%	58,400
10	Total Other Revenues	65,333	4.4%	62,550
11	**TOTAL OF REVENUES FROM ALL SOURCES**	$ 12,155,544	-2.0%	$ 12,403,393
	Expenditures:			
12	Salaries	7,198,543	0.6%	7,156,750
13	Fringe Benefits	2,335,988	1.2%	2,307,899
14	Expenses	3,068,318	2.0%	3,007,101
15	Other	25,000	-6.5%	26,750
16	Fixed Capital Outlay (Construction/Renovation)			
17	**TOTAL EXPENDITURES**	$ 12,627,849	1.0%	$ 12,498,500

(continues)

Table 11-2 Continued

Specific Revenue and Expenditure Breakouts *(The amounts in this section are different breakdowns of the amounts above, not in addition to the above dollar amounts)*

Item Number	Local Public Health Agency (LPHA) Financial Data	Actual 2008	% Change in Actuals from 2007	Actual 2007
	Revenues:			
18	Total Restricted (categorical) Revenues	$ 10,968,484	1.0%	$ 10,860,155
19	One-Time Revenues	$ 175,000	-22.2%	$ 225,000
20	A. County Special Tax Revenue	$ 0		$ 0
	B. Millage Rate			
21	Other Agency Venture Generated Revenues (Ex. wellness programs, mini course grant writing, trainings, etc)	$ 23,600	-75.2%	$ 95,000
22	Total Home Health Revenues	$ 398,000	-24.4%	$ 526,790
23	Total Grant Revenues	$ 960,625	-6.6%	$ 1,028,000
24	Total Environmental Health Revenues	$ 847,000	-13.7%	$ 981,200
25	Total Dental Revenues	$ 78,000	-11.3%	$ 87,951
26	Total Immunization Revenues	$ 213,677	1.3%	$ 210,890
27	Total Medical Services Revenues (exclude Immunizations, Dental, STD, TB, Epi, HIV/AIDS, and Outreach activities)	$ 968,551	-0.9%	$ 977,600
28	Total Revenues in Annual Operating Budget	$ 12,510,000	-0.3%	$ 12,550,000
29	Actual Budgeted Revenues Received	$ 12,003,927	-3.0%	$ 12,371,000
	Expenditures:			
30	Total Administrative Expenditures	$ 5,158,830	1.2%	$ 5,097,000
31	Total Program Expenditures (all Agency Expenditures less Administration)	$ 7,469,019	0.9%	$ 7,401,500
32	Total Laboratory Expenditures	$ 530,690	-4.6%	$ 556,150
33	Total Public Health Preparedness Expenditures	$ 551,170	-14.5%	$ 645,000
34	Total Chronic Diseases Expenditures	$ 478,002	5.8%	$ 451,800
35	Total Home Health Expenditures	$ 551,030	2.4%	$ 538,074
36	Total Medical Services Expenditures (exclude Immunizations, Dental, STD, TB, Epi, HIV/AIDS, and Outreach activities)	$ 1,216,000	11.1%	$ 1,095,000
37	Total Pharmacy Expenditures	$ 273,089	7.4%	$ 254,321

Table 11-2 Continued

Item Number	Local Public Health Agency (LPHA) Financial Data	Actual 2008	% Change in Actuals from 2007	Actual 2007
38	Total Environmental Health Expenditures	$ 1,086,100	5.0%	$ 1,034,760
39	Total Dental Expenditures	$ 258,610	8.4%	$ 238,600
40	Total Immunization Expenditures	$ 325,100	3.0%	$ 315,688
	Fund Balances			
41	General Fund Balance	$ 103,830	-78.3%	$ 479,200
	Other Financial			
42	Accounts Receivable All Payers	$ 696,900	3.9%	$ 670,686
43	Total Amount of Accounts Receivables That Are "Written-Off"	$ 324,555	10.9%	$ 292,670
44	# of Programs with Expenditures That Exceed Dedicated plus Self Generated Revenues	18	63.6%	11
45	# of Programs w/ a Completed Cost Analysis	3	50.0%	2
	Demographic			
46	Total Population	928622	0.2%	926986
47	Median Population age	35.2	0.6%	35
48	Number in Population under 18	176500	0.2%	176222
49	Number in Population over 65	321899	0.4%	320745
50	% of Population below poverty	5.9%	5.4%	5.6%
51	# of residential building permits issued current FY	3325	-32.5%	4923
52	Number of people in county that are covered by Medicaid	9750	-2.3%	9980
53	Number of people in county that are uninsured	48100	3.7%	46388
	Workforce			
54	Total FTE (Full Time Equivalents)	271.00	4.2%	260.00
55	Total Liability Days for Unused Vacation and Sick Leave (Include Comp Time)	15377.00	2.4%	15010.00
56	# of Financial Management Employees with Discipline Specific Training/Education	2.00	0.0%	2.00
57	# of Employees w/Financial Management Responsibilities	12.00	0.0%	12.00
	Mission Critical (Other Financial and Related Indicators)			
58	# of Priority Programs* in Annual Operating Budget (*Identified through Strategic Planning or Community Health Assessment Process)	6	200.0%	2
59	# of Priority Programs Identified in Strategic Plan or Community Health Assessment	6	100.0%	3

(continues)

Table 11-2 Continued

Item Number	Local Public Health Agency (LPHA) Financial Data	Actual 2008	% Change in Actuals from 2007	Actual 2007
60	# of Community Health Outcomes Showing Improvement During a 3-Year Period	2	-60.0%	5
61	# of Community Health Outcomes Monitored Yearly	9	0.0%	9
62	Total Expenditures Targeted to Health Disparity Programs	$ 35,600	0.0%	$ 35,600
63	Total Number of Agency Programs	51	13.3%	45
	NO DATA INPUT REQUIRED BELOW THIS LINE			
	RATIOS			
	Revenue Ratios			
1	Revenues per Capita (Total Revenues/Population)	$13.09	-2.2%	$13.38
2	Federal Revenues as % of Total Revenues (Federal Revenues/Total Revenues)	11.2%	-1.0%	11.3%
3	State Revenues as % of Total Revenues (State Revenues/Total Revenues)	14.2%	1.7%	14.0%
4	County Revenues as % of Total Revenues (County Revenues/Total Revenues)	35.7%	-0.5%	35.9%
5	Medicaid Revenues as % of Total Revenues (Medicaid Revenues/Total Revenues)	17.6%	2.4%	17.2%
6	Medicare Revenues as % of Total Revenues (Medicare Revenues/Total Revenues)	4.1%	2.6%	4.0%
7	Total Grant revenues as a % of Total Revenues (Grant Revenues/Total Revenues)	7.9%	-4.6%	8.3%
8	Total Fees Collected as a % of Total Revenues (Total Clinic, Env, Vital, Other Fees Collected/Total Revenues)	16.6%	-2.8%	17.1%
9	Total Home Health Revenue as % of Total Revenues (Total Home Health Revenue/Total Revenues)	3.3%	-22.9%	4.2%
10	Other Revenue as % of Total Revenues (Other Revenue/Total Revenues)	0.5%	6.6%	0.5%
11	Restricted Revenues as % of Total Revenues (Restricted Revenues/Total Revenues)	90.2%	3.1%	87.6%

Table 11-2 Continued

Item Number	Local Public Health Agency (LPHA) Financial Data	Actual 2008	% Change in Actuals from 2007	Actual 2007
12	Total Margin (Total Revenues—Total Expenditures)/Total Revenues	-3.9%	406.7%	-0.8%
13	Operating Surplus/Deficit (Total Revenues/Total Expenses)	0.96	-3.0%	0.99
14	One Time Revenues as a % of Total Revenues (One Time Revenues/Total Revenues)	1.4%	-20.6%	1.8%
15	Budgeted Revenues Received as a % of Budgeted Revenues in Annual Operating Budget (Budgeted Revenues Received/Total Revenues in Annual Operating Budget)	96.0%	-2.7%	98.6%
16	Days in Accounts Receivable (Accounts Receivables Balance/(Total Payers Revenues/365 days))	55	5.9%	52
17	Accounts Receivables Written Off as a % of Total Fees Collected (Accounts Receivables Written Off/Total Clinic, EH, Vital, Other Fees Collected)	16.1%	16.4%	13.8%
18	General Fund Balance as a % of Total Revenue (General Fund Balance/Total Revenue)	0.9%	-77.9%	3.9%
19	Total Environmental Health Revenues as a % of Total Revenue (Total Environmental Health Revenue/Total Revenue)	7.0%	-11.9%	7.9%
20	Total Dental Revenues as a % of Total Revenue (Total Dental Revenue/Total Revenue)	0.6%	-9.5%	0.7%
21	Total Immunization Revenues as a % of Total Revenue (Total Immunization Revenue/Total Revenue)	1.8%	3.4%	1.7%
22	Total Medical Revenues as a % of Total Revenue (Total Medical Revenue/Total Revenue)	8.0%	1.1%	7.9%
Expenditure Ratios				
23	Expenditures per Capita (Total Expenditures/Population)	$13.60	0.9%	$13.48
24	Employees per 1,000 Population (Number of Full Time Employees/(Population/1000))	0.29	4.0%	0.28

(continues)

Table 11-2 Continued

Item Number	Local Public Health Agency (LPHA) Financial Data	Actual 2008	% Change in Actuals from 2007	Actual 2007
25	Fringe Benefits as a % of Salary and Wages (Total Fringe Benefits/(Total Salary + Wages))	32.5%	0.6%	32.2%
26	Salaries & Wages as a % of Total Expenditures ((Total Salaries + Wages)/Total Expenditures)	57.0%	-0.4%	57.3%
27	Administrative Expenditures as a % of Total Expenditures (Administrative Expenditures/Total Expenditures)	40.9%	0.2%	40.8%
28	Average Accumulated Employee Leave Liability (Total Accumulated Employee Leave Liability/Total FTE)	57	-1.7%	58
29	Laboratory Expenditures as % of Total Expenditures (Laboratory Expenditures/Total Expenditures)	4.2%	-5.6%	4.4%
30	Public Health Preparedness Expenditures as % of Total Expenditures (Public Health Preparedness Expenditures/Total Expenditures)	4.4%	-15.4%	5.2%
31	Chronic Diseases Expenditures as % of Total Expenditures (Chronic Disease Expenditures/Total Expenditures)	3.8%	4.7%	3.6%
32	Home Health Expenditures as a % to Home Health Revenue (Home Health Expenditures/Total Home Health Revenues)	138.4%	35.5%	102.1%
33	Medical Services Expenditures as a % of Total Expenditures (Medical Services Expenditures/Total Expenditures)	9.6%	9.9%	8.8%
34	Pharmacy Expenditures as a % of Total Expenditures (Pharmacy Expenditures/Total Expenditures)	2.2%	6.3%	2.0%
35	Environmental Health Expenditures as a % of Total Expenditures (Environmental Health Expenditures/Total Expenditures)	8.6%	3.9%	8.3%
36	Dental Expenditures as a % of Total Expenditures (Dental Expenditures/Total Expenditures)	2.0%	7.3%	1.9%
37	Immunization Expenditures as a % of Total Expenditures (Immunization Expenditures/Total Expenditures)	2.6%	1.9%	2.5%
38	**Mission Critical Ratios (Other Financial and Related Indicators)** % of Monitored Community Health Outcomes w/ Improvement During 3-Year Period (# of Improved Monitored Community Health Outcomes/ # of Monitored Community Health Outcomes)	22.2%	-60.0%	55.6%

Table 11-2 Continued

Item Number	Local Public Health Agency (LPHA) Financial Data	Actual 2008	% Change in Actuals from 2007	Actual 2007
39	% of Community Priority PH Issues in the Annual Op Budget (# of Community Priority PH Issues in AOB/# of Community Priority PH Issues)	100.0%	50.0%	66.7%
40	County Special Tax Revenue as % of Total Revenues (County Special Tax Revenues/Total Revenues)	0.0%	NA	0.0
41	LPHA Venture-Generated Revenues as % of Total Revenues (LPHA Venture-Generated Revenues/Total Revenues)	0.2%	-74.7%	0.8%
42	% of Financial Staff w/ 100% of Public Health Financial Competencies (# of Financial Staff w/ 100% of PH Financial Competencies/# of Financial Staff)	16.7%	0.0%	16.7%
43	% of Programs with Expenditures that Exceed Dedicated plus Self-Generated Revenues ((# of Programs w/Expenditures that Exceed Dedicated + Self-Generated Revenues) /Total Revenues)	35.3%	44.4%	24.4%
44	% of Programs w/ Completed Cost Analysis (# of Programs w/ Completed Cost Analysis/Total Number of Programs)	5.9%	32.4%	4.4%
45	% of Total Expenditures Targeted to Health Disparities Programs	0.3%	1.0%	0.3%
	Community Statistics			
46	Population Trend	928,622	0.2%	926,986
47	Median Population Age	35%	0.6%	35%
48	% of Population under 18 (Number in Population < 18/County Population)	19%	0.0%	19%
49	% of Population over 65 (Number in Population > 65/County Population)	35%	0.2%	35%
50	% Population Below Poverty (Population × % Below Poverty from US Census)	5.9%	5.4%	5.6%
51	% Population Insured by Medicaid	1.0%	-2.5%	1.1%
52	% Uninsured Population	5.2%	3.5%	5.0%
53	Residential Permits/1,000 Population (# of Residential Permits/(Population/1000))	4	-32.6%	5

Table 11–3   Thad Brewski's Ratio and Trend Analysis of Patriot Public Health Department, August 4, 2009

Categories & Guide	Patriot County Public Health Findings
FINANCIAL	**REVENUES**
This section looks at Items 1–45 on the Public Health Financial Ratios Spreadsheet.	The agency's resources are dwindling as shown with the $247,849 (2%) decrease in revenues during FY 2008 (Item #11). All major sources of revenues have decreased with the exception of Medicare, which has only grown roughly $8,000 (.6%) over FY 2007. The largest % decrease was in Medical Services, down 7.1%.
Revenues establish an agency's capacity to provide services. The following issues are critical to consider when analyzing revenue: growth rate, flexibility, dependability, diversity, major revenue sources.	The major source of revenue for the agency is from the County (Item #3). In FY 2008 County revenues decreased by 2.5% ($113,015).
	The agency does not receive dedicated tax revenues from the county (Item #20).
	Revenues are down in major program categories (e.g., home health, environmental health, dental) except in immunizations. Home health had a significant decrease of 24.4%, $128,790 (Items #22–27).
Expenditures are approximate measures of an agency's service output. Usually, the more an agency spends the more services it is providing. The following issues are critical to consider when analyzing expenditures: expenditure growth rate in comparison to revenue growth rate, future liabilities, administrative costs, types of public health services provided, ability to collect Accounts Receivable, and number of programs with expenditures exceeding allocated or earned revenue. Reference: Evaluating Financial Condition, 2003, ICMA	**EXPENDITURES**
	While agency revenues decreased, the reverse was true for expenditures which increased $129,349 (1.0%) (Item# 17). Even more significant was the fact that the agency was in a deficit position for FY 2008 because total expenditures were $472,305 higher than total revenues.
	In spite of the decrease in revenues, a breakout by specific categories shows that expenditures have actually increased in all categories with the exception of Lab and Preparedness (Items #28–38).
	The Fund Balance was reduced in FY 2008, down to $103,830, as a result of the deficit spending (Item #39).
	Over 50% of the Accounts Receivable balance (Item #40) was written off as "uncollectible." This is an indication that either collection efforts needs to be strengthened or activities

Table 11–3 Continued

Categories & Guide	Patriot County Public Health Findings
	need to be undertaken to seek reimbursement from other sources (qualify more patients for Medicaid/Medicare, etc.). The # of programs in the agency that were not self-supporting is growing, 18, up from 11 in the previous year (Item #42). These programs are maintained by shifting revenues from other sources in order to continue to operate.
DEMOGRAPHICS **This section looks at Items 46–53 on the Public Health Financial Ratios Spreadsheet.** Population change can affect governmental revenues and the need for services. The number of building permits issued, poverty rates, and percent of the population uninsured helps understand the effect of population change on the financing of local public health services.	Population in the county area did not change significantly (Item #44). The housing market downturn probably explains the decrease in building permits (Item #49). An examination is needed to determine if there is a relationship between the drop in residents on Medicaid (2.3%) and the increase in those that are uninsured (3.7%).
WORKFORCE **This section looks at Items 54–57 on the Public Health Financial Ratios Spreadsheet.** Employee costs represent a major part of the agency's budget. Increasing employee costs may signal expenditures in excess of revenue or a decline in personnel productivity. Assessing financial skills will indicate the level of	FTE in the agency increased by 11 people in FY 2008, in spite of decreases in revenues. There was no progress with providing training for staff with fiscal responsibilities.

(continues)

Table 11-3 Continued	
Categories & Guide	***Patriot County Public Health Findings***

financial skills in the workforce and may affect the agency's financial performance.

RATIOS
The above data about an agency's revenues and expenses, workforce, community demographics, and economics are used to create ratios that can be used to monitor changes in financial status and alert agency leaders to future problems. No one ratio is conclusive. All ratios chosen should be examined simultaneously to discern interrelationships that help to explain the trends revealed through ratio analysis.

Examples of questions to consider:
1. Revenue Ratios:
Is the community experiencing general economic decline? Is this temporary? Is it related to changes in the populations? What agency revenue sources are declining? Is the decline a result of the type of revenue upon which the agency depends? Is there a local tax to support Public Health services? Does the agency have flexibility in its

The agency is experiencing a decrease in Revenues per capita (Item #1), while Expenditures per capita (Item #23) continues to increase.

REVENUES
Total Margin is an indicator of how well the organization is managing the control of expenditures given the overall level of revenues. Patriot's Total Margin for FY 2008 is –3.9% (Item #12), a dismal indicator of current year financial health and cause for immediate corrective action.

An indicator below 1.0 is an indicator of an Operating Surplus (Item #13). This is directly related to the negative Total Margin Indicator.

The General Fund Balance (Item # 18) has decreased 77.9%, another dismal indicator and cause for immediate action.

Total Medical Revenues (Item #22) equal 8.0% of the agency's total revenues. However, expenditures in this category (Item #33) represent 9.6% of all expenditures. This situation should be examined closely.

EXPENDITURES
Expenditures per capita increased in FY 2008 (Item # 23). However, money for these expenditures came at the expense of depleting the General Fund Balance since there were not sufficient current year revenues to support the additional expenditures.

Fringe benefits (Item #25) appear to be aligned with national averages, but it has grown slightly. This could be explained by the increase in 11 FTE.

Table 11–3 Continued

Categories & Guide	Patriot County Public Health Findings
use of revenues? Are unrestricted resources supporting restricted revenue programs? Are there differences between operating revenues estimated in the annual budget and revenues actually received? Are the shortfalls due to inaccurate estimating techniques, sharp fluctuations in the economy, or inefficient revenue collection?	57% of the agency expenditures are spent on salaries (Item #26). Additionally, nearly 41% of every dollar spent in the agency is classified as Administrative (Item #27). Both of these seem high; however, there are no datasets of public health financial data and indictors where comparative effectiveness analysis or benchmarking between peer institutions could be conducted.
2. Expenditure Ratios: Do expenditures exceed revenues? Are the increases the result of new services? Which programs are increasing in costs? What specific costs are driving the increases? Is the agency operating efficiently? Have the number of employees increased? Is productivity declining? Are there new contracts?	Home Health expenditures were 138% higher than home health revenues. Also, this has increased roughly 36% over the prior year. This is an obvious contributor to the agency's deficit position. The total # of employees (Item #24) in the agency grew in FY 2008. This requires some examination since revenues are decreasing. 57% of all expenditures are dedicated to salaries (Item #26). Of greater concern is that Administrative spending (Item #27) accounts for 40.9% of expenditures. This appears to be exceptionally high but lacking public health financial dataset makes it difficult to conduct comparative analysis. Especially important is the fact that 40% being spent on administration leaves roughly only 60% of agency funding to be dedicated to public health programs.
3. Mission Critical Ratios: Do priority public health programs appear in the agency's budget? Which program outcomes are not improving? What strategies are in place to assure adequate program funding and the application of quality improvement methods? Are expenses exceeding dedicated and self-generated revenues?	**MISSION CRITICAL** The % of programs showing improvement is low and declining compared to the previous year (Item #38). Patriot does not collect a tax dedicated for public health (Item #40). This could put the agency at greater risk to annual fluctuations of county support. The agency does not create new ventures to generate and diversify its revenue streams (Item #41).

(continues)

Table 11–3 Continued	
Categories & Guide	*Patriot County Public Health Findings*
What are the costs of providing services in major program areas? Are they reasonable or comparable to similar agencies? Are there plans in place to increase revenues or decrease services if revenue shortfalls are detected?	More attention should be given to training of the staff with fiscal responsibilities (Item #42). Another contributing factor to the declining financial status is that 35% of programs in the agency cannot operate on dedicated or self-generated revenues (Item #43). Fiscal resources from other areas of the agency must be transferred to fund these programs. Patriot does not conduct cost analysis on the majority of its programs (Item #44). This could be a contributing factor to the large # of programs that are not self-supporting and also to the declining financial health. The # of agency programs actually grew in FY 2008 (Item #61) in spite of the fact that revenues are declining.
OVERALL FINANCIAL CONDITION	Overall, Patriot County Health Department has a weak financial condition. Significant contributing factors include: 1. Negative Total Margin 2. Expenditures that are greater than revenues 3. Increase in expenditures while revenues are declining 4. Depletion of General Fund Balance 5. Large % of programs that are not self-supporting 6. Increasing # of programs being created while revenues are declining 7. Large % of resources spent on Administration and Salaries

CASE ANALYSIS

This case outlines the weaknesses of many local public health departments in the area of financial management. Because these are often arms of local government, they do not handle many financial functions that a free-standing nonprofit would handle including cash management and accounting functions. Therefore, the top management jobs often do not call for sophisticated financial skills. However, there are still a number of financial processes that need to be handled by management. Try to identify these and see how the ratio analyses in the case relate to those processes. This is just one of the management areas that could be subject to process improvement efforts. Try to identify some others.

ASSIGNMENT QUESTIONS

1. What do you think of Thad Brewski's analysis? Did he identify all the key issues of financial concern for the agency?

2. Dr. Chernow mentioned three possibilities:

   a. Transmitting the material to the quality improvement committee.

   b. Keeping it under his hat and mixing it with other information he had as the agency head.

   c. Some other response.

   What would you recommend he do with the information?

3. Would you consider this approach to be primarily a quality improvement tool or something else?

4. What do you think of the fact that Thad's findings seem to be news to Dr. Chernow?

5. What do you think of the concept of financial management quality?

CLASS EXERCISE

Using one of the texts on healthcare financial management, identify the analyses that Dr. Chernow ought to be reviewing regularly in order to have effective control of the financial status of the department.

Quality in Pediatric Subspecialty Care[1]

William A. Sollecito, Peter A. Margolis, Paul V. Miles, Robert Perelman, and Richard B. Colletti

INTRODUCTION

The American Board of Pediatrics (ABP) is one of 24 certifying boards of the American Board of Medical Specialties (ABMS). ABP awards certificates in the 13 pediatric subspecialties listed in Exhibit 12–1. Certification provides assurance to the public and the profession that a pediatrician has successfully completed an accredited educational program and possesses "the knowledge, skills, and experience requisite to the provision of high-quality care in pediatrics." Historically, certification was based on individual knowledge rather than actual performance in practice. But evidence has shown significant variation in medical care, even among board-certified physicians, indicating that medical knowledge alone is not sufficient to ensure high quality of care. In response to this evidence, the ABMS voted to create a more continuous process of recertification.

By 2010, it was targeted that 75% of U.S. physicians were to be required to participate in ongoing maintenance-of-certificate programs to document competency in performance, practice, and systems-based thinking in addition to the current requirements for medical knowledge,

---

[1]This project was most active during the 2003–2004 period. Some updates are included for interest, but they are not intended to be representative or exhaustive of the outcomes of the project. The learning objectives of the case relate to the project efforts during the active project period.

EXHIBIT 12–1

13 Pediatric Subspecialties

- Adolescent medicine
- Cardiology
- Critical care
- Developmental and behavioral pediatrics
- Emergency medicine
- Endocrinology
- Gastroenterology
- Hematology-Oncology
- Infectious diseases
- Neonatology
- Nephrology
- Pulmonology
- Rheumatology

communication skills, and professional behavior. Substantial progress was made toward that very aggressive goal. For example, by 2010 efforts were underway by all medical specialties to address the need for greater QI knowledge, including making available QI modules and participation in a substantial number of QI collaboratives across a number of specialties. But perhaps the most tangible evidence of progress toward this goal is provided by the American Board of Pediatrics: 2010 was the first year that pediatricians had to complete a QI effort for maintenance of certification and (at the time of the writing of this text) by the end of 2010 it was expected that 8000 would have done so.

As a component of this evolving certification process, ABP launched the Quality in Pediatric Subspecialty Care (QPSC) initiative in the fall of 2003 "to improve the healthcare delivery system for children with complex medical conditions." Based on previous studies of how to apply Continuous Quality Improvement (CQI) principles in individual pediatric practices, ABP decided to use a mass customization approach and extend the lessons learned to each pediatric subspecialty incrementally. The common elements of CQI and mass customization are the sharing of existing knowledge and experiences among peers to achieve mutually agreed-upon improvement goals, using data-driven collaborative learning techniques. This was a multilevel plan to improve performance, not only of individual practitioners but of an entire profession, by first motivating and educating all pediatricians in the principles of CQI and then changing the standards of care by requiring quality improvement principles as part of the continuing education and certification process.

BACKGROUND

Pediatricians and other child healthcare clinicians strive to ensure the health of the children and families they serve. Numerous studies, however, have shown wide and persistent variation in outcomes across providers and communities. In its report, *Crossing the Quality Chasm*, the Institute of Medicine (2001) identified problems in the system of healthcare delivery rather than deficiencies in individual physicians as the major impediment to quality health care for all Americans. In pediatrics, for example, where robust systems have been defined and implemented, the results have been dramatic. The Children's Oncology Group captures information on over 80% of children in the United States with cancer. Children with cancer participate in ongoing clinical trials focusing on new therapies and in studies of how to improve the delivery of existing therapies. Subsequently, the five-year survival rate of children under age 15 with acute lymphocytic leukemia was 85% in 2002 (Leukemia and Lymphoma Society, 2002). This represents a more than doubling of the survival rate in the last quarter of the 20th century. However, such approaches are not widely used, leaving enormous opportunities to improve the care of children with chronic diseases. For example, the staff of the Cystic Fibrosis Foundation estimated that the average 33.5-year life of individuals with CF could be extend by seven years simply by applying current knowledge to every child with this condition (Schechter and Margolis, 2004). Collaborative learning approaches have been developed to spread existing knowledge among practitioners. The efficacy of QI approaches in a controlled setting has been demonstrated by several authors, including Margolis *et al.,* just prior to the initiation of QPSC (2004). While clearly successful, at that point in time the use of QI had been limited to specific clinical areas and/or relatively small numbers of practices. A logical priority, which was identified in 2003, was to increase impact and disseminate the learnings from previous successes by extending these QI methods on a larger scale.

COMPONENTS

The aim of QPSC is to improve the healthcare delivery process for children with complex medical conditions by changing the way that subspecialists practice. This change program relies on a unique process

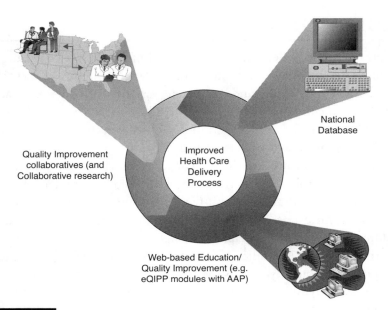

Figure 12–1 QPSC Model

that integrates the three components outlined in Figure 12–1: (1) national databases/registries of key childhood illness (e.g., inflammatory bowel disease) developed and coordinated through a national data coordinating center; (2) subspecialty-wide multicenter collaborative improvement activities among pediatric sub-specialists, and (3) Web-based improvement/educational modules.

The components of this model will be integrated as follows:

- *National databases and a national database support center*: Most conditions managed by pediatric subspecialists are not seen frequently enough to provide a single medical center with sufficient data to study or improve the treatment. Experience with children's oncology, low birth-weight infants, and cystic fibrosis have shown the value of national databases for important but relatively infrequent pediatric problems. National databases are essential for understanding variations in care and outcomes and for providing opportunities to learn from high-performing organizations. Each pediatric subspecialty will identify one or more "key" conditions, surgical procedures, or processes that are central to the specialty.

After the identification of this clinical content, a practical, useful database will be developed around children with that condition, procedure, or process.

- *National improvement collaboratives*: Each subspecialty will design its own collaborative improvement program around the topic selected for its database–registry. These collaborative activities will help identify those process changes with the most potential and specify the sequence in which they will be undertaken. Physicians have shown willingness to collect and submit performance data that is valid and complete when it is clear to them that the aim is to improve care and not to sanction "poor performers."

- *Education–improvement activities*: A major component of the model is the use of online education–improvement activities as exemplified by the eQIPP program developed by the American Academy of Pediatrics. These activities enable individual subspecialists to do self-assessments of how they practice and how they can improve their quality of care for a specific disease entity. Each pediatric subspecialty will develop a Web-based module alone or in conjunction with other subspecialities on subjects of broad application in the pediatric community.

ORGANIZATIONAL STRUCTURE

An important key to success in applying CQI to a large, complex organization such as a subspecialty group is the creation of an organizational structure that motivates learning and improvement. Structures and procedures must be implemented to empower individuals and teams to take responsibility for change and continuous improvement with an outcome focus. Leadership is necessary at multiple levels; in medical care, physician leadership is crucial for the design of change, for developing incentives and opportunities, and for assembling resources. The QPSC seeks to foster that leadership by involving each subspecialty in the design and planning process. Also critical is the creation of a virtual partnership of complementary organizations to lead the process over time; these groups provide an infrastructure that guides each subspecialty through the improvement process and serves as an administrative and data coordination base for the program.

A flexible governance structure is defined by a program charter and managed by a QPSC (leadership) council that includes representatives of each of the partner organizations. The organizational structure of QPSC includes the following organizations:

- The American Board of Pediatrics (ABP): Located in Chapel Hill, NC; this organization has been discussed earlier.

- The American Academy of Pediatrics (AAP): It supports the efforts of some 60,000 health professionals on behalf of the health, well-being, and safety of infants, children, adolescents, and young adults. Members include pediatricians, pediatric medical subspecialists, and pediatric surgical specialists. Most board-certified pediatricians are members of AAP. The Academy's online system, Education in Quality Improvement for Pediatric Practices (eQIPP), will be used to disseminate knowledge and assist subspecialty pediatricians in implementing practice improvements, as well as enabling them to meet recertification requirements.

- The UNC School of Public Health (UNC-SPH): This organization contributes expertise in epidemiology, health behavior, biostatistics, child health at the population level, and public health leadership to QPSC. The UNC-SPH has operated an internet-based data collection system to support collaborative improvement activities and has developed software applications designed to support thousands of simultaneous users. The UNC-SPH Instructional and Information Systems (IIS) group provides the information technology, software development, and database-management systems required for this program. The Public Health Leadership Program's role is to contribute expertise on large-scale organizational design, project management, and continuous improvement.

- The North Carolina Center for Children's Healthcare Improvement (NC-CHI), located in the UNC School of Medicine, has as its mission the elimination of gaps in care for children and adolescents. It is the National Program Office for QPSC. This Center has worked on practice-based improvement since 1992 and supported over 20 collaborative improvement programs over five years prior to the start of QPSC. Its primary role is to provide expertise and guidance in implementing collaborative improvement activities. Its Data Coordinating Center will provide large-scale data management and statistical support, in conjunction with the IIS group at the School of Public Health.

Implementation Teams

Management of the implementation process will involve a team-based matrix program-management structure for each improvement project. The teams interact directly with each subspecialty group and cut across each of the partner organizations to insure optimal knowledge sharing and efficiency. The implementation teams for the initiation of QPSC were:

1. Collaborative learning and improvement

2. Educational module development and implementation

3. Data management and statistics

4. Software systems development and support

5. Research

Each of these teams is represented on the overall coordination team headed by a Program Director. The QPSC Council and the implementation teams are supported further by a set of subcommittees that coordinate design, governance, and fundraising activities. An advisory board is also planned to provide guidance and insure input from all constituencies, including patients and their families.

Collaborative Improvement

The key CQI component of QPSC is the application of Deming's "System of Profound Knowledge" (1993). Each improvement effort within a subspecialty will be framed within a generic model for managing improvement (Langley *et al.*, 1996) asking "What are we trying to accomplish?"; "What changes can we make that will result in improvement?"; and "How will we know that a change is an improvement?" This approach will provide a framework, at a large scale for the use of Shewhart (PDSA) cycles to determine how to implement improvements in care within the network of collaborating provider centers. Successful changes or "best practices" will be identified, summarized by the subspecialty leadership structure, and hopefully deployed across the collaborative network.

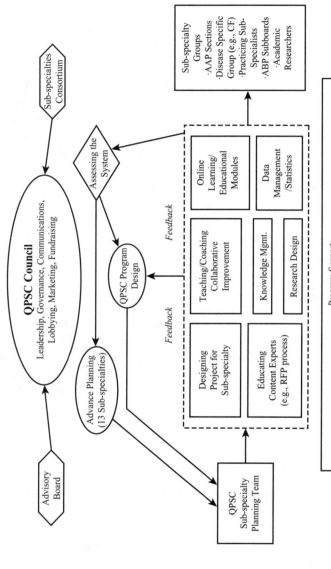

Exhibit 2-3 : QPSC System

System Aim: Improve the health of children by improving the quality of sub-specialty pediatric care

Figure 12-2   QPSC System

Figure 12–2 describes the QPSC application of this system to support sub-specialty societies and physicians including the assignment of functions and feedback loops that allow for system improvement. The system is partitioned into leadership processes such as planning, service activities for subspecialty societies such as collaborative learning, and program support processes. The leadership role of the QPSC Council is also clearly identified. The overall aim of this system is to improve the health of children by improving the quality of pediatric subspecialty care.

Previous Examples

Just prior to the initiation of QPSC, the Cystic Fibrosis Foundation sponsored a very successful application of the QI processes that were to be adopted on a larger scale in QPSC. The Cystic Fibrosis collaborative made a number of between-center comparisons and found centers with life expectancies as much as 50% above the national average. The collaborative noted the potential to improve children's health outcomes by improving nutritional counseling and reducing children's exposure to tobacco smoke, thereby improving lung function. Most pediatric specialists were comfortable with the nutrition intervention, but were less knowledgeable and experienced in getting parents to stop smoking. The team went to work on improvements in both areas and preliminary analyses indicated positive results (Schechter and Margolis, 2004).

AN INCREMENTAL APPROACH

A traditional CQI transitional model of incremental change was adopted by QPSC. This meant working with one subspecialty as a "pilot group"; and through continuous learning building on the experience gained there, expand to all 13 pediatric subspecialities. The improvement targets for each subspecialty were to include measures such as:

- Measurable improvement in children's health

- Percentage of subspecialists contributing data to the national registry

- Percentage of subspecialists participating in the national collaborative

- Percentage of subspecialists successfully completing eQIPP programs

- Number of independent, self-sustaining efforts

The NASPGHAN Pilot

The North American Society for Pediatric Gastroenterology, Hepatology, and Nutrition (NASPGHAN) was selected to be the pilot subspecialty to develop, implement, and evaluate the QPSC model. Its membership includes almost all the 800 pediatric gastroenterologists in North America. NASPGHAN formed a pediatric inflammatory bowel disease (IBD) QI and research network as its first initiative. This Pediatric IBD Network for Research and Improvement (PIBDNet) will conduct collaborative improvement and research on the quality and safety of care delivered by member subspecialists to children with this condition.

Inflammatory bowel disease is the most common chronic and serious pediatric gastrointestinal disorder afflicting children and adolescents. Over 45,000 children and adolescents in North America suffer from IBD and more than 4,500 new cases are diagnosed annually. Yet, there is a lack of evidence as to its optimal management and the safety and effectiveness of available treatments.

Project Objectives for PIBDNet

The Project leadership defined the following objectives of this effort:

1. Engage 200 pediatric gastroenterologists in network activities within the first year.

2. Determine the extent of variation in care of children with IBD who are initiating treatment with 9-mercaptopurine/azathioprine (6-MP/AZA) or with infliximab and identify the predictors of a successful outcome of treatment.

3. Involve 10–15 GI practices in an "innovation community" that will work collaboratively to identify, test, and develop changes that can improve IBD care.

4. Spread to all NASPGHAN members care delivery strategies that will improve the quality and safety of care for children with IBD.

5. Develop an eQIPP module on nutrition to test online education and QI support in the context of other subspecialty improvement activities as a means of supporting ongoing dissemination of activities.

6. Measure the effectiveness of the program in terms of the following outcomes:

    a. reductions in gastrointestinal symptoms

    b. improved growth and nutritional management of patients prior to and during treatment

    c. increased family self-management skills, including adherence to 6-MP/AZA therapy

    d. reduction in medication side effects (e.g., steroid side effects)

    e. appropriate diagnostic evaluation prior to treatment

    f. safe initial 6-MP/AZA administration

    g. surveillance for adverse effects of 6-MP/AZA and infliximab

    h. reporting of serious adverse effects of treatment to the FDA

Program Development Status

By the summer of 2004, NASPGHAN had created the PIBDNet, and approximately 40% of the NASPGHAN membership had volunteered to participate following initial email solicitation. All of the individual components of the QPSC model had been implemented by the partner organizations. However, following the platform testing and pilot initiative, each of the components of the QPSC program would require further financial support to continue to scale them up to the degree necessary to reach all sub-specialists and to meet ABP's aggressive timeline to implement the model in all subspecialities by 2010. Despite limited additional funding directed at QPSC and NASPGHAN specifically, as noted earlier, by this date substantial progress had been made by 10 of the 14 subspecialities toward improving knowledge and implementation of QI processes and initiatives. The seminal work done by QPSC and NASPGHAN played an important role in achieving this progress.

An evaluation of the NASPGHAN pilot program, including an assessment of ways to improve the efficiency of the implementation steps, is currently underway and planning has begun to expand the model to the next subspecialities. Early observations of needed program changes include:

1. Technology improvements for data collection/management systems, including the study of ways to interface with existing electronic medical record systems;

2. Further development of data quality-assurance procedures to accommodate the large number practices to be included and the variety of data to be collected for each subspecialty;

3. New disease-specific eQIPP modules for each subspecialty; and

4. Management changes related to infrastructure growth.

Ongoing fundraising was an important component that was to be managed by the QPSC Council. Costs appeared to be of the order of a million dollars for each subspecialty plus common infrastructure costs.

CASE ANALYSIS

This case presents a very different approach to the improvement of quality in which the responsibility falls on professional societies and board certifying agencies to push the clinical quality agenda forward. At some point in the future, then, all professionals will have to show activity and results in this arena. This is quite different from the institutional roles envisioned in CQI efforts over the recent past. This will not be a rapid change—but likely will be quite controversial.

ASSIGNMENT QUESTIONS

1. What should be the role of professional societies and certifying entities in promulgating the concepts of evidence-based medicine and CQI among its professional cadres?

2. How would one go about developing the business case for CQI in this setting?

3. The data collected on cystic fibrosis clinical outcomes are considered the most complete of any disease in the country (Gawande, 2004). How can the pediatric consortium and other credentialing bodies function where complete outcome data are not so available?

4. Contrast and compare the approaches to transformation and organizational learning in this case with that of Intermountain Health Care (Case 5) or West Florida Regional Medical Center (Case 1). Which is more likely to be effective? Why is this case so different?

CLASS EXERCISE

Review the current requirements of the American Board of Pediatrics for Maintenance of Certification and the alternatives available for pediatricians to meet the Quality Improvement component of Performance in Practice (Part 4). Some of these collaborative efforts were influenced by the project reported in the case. How do you think these experiences are likely to affect quality of care over time?

Assessment, Incentives, and Regulation

With the costs of health care as a percentage of gross domestic production rising in just about every country, payers, including governments, have sought more and better outcomes for their investments. This has created much greater emphasis on assessment, incentives, and regulation. These activities are extremely varied across countries and types of healthcare organizations. We have been able to include a few examples in Part IV, which represent some diversity of settings.

Case 13 examines the decision-making processes as country after country examines proposals to supplement the folic acid intake of pregnant women through mandatory enrichment of bread products. Are these changes healthcare improvements? There is clear evidence that this significantly reduces the incidence of births with neural tube defects. There is, however, concern that there are also potential negative side effects. Some countries have adopted mandatory supplementation and others looking at the same evidence have left it voluntary or not allowed it at all. There are obviously cultural components of these decisions. The case illustrates some of the factors that plague evidence-based decision-making: conflicting studies, offsetting outcomes, shifting evidence, cultural differences, and lack of urgency.

In Case 14, the United Kingdom's National Health Service (NHS) acts to assure that its pay-for-performance (P4P) system continues to emphasize continuous improvement. It relies on an extensive set of performance indicators used to reward each primary-care practice. As the care deliverers respond to the incentives, NHS wants a rational and transparent system for modifying indicators and substituting new ones as evidence

243

changes and as achievements approach an upper limit. One alternative is to mandate performance once widespread maximum achievement is observed. It is also useful to observe in this case the important role that information systems play in making a P4P system practical.

The accreditation of local health departments in the United States discussed in Case 15 has been intended to improve performance quality despite severe measurement problems. However, using an example from North Carolina, it illustrates that in the absence of an electronic medical record system, labor-intensive self-assessments and site visits must be relied on to measure and then evaluate quality improvement. Due to budgetary cutbacks, the implementation of the accreditation effort is slowed down and spread out over a number of years. So how and when do you raise the bar?

With the Lewis Blackman Hospital Patient Safety Act discussed in Case 16, the state of South Carolina has mandated sharing fully and visibly with patients and their families the status of learners and supervisors in the medical hierarchy. Quality-improvement legislation at the state level, especially that empowering patients and families, is still rare. Usually that is left up to professionally-dominated organizations. How effective is a legislative approach to quality improvement? What do such laws imply about the changing status of healthcare professionals?

Governments and others may also look for and publicize outstanding performers to induce quality competition and consciousness in health care. One of the earliest of these efforts was the Baldrige Award for industrial organizations, which was then modified for healthcare organizations. It is awarded to very few organizations. Today, it exists in parallel with mandatory-reporting requirements such as hospital COMPARE and the reporting requirements of The Joint Commission and NCQA. Management in Case 17 asks itself some hard questions about the unique contributions currently possible from a Baldrige evaluation.

The Folic Acid Fortification Decision Bounces Around the World

Curtis P. McLaughlin and Craig D. McLaughlin

INTRODUCTION

At 5 p.m. on July 20, 1991, Dr. Godfrey P. Oakley, Jr., head of the Division of Birth Defects and Developmental Disabilities at the Centers for Disease Control and Prevention (CDC), took a phone call that, he says, "forever changed my life." On the phone was a member of the British Medical Research Council (MRC) Vitamin Study Group, calling to share study results that would be published the following month in *The Lancet* (SerVaas and Perry, 1999).

The MRC study, as it became known, focused on women who had previously had a pregnancy in which the fetus or child had a neural tube defect (NTD), a birth defect of the spinal cord or brain. In April 1991, the MRC halted its study after almost eight years because the data indicated that daily folic acid supplementation before pregnancy and during early pregnancy resulted in a 71% reduction in the recurrence of NTDs (CDC, 1991). It was no longer considered ethical not to provide folic acid to all of the women.

"Until that time," Dr. Oakley told the Saturday Evening Post Society in 1999, "I thought that prevention of neural tube defects by taking folic acid supplementation was certainly no better than 50–50. If you really pressed me on what I would have thought the likelihood that a vitamin would have prevented neural tube defects, I would have said no more than 10% or 20%. But this was the first randomized, controlled trial designed and executed in a way that it proved folic acid would prevent spina bifida—not all but most of it. You could bet the farm that folic acid prevents neural tube defects" (SerVaas and Perry, 1999, p. 3).

The study ignited a policy debate that would continue for many years. In the United States, the question of how to increase folic acid consumption in woman of child-bearing years was contentious in itself, but the issue was complicated further by the controversy that surrounded implementation of the Nutrition Labeling and Education Act (NLEA) of 1990, which required the Food and Drug Administration (FDA) to regulate the health claims of food manufacturers.

Three economic analyses predicted positive net economic benefits from fortifying foods with folic acid. A number of other countries, including Canada, Chile, Ireland, the United Kingdom, Australia, and New Zealand were going through similar processes of evaluating scientific evidence and deciding whether or not to fortify their food with folates. However, they reached a variety of end points for the fortification decision.

TECHNICAL BACKGROUND

NTDs are a class of birth defects that involve the brain and spinal cord. The most extreme form is anencephaly, in which all or part of the brain is missing. Another form is spina bifida, in which the spinal cord is not fully encased in the spine. In the early 1990s, there were typically about 4,000 NTD-associated pregnancies per year in the United States.

Folates are a form of B vitamin that occurs naturally in leafy vegetable, legumes, nuts, and other foods. Folic acid is its synthetic form. Folates help cells replicate quickly. Reports that increased folic acid intake could help prevent birth defects date back to 1965 (Hibbard and Smithells, 1965). Vitamin manufacturers learned how to add it to their supplements in 1970s. The Saturday Evening Post Society launched its campaign to promote folic acid supplementation in October 1982 in the wake of a report that women who took a vitamin supplement with 400 micrograms (mcg) of folic acid experienced fewer NTD-affected pregnancies. In the late 1980s, the CDC held a workshop to discuss emerging research linking folic acids to reductions in the numbers of NTDs, which renewed interest among supplement manufacturers.

Support for folic acid was limited, however; Post writers Cory SerVaas and Pat Perry (1999) reported that they were ridiculed for their efforts. Scientific evidence was sparse, inconclusive, and based on observational epidemiological studies. Around the time of the CDC workshop, in fact, the National Research Council advised the U.S. FDA that it should lower the recommended daily allowance. A 1990 report by the Institute of Medicine's Food and Nutrition Board called taking vitamin supplements to prevent NTDs "unjustified." The National Academy of Sciences also discounted the link between NTDs and folic acid in its 1990 *Report on Nutrition and Pregnancy.*

In the midst of this debate, the NLEA skated through Congress and was signed by President Bush. The act directed the FDA to establish standards for nutrition labels and define how certain terms such as low fat and low cholesterol could be used on food packaging. Congress also directed the FDA to investigate 10 specific health claims and develop language food manufacturers could use to convey any valid claims on their packaging. One of those claims, to the surprise of many, was that folic acid reduced the risk of neural tube defects. The FDA was hard at work on its proposed rules when *The Lancet* published the MRC study (MRC Vitamin Study Research Group, 1991).

The MRC study involved more than a thousand women in 33 centers across 17 countries. Researchers divided the subjects into four groups: Those in the first group received 400 mcg of folic acid. Those in the second group received the same amount of folic acid plus a multivitamin supplement. Those in the third group received neither the multivitamin supplement nor folic acid, and those in the final group received only the multivitamins. NTDs recurred 1% of the time when mothers received folic acid, with or without other vitamins, and 3.5% of the time when they received nothing or only the multivitamin supplement.

The MRC study did not settle the debate. It studied women who had already had an NTD-associated pregnancy and therefore might be predisposed to having another, so the results were not necessarily applicable to the general population. An FDA-contracted study released in

November 1991 said that it was not possible to positively conclude that folic acid prevented NTDs, but it criticized the Institute of Medicine and National Academy of Sciences reports. The FDA draft rules issued later that month rejected claims that high-folate foods prevented NTDs, but it called its conclusion "tentative" and left open the possibility of further review.

The CDC, however, was less equivocal. At a conference on "Vitamins, Spina bifida, and Anencephaly" that same year, participants had generally accepted the notion that women who were pregnant or might become pregnant required more folic acid. They began to wrestle with what FDA Commissioner David Kessler would call "one of the most difficult issues" of his tenure—exactly how to go about providing that folic acid.

ALTERNATIVES

There were only a few ways to ingest more folic acid at the time: consume more foods naturally high in folates, take vitamin supplements, take folic acid pills, or eat fortified foods. Each option brought its own challenges. Working against the natural nutritionists was the fact that natural folates have lower bioavailability than folic acid and break down during cooking. A typical U.S. woman ingested only 25 mcg of naturally-occurring folates daily, and thus, it was hard to envision women ingesting 400 mcg through dietary changes.

Folic acid by itself was only available in a 100-mcg prescription formulation. The level of folic acid in most multivitamin supplements was so low that a woman trying to hit the 400-mcg target would have to ingest toxic levels of other vitamins. One option was to make folic acid more readily available in larger doses. Another was to reformulate multivitamins. Both of these options suffered from the same problem. To be effective, folic acid had to be taken before pregnancy and during the first few weeks after conception. Yet, roughly half of all pregnancies occur without early prenatal care. You would have to convince all women to take pills to supplement their folic acid intake throughout their childbearing years or risk missing more than half the pregnancies.

That left the possibility of fortification (adding a nutrient to food that does not otherwise contain it). This approach would reach everyone, including all women who are or might soon become pregnant. Food fortification and enrichment (increasing the levels of a nutrient already in a food) has a long history in the United States, beginning in 1924 with the decision to add iodine to salt to prevent goiter and other iodine-deficiency disorders. Vitamin D was added to milk in the 1930s (much later, Vitamin A was added to low-fat dairy products). Flours and bread have been enriched with various nutrients—1938 through 1942 saw the addition of thiamine, niacin, riboflavin, and iron.

Four hundred micrograms of folic acid, however, struck many as a pharmacological dose. Best-selling longevity authors Durk Pearson and Sandy Shaw called it unethical and equivalent to medicating competent adults without informed consent (Junod, 2006). Scientists worried about adverse reactions. One issue was that at daily doses of a microgram or more of folic acid could mask vitamin B_{12} deficiency, particularly among the older population, prompting some scientists to worry that fortification would simply shift risks from developing embryos to adults with pernicious anemia (Gaull *et al.*, 1996).

SUPPORT BUILDS

Fortification gained more adherents after the MRC study appeared, however, and supporters' ranks swelled as people became aware of two studies, as yet unpublished, conducted on women with no previous history of NTD-affected births. One, conducted in Hungary by Andrew Czeizel and his colleagues, showed benefits in the general population from consuming 800 mcg per day. Another, the "Werler study," studied women in Boston, Philadelphia, and Toronto. Although Werler and her colleagues recommended 400 mcg daily, they found that even 250 mcg offered some protection. In May 1992, Dr. Walter C. Willet argued in an *American Journal of Public Health* editorial that "fortification should be the long term goal" and criticized the tendency to disregard observational epidemiological studies (Junod, 2006).

PUBLIC RECOMMENDATION CHANGES

In September 1992, the Public Health Service announced that women of child-bearing age should get 400 mcg of folic acid every day, a decision touted by the CDC but soft-pedaled by the FDA and the National

Institutes of Health (Palca, 1992). The announcement did nothing to satisfy the two policy questions in the FDA's lap: whether to allow food products to promote their folic acid levels on their labels and whether to require that certain foods be fortified with folic acid.

The FDA's folic acid advisory committee recommended against a folic acid health claim after a November 1992 meeting. In early 1993, the FDA, working under tight deadlines, adopted an NLEA rule that reflected this position and disallowed a health claim; however, the committee expressed an interest in fortification, and it reconvened in April 1993 to look at a variety of unresolved issues, including fortification. By October, the FDA had reversed its position, publishing a draft rule that would allow health claims for foods containing folic acid. There were many aspects of the rule, but its core was a provision that would allow health claims for foods that contained 40 mcg or more of folic acid per serving. On December 31, 1993, the rule became final.

The October 1993 draft rule contained provisions about fortification, but fortification was not mandated as part of the New Year's Eve ruling. The FDA and its folic acid advisory committee continued to struggle with a variety of implementation questions.

COST–BENEFIT ANALYSIS

U.S. federal agencies are required to conduct regulatory impact analyses as part of rule making and starting in 1993 were required to assess expected costs and benefits of significant rules. FDA staff conducted a cost–benefit analysis and estimated that fortification with 140 mcg of folic acid per hundred grams of cereal grain products would prevent 116 NTD-affected births per year. This analysis tallied direct savings, notably medical care avoided, and estimated a savings of $5 million for each case averted, resulting in economic benefits of $651 million to $786 million annually. The annual cost of fortification would be $27 million, and thus, the annual net economic benefit would be $624 million to $750 million (FDA, 1993).

In 1995, University of California researchers published a second cost–benefit analysis. They estimated that 304 NTD-associated births would be avoided through fortification. Using a different method that looked at lost productivity, they put the value of a case avoided at $342,500.

The economic benefit came in at $121.5 million. From this, the researchers deducted not only the cost of fortification, which they put at $11 million, but the cost of adverse events—namely 500 cases of neurological damage annually at a cost of $16.4 million. There calculations resulted in an estimated net benefit from fortification of $93.6 million (Romano *et al.*, 1995).

These two studies were before the advisory committee as it debated folic acid implementation and they played a role in the shaping the draft folic acid fortification rule published on March 5, 1996. A third analysis, published by the CDC that same year, was not influential. The CDC estimated 89 averted NTDs at a total benefit of $16.1 million annually. That was largely offset by the $11 million cost of fortification and an estimated $350,000 in health costs related to 89 cases of neurological damage. That left a net benefit of $4.7 million.

The FDA ultimately adopted a rule requiring fortification of cereal grain products with 140 mcg of folic acid for every 100 g of grain. The rule went into effect in January 1, 1998. Between October 1998 and December 1999, the prevalence of reported cases of spina bifida declined 31%. Anencephaly declined 16%. Various studies over the years have put the total reduction of cases of spina bifida and anencephaly at 20% to 30%, much more than were reflected in the three *ex ante* economic analyses. (Not all of the improvement can be attributed to fortification, as women of childbearing age can expect to get only about a quarter of their recommended intake through fortified grains, and public education campaigns continue to promote consumption of folic acid through vitamin pills.)

THE RESULTS COME IN

Studies in Chile and Canada also reported the effectiveness of folate fortification programs. Three Canadian population-based studies showed reductions in the incidence of NTD-related births of 50%, 54%, and 43%, respectively. The Chilean study included measures of increased folate blood levels from fortification and reported a 43% reduction in the NTD rate within six months. Differences among these studies included differences in fortification levels and differences in measurement and reporting regarding the inclusion or exclusion of stillbirths and terminated pregnancies.

The CDC published a before and after epidemiological study in 2004, which reported that between 1995 and 1996 (prefortification) and 1999 and 2000 surveillance-based population studies showed a reduction in estimated number of NTD-affected pregnancies declined from 4,000 to 3,000. These results are summarized in Table 13–1. An editorial note in the *Morbidity and Mortality Weekly Report* noted that a 26% reduction was somewhat less than earlier studies had indicated and short of the national goal of a reduction of 50% (CDC, 2004).

For systems with prenatal ascertainment, estimated total pregnancies included live births, stillbirth, prenatally diagnosed cases, and elective terminations. For systems without prenatal ascertainment[1], estimates included live births, stillbirths, and fetal deaths through 20 weeks. Fetal deaths and elective terminations were calculated as the difference between systems with and without prenatal ascertainment. The numbers of NTD-affected pregnancies and births were determined as prevalence multiplied by the average total number of U.S. births during the respective periods, as derived from the U.S National Vital Statistics System.

Table 13–1 Estimated Average Annual Numbers of Spina Bifida and Anencephaly Cases Based on Prevalence Per 10,000 Live Births from Surveillance Systems—United States 1995–1996 and 1999–2000

	Systems With Prenatal Ascertainment		Systems Without Prenatal Ascertainment		Fetal Deaths and Elective Terminations
	Prevalence	No.	Prevalence	No.	No.
Prefortification					
Spina bifida	6.4	2,490	5.1	1,980	
Anencephaly	4.2	1,640	2.5	970	
Total		4,130		2,950	1,180
Postfortification					
Spina bifida	4.1	1,640	3.4	1,340	
Anencephaly	3.5	1,380	2.1	840	
Total		3,020		2,180	840

Source: CDC (2004, p. 364)

---

[1]Programs with prenatal ascertainment use specific case finding technologies to identify prenatally diagnosed and electively terminated cases.

THE NEW U.S. ECONOMIC STUDY

In 2005, Grosse *et al.* published an ex-post economic study. It estimated 520 averted cases of spina bifida and 92 cases of averted anencephaly annually, which led to economic benefits per case of $636,000 and $1,020,000, respectively. That translated into $425 million in economic benefits ($146 million in direct costs, mostly medical) against an annual cost of fortification of $3 million. The authors did not identify any documented adverse health effects from fortification. Of the $636,000 savings per spina bifida case avoided, $279,000 were in direct costs, mostly medical, with the rest apparently indirect costs for nonmedical care giving. For the anencephaly cases, almost all of the $1,020,000 in costs were indirect. The authors observed that the benefits were exceptionally large and noted that "few public health interventions beyond immunization and injury prevention are cost saving" (p. 1921).

Hertkampf (2004) estimated that in Chile the fortification process costs approximately U.S. $280,000 annually. For spina bifida, she estimated the cost of surgery and rehabilitation for each of the 110 cases avoided annually at U.S. $100,000. She noted that bread is more of a staple of the Chilean diet. Commenting on the low priority given to folate fortification in most developing countries, she noted that prevalence data are lacking and that NTDs are not recognized as an important cause of morbidity and mortality.

New Concerns About Adverse Effects of High Dosages

The earlier concerns about the masking of B_{12} deficiencies in the elderly have not been supported with reported cases. However, new concerns surfaced by 2007 about the impact of high doses of folates on colorectal cancer (CRC). Animal studies suggested that high doses led to two conflicting effects. Doses higher than those normally introduced by fortification protected against the onset of CRCs, but also seemed to stimulate the growth rates of existing neoplasms.[2] Figure 13–1 shows data from

---

[2]"Time trends for colorectal cancer (CRC) incidence in the USA and Canada show that mandatory fortification of foods with folic acid occurred about the same time as non-significant increases in CRC incidence. If this was caused by folic acid fortification, the effect of folic acid on cancer progression would have to have been immediate, which may not be plausible. The increase in rates occurred at different times for men and women and in different age groups. The timing of changes in average blood folate concentrations of the USA population was also not clearly consistent with changes in CRC incidence." SACN, 2008. Paper for Information: Briefing for review of SACN recommendations for mandatory fortification. SACN/08/00

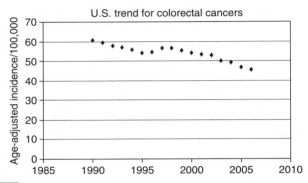

Figure 13–1 U.S. Trend for Colorectal Cancers

Source: National Institutes of Health, National Cancer Institute, Sampling of invasive cancer incidence rates in 9 jurisdictions, all races.

the United States. These observations, reported by Mason *et al.* in 2007, were not followed up by randomized controlled trials, which led the British Scientific Advisory Council on Nutrition (SACN) to report in January 2008: "The evidence for an association between folic acid and increased or reduced cancer risk is equivocal."

Then a 2009 report on two Norwegian clinical trials with high doses of folic acid and vitamin B_{12} in patients with ischemic heart disease showed significant increases in overall cancer rates (Ebbing *et al.* 2009). Folic acid was considered to have a preventive effect toward heart disease and stroke (Wang *et al.,* 2007).

Table 13–2 Tedstone (2007) summarized the evidence up to that time as follows:
Problem: Need for Risk Benefit Analysis

	Benefit	*Harm*
Folate status	yes	
Neural tube defects	yes	
Cancer	??	??
Heart disease	??	??
Clinically manifest vitamin B12 deficiency		yes

Source: Tedstone, A. 2007. Folic acid: UK Position, Nutrition Division, Food Standards Agency, January 11, 2007.

The Food Standards Australia New Zealand Decision

Mandatory fortification of bread began in Australia on September 13, 2009. Voluntary fortification had been allowed for more than 10 years. The Food Standards Australia New Zealand (FSANZ) made its original recommendation in 2006 following an extensive review begun in 2004. The recommendation triggered a public comment period followed by approval of the Australia and New Zealand Food Regulation Ministerial Council, which is made up of the food and health ministers of the two countries. A twelve-month phase-in period followed. The mandate was anticipated to avoid about 14% of the 300-350 NTD-affected pregnancies annually. New Zealand, however, delayed implementation of the mandate pending further study (FSANZ, 2009).

Ireland's Derailed Fortification Plans

In 1990, Ireland had one of the highest rates of NTDs in Europe, one to 1.5 NTDs per 1000 births. Voluntary fortification and nutritional education were only marginally successful, so in 2002 the Department of Health turned to the Food Safety Authority (FSA) of Ireland. In 2003, FSA recommended fortification and the health minister established a National Committee on Folic Acid Food, which consulted the parties involved and in July 2006 recommended mandatory fortification. The successor health minister supported the recommendation. An Implementation Group on Folic Acid Fortification formed with the expectation of final implementation in 2007. However, that group never made its recommendations and as of late 2009 the decision was stalled. The Department of Health reported it was still monitoring the situation (Lynch, 2009).

Meanwhile, Back in the United Kingdom

On April 6, 2006, the U.K. Food Standards Agency Board "agreed to consult on options for improving the folate status of young women." When the board first discussed the issue in 2002, concerns were raised about possible risks to the health of older people. Then the Scientific Advisory Committee on Nutrition (SACN), an independent expert panel, reviewed the evidence and tracked the emerging science. A SACN report issued in draft form in November 2005 and released as a final report in December 2006 recommended mandatory fortification of flour.

The Food Standards Agency Board (2006) agreed that it would consider four options:

- Do nothing

- Increase efforts to encourage young women to change their diets and take supplements

- Further encourage voluntary fortification of foods

- Implement mandatory fortification of "the most appropriate food vehicle"

The board announced December 12, 2006 that it would consult with consumers, stakeholders, and industry over a 13-week period. It was expected to make recommendations following its May 2007 meeting. The board's announcement highlighted the following: "The Food Standards Agency is committed to policy-making that will benefit people's health and we do this on the basis of weighing up the evidence in relation to risks and benefits."

A SACN briefing paper issued in January 2008 recommended fortification of flour but also noted:

> The establishment of a new baseline for folic acid intakes and blood folate concentrations will be required prior to fortification to ensure that mandatory fortification does not lead to substantial increases in folic acid intake/status and so trends can be monitored in future surveillance programmes. The adoption of a common standard analytical method to measure folate status at baseline and all future surveillance studies will also be required as well as the establishment of suitable reference ranges to predict folate adequacy and deficiency. (SACN 2008)

CASE ANALYSIS

So far no European country has adopted *mandatory* folic acid fortification. Yet, voluntary fortification is widely practiced in the EU under the regulation 1925/2006/EC on the addition of vitamins and minerals and of certain other substances to foods. This regulation allows the fortification of all foods except unprocessed foods and alcoholic beverages. Foods fortified with folic acid are widely available on the European market, except in Sweden where fortification is not practiced, and in Denmark and Norway, which require approval. The range of product categories that are fortified on a voluntary basis includes dairy products, breakfast cereals, cereal bars, fruit juices, fat spreads, bread and beverages. Maximum levels for the addition of folic acid to foods are not yet set in European regulations. The levels vary widely, with the highest levels added to spreads. Mandatory fortification with folic acid has been introduced in some 50 countries worldwide as a strategy to help women increase their intake of folate (European Food Safety Authority, 2009).

Meanwhile blood folate levels among non-pregnant women in the United States have fallen somewhat, perhaps related to increased obesity and/or to reduced bread intake (CDC, 2007).

Even when the effects are measured, reported, and confirmed, different decision makers have come up with very different conclusions and actions. Certainly, these have a lot to do with cultural and national attitudes to food supplementation in general and how to handle the risks of side effects. Health care is a social activity as well as a social good and factors other than science are involved in the conduct of continuous quality improvement efforts. Think about what might be necessary in the way of research to get the best outcome for all concerned.

ASSIGNMENT QUESTIONS

1. How do these various countries come up with such different conclusions about the same policies with access to the same information?

2. Would you want to change the policies and procedures of the United States after reading this case?

3. What should be the influence of the cost-benefit studies in this and similar analyses? What are the strengths and weaknesses of quality-adjusted-life-years as a metric in this situation? What other metric, if any, would you prefer?

4. What have you learned from this case about quality-improvement efforts at a national level?

CLASS EXERCISE

Find out what has transpired lately with this decision. Check on the research studies about the side effects of folic acid fortification. Have other countries considered fortification? What was their decision and why? Was it consistent with the experiences cited in this case?

Continuing Improvement for the National Health Service Quality and Outcomes Framework

Curtis P. McLaughlin

INTRODUCTION

In April 2004, the United Kingdom's National Health Service (NHS) launched a nationwide pay-for-performance (P4P) effort for General Practitioners (GPs) called Quality and Outcomes Framework (QOF). This was a component of the five-year contract negotiated between the NHS Employers (acting on behalf of the Department of Health (DoH)) and the General Practitioners Committee (GPC) of the British Medical Association. Payment was based on a set of indicators for the QOF developed by a consortium of academic healthcare and information technology experts coordinated by the National Primary Care Research and Development Centre (NPCRDC), a joint effort of the universities of York and Manchester based at the University of Manchester. The NPCRDC recommendations remained confidential during contract negotiations and were published on the Centre's website after the negotiations. By 2009, the Framework had cost the NHS at least £1.8 billion. This was such a large portion of the NHS budget that both the Government and Parliament were concerned about how to maintain and improve its effectiveness going forward. They were also concerned about the lack of transparency in the process developing and selecting those indicators.

THE INDICATORS

The 2004 contract called for indicators in four domains: clinical, organizational, patient experience, and additional services (cervical screening, child-health surveillance, and contraceptive and maternity services).

The clinical indicators were of two types: 0-1 indicating the presence or absence of something such as a diabetes patient registry or linear across an interval allocating the allowed points between a minimum acceptable value and a maximum compensated threshold. For example, in 2007 there were 16 indicators for diabetes mellitus care set by NHS Quality Scotland and NHS England and Wales in cooperation with NICE. A GP received six points if he or she had the appropriate registry or nothing at all if it was lacking. If the practice recorded retinal screening of more than 40% of its diabetes patients in the last 18 months, it could receive up to 5 points depending on where its percentage was in the 40% to 90% range.

Clinical indicators could be for screening, treatment, and/or control. Other diabetic screening indicators included Body Mass Index and cholesterol levels recorded and screening for kidney problems. Treatment indicators included percentage of diabetic patients receiving influenza vaccine and percentage with micro-albuminuria or proteinuria receiving appropriate ACE inhibitors or A2 antagonists. The biggest potential payments were for control variables including percentage of diabetics with Hb41c controlled at the 10 or less and 7 or less levels, blood pressure at 145/85 or less, and cholesterol at 5 mmol/l or less.

In the case of indicator DM18 the GP would receive 0 points if less than or equal to 40% of the relevant patients had been immunized, with the three available points spread over the range 40% to 85%. Values higher than 85% still earned 3 points. For DM18, the practices received 98.5% of the possible points; however, the actual coverage was 90.2% after an exception rate of 14.3%, the highest for any of the diabetes indicators, presumably because many patients declined the immunization (Health and Social Care Information Centre, 2009).

The values for most of the clinical variables were determined by the NHS computerized patient record system. Variables that were not recorded in that system, such as the presence or absence of a registry or the amount of time scheduled per visit, were determined annually by assessors who would visit each site. Some variables were also determined by patient surveys. Practices were required to administer post-visit surveys annually to 25 patients for each 1000 patients registered with the practice. The practices were incentivized to act on these results and take steps to improve their performance. For example, achievement of the third level worth 30 points on Patient Experience Indicator 6 that related to the surveys required that:

- The practice will have undertaken a patient survey each year and, having reflected on the results, will produce an action plan that:

  1. Sets priorities for the next 2 years.

  2. Describes how the practice will report the findings to patients (for example, posters in the practice, a meeting with a patient practice group, or a Primary Care Organization approved patient representative).

  3. Describes the plans for achieving the priorities, including indicating lead persons in the practice.

  4. Considers the case for collecting additional information on patient experience, for example, through surveys of patients with specific illnesses, or consultation with a patient group. (NHS, 2008, p. 142)

NHS Principles Concerning the QOF

The Department of Health had specified its principles concerning the QOF in its contract with the GPs called Statement of Financial Entitlements as follows:

1. Indicators should, where possible be based on the best available evidence.

2. The number of indicators in each clinical condition should be kept to the minimum number compatible with an accurate assessment of patient care.

3. Data should never be collected purely for audit purposes.

4. Only data that are useful in patient care should be collected. The basis of the consultation should not be distorted by an over-emphasis on data collection. An appropriate balance has to be struck between excess data collection and inadequate sampling.

5. Data should never be collected twice: data required for audit purposes should be data routinely collected for patient care and obtained from existing practice clinical systems. (DoH, 2009, p. 123)

The NHS information system for general practice was a considered successful, although the parallel information system for hospital services was still going through a rocky course of development.

The Takeoff

The 2004 version of the QOF started with 146 quality indicators related to clinical practice, practice organization, patient perceptions of service, and additional services. Seventy-six of those indicators were clinical. Of the 1050 possible points earning an average of £77.5 each, 550 points were clinical. For 2006–2007 the possible number of points was reduced to 1000, some thresholds increased, and the proportion in the clinical domain increased at the expense of the organization domain. The incentives for the GPs were substantial. Campbell *et al.* (2009) reported that QOF incentives amounted to roughly 25% of GP incomes and that, while the program was voluntary, 99.6% of GPs participated. Any additional costs for personnel needed to improve quality were borne by the practices.

Doran *et al.* (2006) reported that the overall achievement of the indicators for England during the first year was 83.6%. By 2008–2009 that overall achievement had risen to 95.4% with the clinical domain indicators at 97.8% and the patient experience domain at 84.2%.

The indicators were to be updated annually. The payment per point was also increased toward an anticipated level for fiscal year 2009–2010 of £126.77 per point. Development and approval of each new or modified indicator was expected to take about two years.

In the 2006–2007 fiscal year indicators were added with respect to dementia, chronic kidney disease, and other problem areas, and many minimum achievement thresholds were raised. Certain existing indicators were also modified.

The New Process of Indicator Development

In May 2009, the National Institute for Health and Clinical Excellence (NICE) took over the development of the QOF indicators from the Department of Health. The NHS had signaled this in its NHS Next Stage Review: *Our Vision for Primary and Community Care*, in July 3, 2008, which had outlined a number of proposed changes as follows in the next section.

Developing the Quality and Outcomes Framework

6.13 We will create a fresh strategy for developing the Quality and Outcomes Framework, which will include an independent and transparent process for developing and reviewing indicators. We will discuss with the National Institute for Health and Clinical Excellence (NICE) and with professional and patient groups how this new process should work.

6.14 We propose to discuss with the profession how to reduce the number of organisational or process indicators in the Quality and Outcomes Framework so that we can focus resources on new or enhanced indicators to promote health and greater clinical quality. We will explore how to give greater flexibility to the local NHS to work with local GP practices to select quality indicators (potentially from a national menu) that reflect local health improvement priorities. We will explore the use of patient reported outcome measures (PROMs) to enhance overall indicators of quality. (DoH, 2008, pp. 45–46)

The NHS also announced that it would move forward with an accreditation scheme.

Accrediting High-Quality Primary Care

6.19 We are committed to promoting the use of accreditation schemes to drive quality improvement. We are currently supporting the Royal College of General Practitioners to develop an accreditation scheme for GP practices, which will be rolled out nationally by 2010. This scheme will involve mixed teams (drawn from GPs, other professions and lay assessors) to undertake a rigorous assessment of the systems used by GP practices to ensure safety and quality of practice. As well as assessing compliance with minimum criteria, it will pinpoint areas where practices have most scope to improve quality. This will act as a spur for continuous improvement. (DoH, 2008, pp. 46–47)

That fresh strategy for the QOF was outlined in a DoH publication "Developing the Quality and Outcomes Framework: Proposals for a New,

Independent Process," published October 30, 2008, and subsequently in a "Consultation Response and Analysis." Shortly thereafter, NICE issued a "process document" outlining how it was proposing to manage the revised process and how new and current indicators would be assessed. A newly appointed Primary Care QOF Advisory Panel was to be convened in June 2009 to consult on recommended priorities for revised indicators and the development of new indicators for FY 2010–2011. These proposals would be published in the summer of 2009 and NICE would work on developing proposals for FY 2011–2012. However, a new contractor was to be appointed for developing and piloting indicators for the FY 2011–2012 and onwards. NICE published its "Interim process guide" in May 2009.

The suggestions about the development of QOF indicators to meet local priorities or to change the weightings for that purpose did not gain much traction in this process. There was the possibility that local trusts might develop their own and pay providers directly, but NICE and NHS seemed to think that nationally consistent set of indicators would help smooth out inequities in services and variations in quality.

About NICE

The National Institute for Health and Clinical Excellence is an independent, government-funded organization, established in 1999 to advise the National Health Service. It was responsible for evidence-based guidelines for England, Wales, and Northern Ireland. Since 2002, NHS organizations in England and Wales have been required to pay for medicines and treatments recommended in NICE's technology appraisals. Prior to accepting the QOF assignment NICE was organized around the following:

- Centre for Public Health Excellence providing public health guidance on promotion of good health and prevention of illness.

- Centre for Health Technology Evaluation with two functions: (1) technological appraisals of the use of new and existing drugs and treatments within the NHS, and (2) intervention procedure guidance evaluating the safety and efficacy of procedures of diagnosis and treatment.

- Centre for Clinical Practice which develops clinical guidelines based on the best available evidence.

- Supporting implementation by estimating local costs and helping practitioners implement its findings.

It was the Centre for Clinical Practice that was taking on the management of the indicator development task.

The Health Technology Evaluation function has attracted worldwide attention. "NICE can be viewed as either a heartless rationing agent or an intrepid and impartial messenger for the need to set priorities in health care" (Steinbrook, 2008, p. 1978). The most greatly debated aspect of its methods is its extensive use of the incremental cost-effectiveness ratio also called the cost per quality adjusted life year (QALY). NICE does not use a fixed cut-off ratio, but it is generally perceived that operationally the cut-off has been between £20,000 and £30,000. There is some feeling that, while NICE is comfortable working at the high end of that range, some healthcare trusts that are at risk for payment look to or below the low end for treatments not assessed by NICE (Appleby, Devlin and Parkin, 2007). NICE has approved several more expensive cancer treatments. The NHS has also accepted deals with manufacturers of more expensive multiple sclerosis drugs to a 10-year trial of their treatments on a pay-for-performance basis with the companies paying back NHS if their incremental cost-effectiveness is less than £36,600 per QALY. Dr. Michael Rawlins, a physician and the only chair that NICE has had, admits that "The big problem is why we have chosen £20,000 to £30,000 per quality-adjusted life year. I have always been honest about this. There is really no empirical research that tells us where the boundaries ought to be. It is really a judgment of the economic community that has provided that sort of number" (Steinbrook, 2008). NICE has found itself in court over specific decisions concerning guidelines a number of times.

A 2007 review by the House of Commons Health Committee was strongly supportive of NICE and its rationing role, but urged it to act more quickly and undertake more studies, especially those resulting in guidance against accepted medical technologies that were not cost-effective. "We also recommend that elements of clinical guidelines be made mandatory. A suitable example would be risk assessment for all patients at risk of developing venous thromboembolism" (Health Select Committee, 2007). However, the Health Select Committee argued that "an independent review of the threshold should be undertaken by an independent body, it also—somewhat arbitrarily— recommends that a lower threshold is used for brief product assessments at launch" (Noble, 2008).

Proposed Interim Process for Developing Indicators

Indicator Prioritization

NPCRDC was to stay active in the process, especially its York Health Economics Consortium (NPCRDC/YHEC). It was to prepare the calendar of indicators to be reviewed for the period 2009 through 2012 for a June 2009 committee meeting. Approximately 20–30 indicators annually were suggested for review as to whether to continue them and at what incentive levels. The evidence on each reviewed indicator would be assembled by NICE. The review would consider:

- Current levels of achievement, trends in achievement and current levels of incentivisation.

- The potential for further increases in performance.

- Net patient and population benefit of estimated future increases in performance.

- Any changes in the evidence base behind the indicator.

- The potential effect on other indicators of retiring an indicator.

- Variation in performance among practices including their demographics and history of exception reporting. (NICE, 2009, p. 15)

The Committee was specifically instructed to consider indicators already included in the QOF schema in terms of whether:

- They have been embedded in practice and therefore do not require incentivisation and could be retired.

- They have been embedded in practice, but achievement levels suggest that the current thresholds may need amending.

- They have been only partly achieved and should continue to be incentivized.

- They have been only partly achieved and, based on consideration of cost-effectiveness information, the level of incentivisation or the thresholds may need to be adjusted to be consistent with other indicators. (NICE, 2009, p.17)

If the evidence base for an indicator changes significantly, NICE could request a review earlier than previously scheduled.

NICE Staffs the Review

Once NPCRDC/YHEC had recommended an indicator for review and the Primary Care QOF Advisory Panel (The Committee) had approved its immediate priority, NICE would assemble the required data to meet decision criteria suggested by the DoH and those used by NICE in its guidance (protocol) reviews. To assure a rigorous and transparent new process, NICE would first present a short briefing paper for The Committee. That paper would outline the epidemiology of the condition, determine whether it is a priority condition where key management variables are directly influenced by general practice staff, and/or whether guidance/incentives would be timely. NICE would review the strength of the evidence base behind current treatment guidance recommendations, summarize clinical effectiveness and cost-effectiveness information, and establish how the recommendations would lead to reduced health inequalities and/or improved cost-effectiveness. NICE would also determine whether the recommendations are feasible, measurable in the practice setting including the primary-care information system. This process would involve the QOF Indicator Programme team and relevant experts and consultants.

Rating Indicators

The Committee was to rate each proposed indicator change using a specific scoring system that was also used in prioritizing guidelines. Its elements were as follows:

- Criterion 1: (Scored 1 to 3) relevance to primary care—prevalence, referral, or management normally under primary care, and delivered by personnel under the QOF. All had to apply or the evaluation ceased.

- Criterion 2: (Scored 1 to 4) disease severity, focusing primarily on quality of life (QOL):

  a. Minor QOL impact, no disability = 1

  b. Definite QOL impact, but not significant mortality impact = 2

  c. QOL impact, some disability or modest increase in mortality risk = 3

  d. Intermediate mortality impact or significant mortality = 4

- Criterion 3: (Scored 1 to 3) healthcare priority and timeliness considered together

- Criterion 4: (Scored 1 to 3) likelihood of reducing health inequities

- Criterion 5: (Scored 1 to 3) strength of the clinical evidence concerning impact

- Criterion 6 (Scored 1 to 3) clinical effectiveness in terms of outcomes (mortality, morbidity, disability, QOL)

- Criterion 7: (Scored 1 to 3) extent to which recommendations would lead to a shift in practice behaviors leading to cost-effective delivery of care

- Criterion 8: feasibility in the practice setting, a go, no-go measure

Testing Indicators

Following the priorization process, NPCRDC/YHEC was to develop and pilot test the high-priority indicators. This included conducting a survey of a panel of experts using a Modified RAND/UCLA Appropriateness Method in which a package of relevant current and proposed indicators for a condition would be presented. The first round would be by mail and the second would involve a face-to-face meeting. After reviewing the evidence, the panelists were asked to rate each indicator on a 1 to 9 integer scale each for clarity, feasibility, and validity. Validity was defined as the extent to which the indicator statement represents high-quality care and would therefore be a valid indicator of quality. For each statement there is sufficient evidence and/or professional consensus to support it, and there are clear benefits to the patient (or the benefits significantly outweigh the risks). Clinicians/practice staff adhering to the statement would be providing a higher quality of care/service than those who are not doing so. Valid indicators must be within the control of the clinician/practice (NICE, 2009, p. 45).

New indicators achieving high and consistent rankings would then be pilot tested in 30 representative practices. During this process NPCRDC/YHEC would collect data from those practices using a workload diary and structured interviews. It might also conduct patient-level interviews about the indicator and its related QOL impact.

After a successful pilot, NICE was to consult on the developed indicators with stakeholders (patients and professional groups) across the UK. Following that internal review, the successful candidate indicators were to be presented to The Committee for approval.

Decision and Final Consultations

Once a new or modified indicator was approved by The Committee it was to be published on the NICE Web site. Then DoH would begin a process of consultation followed by negotiation with the GPC. Each year the agreed-to indicators would be included in full in the revised Statement of Financial Entitlements. A proposed or revised indicator is considered cost-effective when the net benefit (as defined as follows) is greater than zero; therefore, a minus figure will indicate the indicator is not cost-effective at the proposed range of incentives and anticipated level of implementation: Net benefit = monetized benefit – delivery cost – QOF payment.

Exception Reporting

One important way that the British pay-for-performance system differs from most pay-for-performance systems in the United States is in its policy of allowing GPs to exclude patients without penalty from patient registers or from specific QOF denominators when certain conditions are met (McDonald and Roland, 2008). For example, the 2007 Statement of Financial Entitlements listed the following criteria for exclusion:

A. patients who have been recorded as refusing to attend review who have been invited on at least three occasions during the preceding twelve months

B. patients for whom it is not appropriate to review the chronic disease parameters due to particular circumstances, e.g. terminal illness, extreme frailty

C. patients newly diagnosed within the practice or who have recently registered with the practice, who should have measurements made within three months and delivery of clinical standards within nine months, e.g. blood pressure or cholesterol measurements within target levels

D. patients who are on maximum tolerated doses of medication whose levels remain sub-optimal

E. patients for whom prescribing a medication is not clinically appropriate, e.g. those who have an allergy, another contraindication or have experienced an adverse reaction

F. where a patient has not tolerated medication

G. where a patient does not agree to investigation or treatment (informed dissent), and this has been recorded in their medical records

H. where the patient has a supervening condition which makes treatment of their condition inappropriate, e.g., cholesterol reduction where the patient has liver disease

I. where an investigative service or secondary care service is unavailable.

The reasons for the exceptions do not have to be reported through the IT system, but GPs must enter the reasons into the medical record for audit purposes. Early exception rates were relatively low overall, but highly variable between practices (Doran *et al.*, 2006).

While most practices seemed to honor the spirit of the exception reporting system, some practices were considered out of line. Increasingly, these were audited and their QOF earnings reduced by the local trusts with the encouragement of the NHS (Anekwe, 2008).

Trends and Concerns

Campbell *et al.* (2009) studied the quality of care for asthma, heart disease, and diabetes before and after the introduction of the QOF. They found that there had been an improvement trend prior to 2004, but that the introduction of incentives appeared to speed up the improvements in asthma and heart disease care for at least a year, but then reached a plateau. The quality of treatment for diabetes did not seem to deviate much from its pre-incentives upward trend. They offered several possible explanations for the plateau:

1. Subsequent gains were more difficult to achieve.

2. Once targets were achieved there was no reward for further achievement.

3. Given their already substantial increase in income, GPs were not interested in further improvements.

They suggested that the NHS seemed to be responding to this plateau by increasing the thresholds for maximum clinical indicator payments and by adding more clinical areas in 2006. Still, overall achievement had risen from 91.3% to 95.3–96.8% in the four subsequent years. They also observed indications that some aspects of quality of care not associated with specific indicators had been dropping. An example they gave was continuity of care that may have suffered in trying to meet an under-48-hour appointment waiting period or were switched to nurse-led clinics for delivering incentivized follow-up of specific diseases. McDonald and Roland (2008) reported from interviews with 20 UK GPs that there had been changes in the nature of the office visit due to the Framework: "The requirement to enter data into the electronic medical record to respond to the large number of targets was described as reducing eye contact, increasing time spent on data collection in the office visit, and potentially crowding out the patient's agenda" (p. 123). Doran *et al.* (2008) did report that the QOF had helped deal with issues of inequalities in care in England, one of its objectives.

CASE ANALYSIS

As more and more payers focus on measuring and rewarding performance, issues arise about how to use that process to motivate continuous quality improvement. The National Health Services has had the world's largest implementation of pay-for-performance. General practitioners have responded rapidly to the incentives, driving most values rapidly toward their maxima. This case considers how the UK has addressed this "now what" question. This is a political environment, so the pacing and the apparent fairness and rationality of the process for continually raising the bar are very important to continued success.

ASSIGNMENT QUESTIONS

1. What do you consider to be the key issues for quality improvement in the NHS quality-improvement program as it goes forward?

2. What do you consider to be the strengths and weaknesses of the effort to improve the development of QOF indicators over the next couple of years?

3. The program appears to be using QALY metrics to justify the choices of future quality and outcome indictors. What are the strengths and weaknesses of such an approach to valuing quality?

4. Some researchers have expressed doubts about the improvement effectiveness of indicators in the high 90% range. What is your evaluation of this concern and what alternatives do you recommend?

5. Most U.S. P4P efforts do not allow for exclusion of a significant numbers of patients. What are the pros and cons of this approach and the one used by NHS?

6. NHS is a single payer system. How does this affect its design of the QOF system and its efforts to implement it? How do the much more complex U.S. payment systems affect its utilization of P4P systems?

7. The NHS QOF effort is obviously full of very specific point systems for evaluation. What are the strengths and weaknesses of such quantification of decision rules in a healthcare environment?

CLASS EXERCISE

A new government came to power in Britain in mid-2010. Find out how it has proposed to change the NHS and especially the role of NICE. How has this change influenced the selection of a successor contractor to NICE to manage the indicator selection process?

North Carolina Local Health Department Accreditation Program

David Stone and Mary V. Davis

INTRODUCTION

Accreditation in public health is a recent development. With the exception of the Missouri and Michigan accreditation programs, local health department accreditation has only received wide attention since the turn of the 21st century. Accreditation of local public health departments in North Carolina started in 2005, following development and pilot testing, which began in 2002, although a study of accreditation had been undertaken in the late 1990s.

In North Carolina, local health department (LHD) accreditation is a mandatory process. It is conferred by the North Carolina Local Health Department Accreditation (NCLHDA) Board housed within the NC Institute for Public Health (NCIPH) at the University of North Carolina at Chapel Hill Gillings School of Global Public Health. It has two fundamental purposes: to certify the capacity of local health departments to deliver the ten essential services and to encourage performance improvement at the local level. Accreditation status is granted when a LHD has been found to meet or exceed stated criteria of capacity and quality as determined by an on-site assessment.

The accreditation process and system had developed steadily since the North Carolina legislature established and funded the program in 2005.

However, its legislative budget was reduced, together with many others for the 09–10 fiscal year, due to revenue shortfalls. Even though many local health directors have stated that the process is beneficial, there has been little tangible evidence so far to validate that LHDs have improved as a result of accreditation. The Board is just beginning to conduct research on the impact of the accreditation program.

BACKGROUND

In 2002, the Division of Public Health (DPH), the North Carolina Department of Health and Human Services (DHHS) under the leadership of Dr. Leah Devlin, the State Health Director, and the North Carolina Association of Local Health Directors (NCALHD), under the leadership of Wayne Raynor, its president, explored the development and adoption of a standards-based system for accrediting local health departments. The NCALHD, partnering with the DPH, convened a "blue ribbon" task force to address public health reform and local public health organizational issues. The task force was chaired by Dr. Devlin and Dr. Dorothy Cilenti, then the Health Director for Chatham County. The task force, referred to as the Standards and Efficiencies Task Force, was subdivided into three committees: best practices, demonstration projects, and local public health accreditation. The best practices committee focused on accountability, partnerships with community-based organizations, administrative flexibility, and effectiveness in addressing health disparities. The demonstration projects committee identified successful collaborations generated using a functional partnerships concept and recommended strategies for replication. The accreditation committee focused on local public health infrastructure and capacity issues.

The NCALHD also formed an Accreditation Committee composed of local health directors from across the state and DPH representatives, which was co-chaired by local health directors Barry Bass and Rosemary Summers and Dr. Joy Reed, head of public health nursing at the DPH. Sheila Pfaender of the NCIPH provided research support to the Committee. The Committee co-chairs made presentations and distributed written reports on the Committee's work to the Standards and Efficiencies Task Force and to the Executive Committee and the general membership of the NCALHD.

In addition, the NCALHD Accreditation Committee, along with the NCIPH staff, began reviewing both proposed and existing models of accountability from a number of states and one Canadian province. Based on this review, the Committee selected the Missouri Local Public Health Agency Accreditation Program as its model framework. Like North Carolina, Missouri has a large decentralized public health system with over 100 autonomous local health departments.

The Committee developed a basic set of accreditation recommendations based on a trial assessment of the Missouri Local Public Health Agency Accreditation Program Self-Assessment Instrument. These recommendations were discussed at regional NCALHD meetings in early 2003. Based on the reviews, the trial assessment and the Committee's findings, the NCALHD Accreditation Committee presented its final report and recommendations for a North Carolina Local Health Department Accreditation program in June, 2003.

Later in 2003, DHHS Secretary Carmen Hooker Odum convened a group of North Carolina public health system stakeholders known as the Public Health Task Force 2004 (PHTF 2004). Their task was to develop recommendations on how to strengthen the state's public health system, improve the health status of the people, and eliminate health disparities. There were six committees established within the PHTF, one of which focused on Accreditation. The Accreditation Committee of PHTF 2004 began work on the North Carolina Local Health Department Accreditation process starting with the recommendations in the NCALHD's June 2003 report. A key accomplishment of the PHTF 2004 Accreditation Committee was the development of a complete set of accreditation standards for North Carolina's local health departments. These standards are now known as benchmarks.

In January 2004, six local health departments that volunteered to participate (Appalachian District, Buncombe, Cabarrus, Chatham, Dare, and New Hanover) piloted the proposed standards and process. Each tested the self-assessment instrument and the proposed accreditation standards and hosted an agency review by a Site Visit Team. An Accreditation Board was appointed under the direction of Moses Carey, an Orange County commissioner, health administrator, and Gillings School of Global Public Health faculty member who has since become NC Secretary of Administration. The pilot also included a trial of the Accreditation Board process and appeals process. At the conclusion of the pilot, each of the participating departments was awarded "Accredited" status. The NCIPH served as the administrator of the pilot and conducted a thorough evaluation of the exercise. Evaluation findings were used to revise both the self-assessment instrument and the proposed processes.

Upon conclusion of the pilot, the PHTF 2004 Accreditation Committee put forward its revised set of recommendations, incorporating most of the previous committee's work and recommending funding from the North Carolina General Assembly to fully implement the program. In June 2004, the General Assembly appropriated funds to implement a continuation of the pilot study in four additional local health departments, again under the administration of the NCIPH (Pilot II—Cherokee, Craven, Harnett, and Pamlico). These four additional local health departments received accreditation in May 2005. The ten health departments accredited in 2004 and 2005 included rural and urban, large and small health departments, and a district that included three counties and a community health alliance.

A program director, Craig Michalak, was hired in March 2005. He was charged with implementing the program, developing relationships among the partners, and developing the practices and processes of the system. Building off of the previous work, the General Assembly established an accreditation system for local health departments effective October 1, 2005, as recommended by the Public Health Task Force 2004. The Commission for Health Services, as required by the accreditation legislation, met and approved the temporary accreditation rules on December 9, 2005. The state's Rules Commission met on December 15, 2005 and adopted the temporary accreditation rules. Later, the Permanent Accreditation Rules were adopted by the Rules Commission on September 21, 2006, with an effective date of October 1, 2006.

WHY ACCREDITATION IN NORTH CAROLINA?

One major point of discussion for the Standards and Efficiencies Task Force was accountability for local health departments. The Task Force was aware that the legislature was examining the organizational structure of local public health. Local health directors wanted to devise a system without structural changes that would show effective use of resources in providing services, offer accountability to communities and elected officials, and provide a basic level of competent services in every local health department. Among the many reasons that such an accreditation system was developed and implemented were:

- The perception of service variability—study after study debated what services a health department should provide. There was a perception that there was tremendous variation from health department to health department.

- A changing model of governance over many years—there was a history of multi-county district health departments throughout the past, as many as 18 counties at one time, but they were increasingly coming apart and struggling financially.

- The perception that some existing health departments were too small—that they didn't have the resources needed to be a viable department.

- The perception that there were too many health departments—there were many conversations, particularly among legislators, that 85 local health departments were too many and that there were unnecessary administrative costs as a result. Another point was the difficulty of the state Division of Public Health having to work with 85 administrative units.

- The need for increased accountability—there was an increasing concern about accountability to communities and the legislature, and a desire to provide more accountability to stakeholders and the public health system itself.

- The impact of mental health reform—North Carolina's mental health system was undergoing reform that was not viewed by the public health community as a success. The mental health reform movement was threatening to spill over into public health and the health directors wanted means to avoid such a result.

- The inability to communicate with the public—public health suffers from an ongoing inability to communicate with the citizens and legislature about what it does and even how to define what an LHD is.

- The recognition that all other healthcare systems are accredited—local health directors wanted this familiar framework and brand recognition for citizens and other providers.

- The recognition that accreditation provided opportunities for being a provider of more services—possible funding sources and grants might become available to or even be limited to accredited agencies.

- The History of Turning Point—Turning Point was an initiative of The Robert Wood Johnson Foundation to transform and strengthen the public health system. NC participated and pursued social marketing over accreditation in 1999, but had yet to develop the concept and readiness with any large stakeholder group.

- A legislative champion that wanted to reform the public health system through accreditation—working with public health partners on codifying an accreditation system as explored with the legislature during passage of the bill in 2005.

PROGRAM STRUCTURE AND DESIGN

Accreditation strives to guarantee that a citizen of NC can walk into any local health department in the state and be assured that defined services will be competently delivered. One goal has been to take 85 independent local health departments and create a state-wide public health system. The program is managed and facilitated by the Program Administrator at the NC Institute for Public Health, and oversight is by an independent entity—the NCLHDA Board. The Board is established by statute, and board members are appointed by the Secretary of the NC DHHS. Yet, the NC program takes a very collaborative approach to the process. There is an Accreditation/Quality Improvement (QI) Liaison Committee of the NCALHD that provides input and feedback. The Division of Public Health provides Board members, input, and funds the public health nurse consultants who work with the LHDs for 6 to 18 months to prepare for accreditation and the Site Visit.

Functional Components

The NCLHDA program entails three functional components with supporting functions:

- **A self-assessment completed by the local health department**
  The health department assesses and reports how it thinks it conforms to the documentation requirements of the activities of accred-

itation. The health department completes the Health Department Self-Assessment Instrument (HDSAI). This, along with other specified information, is submitted to the Accreditation Administrator.

* **A Site Visit by a multidisciplinary, trained team of peer volunteers**
A Site Visit is scheduled and is managed by staff of the program. The typical visit is three days. The State Accreditation Coordinator serves as the liaison with the health department, with consultants, and with site visitors.

* **The determination of accreditation status by an independent accreditation board**
The Board meeting is supported by program staff. Working with the Board Chair, an agenda is developed that is emailed to Board members along with the documents prepared for the meeting.

There are a variety of support functions delivered by the administrator's office including:

* Orientation to the accreditation process is given to local health departments and boards of health. This is provided by webinar at least annually and is also conducted on request.

* Required training of site visitors is conducted annually.

* A Web site is maintained containing various elements of the process and system documents.

* Development, implementation, and maintenance of system documentation, such as policies, protocols, guidance, and interpretation.

There are two full-time staff persons—David Stone, the Accreditation Administrator, and a State Accreditation Coordinator, Brittan Wood. There is also another state accreditation coordinator position that has been unfilled for almost two years. Part-time clerical support is offered through other NCIPH staff. A part-time clerical position was terminated May 30th, 2009, due to funding cuts. Evaluation Services for the program are directed by Mary Davis.

All scheduling has been voluntary. Initially, a LHD would notify the Accreditation Administrator (AA) of its readiness to undergo accreditation. David and Brittan then draft a schedule based on the requests submitted from LHDs, and the Board determines the final Site Visit schedule. Due to funding, the Site Visit calendar for LHDs undergoing initial accreditation was limited to ten per fiscal year. The 2005 legislation stated that all LHDs must be scheduled by the end of 2014. All 85 LHDs were scheduled and the calendar extended through FY 2013. Once the current fiscal year is selected for the Site Visit, the Division of Public Health assigns a public health nurse consultant to the applicant agency to provide consultation and technical assistance throughout the process. Regional program consultants from the Division of Environmental Health and the Division of Public Health are available for consultation as requested. The AA provides training to the staff of the participating health departments on the accreditation process and how to use the HDSAI. The DPH consultants usually participate in this training. On-going conference calls are available to the applicant agencies. Figure 15–1 provides a summary flow chart of the accreditation process.

Each health department usually assembles a multidisciplinary Accreditation Management Team (AMT) to lead the accreditation process in the agency. The LHD determines who will be on the team, and many times it is or starts with the agency's management team. One member of this team is designated as the health department's "Agency Accreditation Coordinator" (AAC); this person serves as the primary contact for the consultants and as the agency's liaison to the AA. The AA strongly recommends that an LHD have an AMT and the agency must name an AAC.

Self-Assessment

Each health department must complete a self-assessment based on available evidence and documentation about the benchmarks and activities. The LHD submits the self-assessment to the AA within 90 days after notification that the accreditation process for the department has begun. The self-assessment, documented through the completion of the Health Department Self-Assessment Instrument, is an internal review of the agency's ability to meet benchmarks and the delivery of essential services as indicated by the agency's performance of a set of prescribed activities. The self-assessment also indicates the availability and qualifications of core staff and the adequacy of physical facilities and administrative services. It assists the local health department in identifying areas for improvement and prepares the department for the on-site review.

The self-assessment instrument contains a total of 41 benchmarks and 148 related activities. There are three sections in the HDSAI. The first

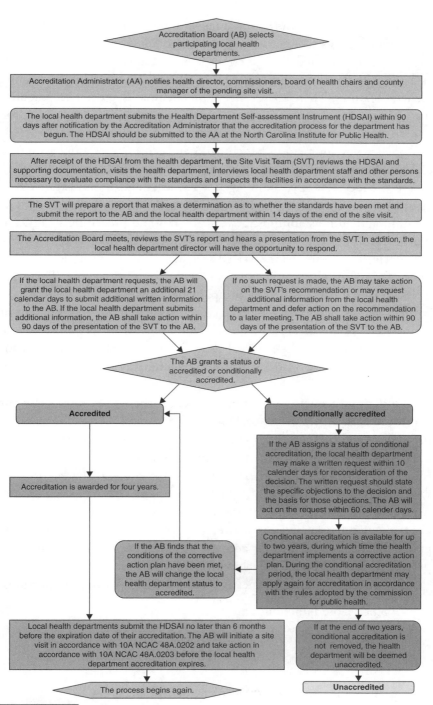

Figure 15-1   A Basic Flowchart of the NC Accreditation Process

section covers Agency Core Functions and Essential Services (CF&ES). These benchmarks represent minimum standards of capacity to perform the nationally-accepted core functions, essential services for public health, and the Mandated Services for LHDs specified in the North Carolina General Statutes. There are 29 CF&ES benchmarks and 93 accompanying activities here, and they are divided into three groups, based on the core functions of public health: assessment (8 benchmarks and 29 activities), policy development (7 benchmarks and 26 activities), and assurance (14 benchmarks and 38 activities).

The second section is about Agency Facilities and Administrative Services (F&AS). These benchmarks pertain to the agency's general administration and address administrative structures and procedures. LHDs in North Carolina are autonomous and demonstrate a wide variety of internal administrative structures, yet all should be able to demonstrate clear lines of responsibility and definitive reporting relationships. There are 4 F&AS benchmarks and 27 accompanying activities.

The final section is on Governance and relates to the development of the agency's Board of Health. The benchmarks in this section recognize the Board of Health's scope of legal authority and overall responsibility for the agency. There are 8 Board of Health benchmarks and 28 accompanying activities.

In order to designate a benchmark as "met," the agency must carry out and meet all activities prescribed for that benchmark. A benchmark may have from one to 10 activities associated with it. Failure to meet any one activity associated with a benchmark means that the entire benchmark is "not met." At the present time, there are no benchmarks that are universally required. The choice of which benchmarks to meet within the required number is up to the local health department. The local health department must satisfy thirty-three (33) of the forty-one (41) benchmarks to be recommended for accreditation. Exhibit 15–1 illustrates this process with some sample benchmarks and activities.

The benchmarks must be met according to the following proportions:

- Agency Core Functions and Essential Services

  - Assessment Function = 6 of 8 benchmarks

  - Policy Development Function = 5 of 7 benchmarks

  - Assurance Function = 11 of 14 benchmarks

EXHIBIT 15–1

A Selection of Standards and Activities from the NC Accreditation System

Standard: Agency Core Functions and Essential Services

FUNCTION: ASSESSMENT
ESSENTIAL SERVICE 1: Monitor health status to identify community health problems.

Benchmark 1: A local health department shall conduct and disseminate results of regular community health assessments.
Activity 1.2: The local health department shall update the community health assessment with an interim "State of the County's Health" report (or equivalent) annually. The report shall demonstrate that the local health department is tracking priority issues identified in the community health assessment, identifying emerging issues, and shall identify any new initiatives.
Documentation: Copy of State of the County's Health (SOTCH) report, *dated within the past 12 months* AND letter of SOTCH receipt by Office of Healthy Carolinians/Health Education. If the Community Health Assessment was completed within the past 12 months, the SOTCH must be dated within the past 24 months.
Re-Accreditation Documentation: Since the previous Site Visit, provide copies of the three State of the County's Health (SOTCH) reports produced AND The three letters of SOTCH receipt by Office of Healthy Carolinians/Health Education.

Standard: Agency Core Functions and Essential Services

FUNCTION: POLICY DEVELOPMENT
ESSENTIAL SERVICE 4: Mobilize community partnerships to identify and solve health problems.

Benchmark 11: The local health department shall convene key constituents and community partners to identify, analyze, and prioritize community health problems/issues.
Activity 11.1: The local health department shall participate in a collaborative community steering committee to identify health issues and needs.

(continues)

EXHIBIT 15-1

Documentation: Steering Committee membership list AND *one of the following*: meeting minutes, action plan, or report from steering committee demonstrating the local health department's role.

Standard: Facilities and Administrative Services

Benchmark 30: The local health department shall provide safe and accessible physical facilities and services.

Activity 30.4: The local health department shall ensure privacy and security of records containing privileged patient medical information or information protected by the federal Health Insurance Portability and Accountability Act.

Documentation: Medical records policies AND proper handling, storage and transport of medical records. To be verified through observations by Site Visitors.

Standard: Governance

Benchmark 38: The local board of health shall participate in the establishment of public health goals and objectives.

Activity 38.3: The local board of health shall assure that individuals, agencies, and organizations have the opportunity to participate in the development of goals, objectives, and strategies for community health improvement.

Documentation: Board of health policy regarding public participation in the development of goals, objectives and strategies for community health improvement AND board of health minutes reflecting that public participation occurred or agenda indicating allocated time to encourage public participation.

- Facilities and Administrative Services = 3 of 4 benchmarks
- Board of Health/Governance = 6 of 8 benchmarks
- Two additional benchmarks from any of the three (3) standards.

Compliance with activities must be documented with appropriate evidence. All documentation presented by the health department should be the most recent available and must be dated within 24 months of the date of the official notification, unless otherwise defined per activity. The HDSAI suggests examples and quantities of appropriate documentation. Except where certain documentation is noted to be *specifically required*, a health department may offer alternative/substitute evidence to document compliance with an activity, providing it offers an explanation of its substitution and provides copies of the alternative evidence. While the evidence that the LHD will be proposing must be listed in the HDSAI, it is not required to be submitted prior to the Site Visit.

Along with the completed HDSAI, the agency must submit the following:

- A completed, signed HDSAI cover page and summary checklist

- The agency's mission statement, strategic plan, and organizational chart

- A roster of the agency's Management Team and the full staff

- The most recent Community Health Assessment (CHA) and the most recent update of the CHA—State of the County's Health report

- A two-page double-spaced narrative about the local health department

The HDSAI and other information is sent electronically to the AA whenever possible. All documentation collected to meet benchmarks and activities is retained in a resource file set aside for examination by the Site Visit Team (SVT). Some LHDs choose to develop an electronic HDSAI in which the evidence is viewed electronically using laptop computers.

Site Visit Teams

Each Site Visit Team (SVT) is comprised of not fewer than four individuals with expertise or experience in local public health, including environmental health, public health nursing, and public health administration or policy development/governance. The SVT usually includes:

- A Local Health Administrator

- A Public Health Nurse

- An Environmental Health Specialist

- A Board of Health Representative

- A State Accreditation Coordinator (program staff)

Applicant agencies are advised of the proposed composition of the SVT in advance. They then have an opportunity to identify any conflicts of interest that might disqualify a site visitor, in which case the AA will provide a replacement. Due to the possibility that a SVT member may need to withdraw, an alternate team is selected when the primary team is appointed.

Team Organization

The AA designates one person on each SVT to serve as the Lead Site Visitor (LSV). The LSV is responsible for coordinating the activities of the team when on-site and is the spokesperson for the group. The LSV is the point-of-contact with the State Accreditation Coordinator who will convey questions or requests for additional documentation to the AAC. Throughout the Site Visit, the LSV evaluates the progress of the team and makes additional or revised assignments. The LSV is responsible for achieving consensus among the site visitors and for completing the Site Visit Team Report. Although each member of the SVT contributes to the final Site Visit Team Report, the LSV is responsible for collecting the information, completing the report, and submitting it to the AA.

Prior to the Site Visit, the SVT reviews the following: the completed Health Department Self-Assessment Instrument (HDSAI) and summary checklist and additional LHD documents, site visitor interview guide, site visitor operational guidelines, the HDSAI Interpretation Document, and the site visitor report form. The SVT should also be familiar with NC Public Health Laws. Prior to beginning the visit, the SVT gathers for a mandatory meeting, either by phone or in person, to:

- Discuss observations made from their individual study of the Health Department Self-Assessment Instrument (HDSAI) and other previously circulated material;

- Discuss specifically any deficiencies or ambiguities noted by analysis of the HDSAI;

- Review any new information from the AA about the agency or about interpreting the benchmarks;

- Review the Site Visit schedule and make any last minute adjustments in SVT assignments for document review or interviews;

- Review the agency's organizational chart and any other basic information that describes how the agency conducts its work; and

- Discuss the methodology for preparing the Site Visit Report.

Site Visit

A few weeks after submitting the completed HDSAI, the LHD hosts an on-site visit by a Site Visit Team. A "typical" Site Visit lasts for three days. The duration of the visit may be longer if special circumstances (such as those encountered in very large, complex health departments or in multi-county district health departments) dictate the need for more time, or shorter, in the case of a very small agency. A sample three-day schedule is provided, but each participating agency can alter it to meet local needs.

The primary task of the SVT visit is to amplify, clarify, and verify the HDSAI in order to evaluate the health department's degree of compliance with the benchmarks and associated activities. To accomplish this task, the SVT:

- Reviews the Health Department Self-Assessment Instrument and supporting documentation;

- Tours the local health department facilities and inspects in accordance with the benchmarks; and

- Interviews local health department staff, Board of Health members, and other persons necessary to evaluate compliance with the benchmarks and the team may request additional supporting documentation or other evidence as necessary to evaluate compliance with the benchmarks.

A typical Site Visit schedule is comprised of the following elements:

- An Entrance Conference on the first morning of the Site Visit, at the main office of the health agency. Representatives from the senior administration of the agency meet with members of the SVT. A sample entrance conference agenda is provided, and the agency should ask all site visitors to sign a confidentiality agreement. Immediately following the Entrance Conference, the Local Health

Director, or designee, will lead the SVT on a general tour of the health agency. One or more pre-planned trips off-site may be required for visits to the agency's satellite facilities.

- Each Site Visitor will have primary responsibility for verifying one or more sections of the HDSAI. This task requires examination of materials provided by the health department in the on-site Resource File (or Files). A site visitor may request additional information or evidence not presented in the Resource File.

- The SVT interviews staff of the agency, members of the Board of Health, and representatives from local government and community agencies to ascertain their understanding of the agency and their role in or with respect to the agency. Interviews also allow for confirmation of evidence provided in the documents. During a typical Site Visit there are 13 interviews.

- At the end of each day of the Site Visit, the SVT meets in executive session to discuss the outcomes of the day's work, to list general impressions, and to identify questions they would like to ask or additional documentation they would like to review.

- The Exit Conference, led by the State Accreditation Coordinator and the LSV, is conducted at the end of the Site Visit and may be attended by any staff that the Local Health Director chooses to have present. The purpose of the Exit Conference is to offer general impressions of the Site Visit as well as any findings available as of the conclusion of the Site Visit, which may include any "not met" activities and potential areas for quality improvement.

Site Visit Team Report

In the Site Visit Team Report the SVT summarizes information it has gathered. The report includes a summary score sheet and a narrative that contains findings, recommendations, and suggested improvements. Time permitting, the SVT begins to compile its report during the Site Visit. The LSV is responsible for completing the report and submitting it to the AA within 14 days of the completion of the Site Visit. The AA reviews the report with the LSV prior to sending it to the Accreditation Board, the LHD, the AAC, and the Board of Health Chair.

Local Health Department Accreditation Board

The purpose of the Accreditation Board (the Board) is to contribute to the improvement of public health programs and services throughout North Carolina by defining, endorsing, and upholding standards of minimum performance for the state's local health departments. The Board is the official entity that assigns accreditation status to a local health department participating in the health department accreditation process.

By statute, the Board is composed of 17 members appointed by the Secretary of the DHHS as follows:

- Four county commissioners

- Four members of a local board of health

- Three local health directors

- Two staff members from the Division of Public Health

- One staff member from the Division of Environmental Health

- Three at-large members

Upon receipt of the Site Visit Report, the AA arranges for the agency's assessment to be reviewed by the Board. David Stone meets with Dr. Betty Alexander, the current Board Chair, prior to every board meeting to review the agenda and the Site Visit reports that will be presented. The Board meets to examine and discuss the health department's self-assessment and supporting evidence, the Site Visit Team Report and the SVT's recommendation for the LHD's accreditation status. The Board considers each agency separately. At the Board meeting, the Lead Site Visitor (LSV) from the SVT presents the report and the recommendation for accreditation status. The LHD representatives (Health Director and AAC) are given the opportunity to respond to the Lead Site Visitor's (LSV) presentation and recommendation for accreditation status. Usually the Board renders a decision upon the conclusion of the SVT report and any questioning.

Accreditation Status

The Board assigns an accreditation status to each LHD that is applying for initial accreditation or re-accreditation from the following options:

- Four-Year Accreditation Status—a rating which indicates that the local health department satisfies the accreditation benchmarks adopted by the Accreditation Board. The initial period of accreditation expires four calendar years after initial accreditation is granted.

- Conditional Accreditation Status—indicating that the local health department has not met the minimal requirements for accreditation and has therefore been granted conditional accreditation subject to conditions specified by the Board. The Board provides to the LHD a written statement of the conditions that must be satisfied in order to be accredited. That LHD must develop a corrective plan of action, which must be completed within two years, and submit it to the AA within 90 days of notice of the Board's decision. The period of Conditional Accreditation expires two calendar years after Conditional Accreditation is granted. During the Conditional Accreditation period, the LHD may apply again for Accreditation. If the Board finds that standards have been met, the Board shall change its status to Accredited with the accreditation period to expire four calendar years after the Conditional Accreditation was initially granted. If the Board finds that the conditions have not been satisfied, the LHD shall continue under its grant of Conditional Accreditation.

- Unaccredited Status—indicating that the LHD has failed to meet one or more accreditation benchmarks after a period of conditional accreditation.

ACCREDITATION PROGRAM STATUS

As of July 17, 2009, 50 of North Carolina's 85 local health departments were accredited. The remaining thirty-five agencies were scheduled for their Site Visits, with the calendar planned through 2013. During 2009, David Stone distributed two status statements to inform partners and stakeholders on the standing of the program due to current budget projections. The June 11th status statement listed program activities for the upcoming fiscal year based upon the projected budget allocation. The projected 85% cut to the state FY 09–10 allocation of funds did hold. As of July 1, 2009, program operations were placed on hold until funding could be restored. A second status statement was distributed in September to affirm the scope of work for the year and some projections for the following year should the funding be restored. As of the writing of this case study, the allocation was in the FY 10–11 budget. The allocation for FY 10-11 was half of the previous amount. The program was being reinstated without any funds being given to local health departments for preparation.

Lessons Learned

The 2009–2010 FY program suspension allowed the remaining Accreditation staff to review the lessons learned from eight years of planning, program development, implementation, and evaluation. Especially important for the future would be the provision of summary data from program evaluation and research that could inform program implementation and assess its impact.

Reflections on Program Planning and Development

The NC system did not begin with the intention of being mandatory, but the 2005 legislation made it so. While this showed support to the program and provided base funding, it came with expectations that were at best unrealistic. While the intent was to improve the level of public health services in every health department in NC, some stakeholders felt that accreditation should pinpoint those agencies that should not be providing services as a stand-alone agency. Some felt that accreditation should drive consolidation of agencies. The approach actually used has been to support a period of preparation prior to the site-visit so that all health departments could be successful in the accreditation process and to provide a basis for quality improvement in the agency.

The Pilot Process in NC yielded a number of lessons. These are outlined in Figure 15–2 together with a summary of the issues identified and the solutions adopted at each stage along the way. The pilot LHDs were given accreditation status as an incentive to participate. This was due in part to the short preparatory time period and lack of available resource support. However, an unintended consequence was that gaining accreditation status became the goal, rather than the pilot testing of the standards and the process. The benchmarks and activities and the process were *de facto* accepted. The LHDs did not focus on whether the requirements of the standards, as provided, were appropriate for public health. Where this type of assessment did occur, it was a secondary outcome. Of the ten pilot LHDs, four were recommended for conditional accreditation.

Pilot 1 Jan–April 2004

Key issues
1. Assessment instrument duplicative, standards unclear
2. Site visitor selection
3. Timeline for assessment too short
4. Accreditation board selection and process
5. Inadequate training

Program solutions
1. Revised, revamped instrument
2. Revised site visitor selection criteria, expanded pool
3. Lengthened timeline for assessment to 3 months
4. Updated accreditation board member selection criteria and processes
5. Modified training

Pilot 2 FY 04–05

Key issues
1. Assessment instrument governance section did not meet all models
2. Need for more specific site visit policies
3. Need for enhanced communication methods

Program solutions
1. Convened committee to improve governance activities
2. Updated site visit policies, e.g., requests for additional documentation and exit interview
3. Created program Web site with FAQs, resources for health departments, etc.

Implement Year 1 FY 05–06

Key issues
1. Partner roles unclear, particularly around interpreting standards
2. Certain accreditation board procedures not clear
3. Consistency between site visit teams in interpreting benchmarks

Program solutions
1. Standardized interpretation procedures among partners
2. Created accreditation board procedures on introducing additional documentation
3. Provided interpretation training for site visitors

Implement Year 2 FY 06–07

Key issues
1. Policy adoption among health departments not tailored appropriately
2. Continued perceived need to increase site visitor interpreting reliability
3. Reaccreditation policies

Program solutions
1 and 2. Enhanced training for agency staff and site visitors
2. Credentialing of site visitors under discussion
3. Partners analyzing reaccreditation policies and procedures

Figure 15-2   Summary Learnings Along a Time Line

Due to limited funding, only ten initial Site Visits of LHDs per year could be conducted. With ten LHDs having undergone assessment in the two pilots, this meant it would take eight years to complete an initial cycle of all 85 agencies. Thus, while some agencies would be having their third Site Visit, others would be undergoing their first. This slowed down the program objective of assuring all citizens competent services across the state. It also hampered the development of the program as there was debate about revising the requirements for re-accreditation, while there were still agencies that had yet to go through the process initially. A better approach would have been to have all agencies complete the process in a four-year timeframe, since that is the time period granted for accreditation status; however, lack of resources and staff made this option impossible.

There was a lack of interpretation and policy guidance in the early years of the program. Many aspects of policy and interpretation of the activities and documentation were conversational. It was not until 2008 that any program policies were written and approved by the Board. An interpretation document to guide LHDs, consultants, and site visitors was not released for use until 2009.

Agency Preparation and Performance

Goals of the accreditation program include increasing agency accountability and reducing variation in service among local health departments. To meet accreditation standards, NC local health departments needed to create new policies or update policies and practices. All 48 LHDs that participated in the NC program from 2006–2009 were awarded accreditation, but to achieve accredited status all LHDs needed to write policies on existing practice, update existing policies, or create entirely new policies or practices. Many LHDs wrote multiple new policies and practices. The considerable policy and practice work that agencies engaged in to prepare for accreditation resulted in most agencies meeting nearly all accreditation activities.

During the initial assessments of the 2006–2009 (thru June) period, 7104 accreditation activities were evaluated and only 60 were missed, involving 25 different benchmarks. These were widely distributed, however, with only 14 agencies meeting all the benchmarks and 15 missing two to four benchmarks. The three activities missed by five or more health departments are listed in Table 15–1.

Table 15–1	Three Activities Missed by Five or More Health Departments

Activity	Occurrences	
7.3	9	The local health department shall investigate and respond to environmental health complaints or referrals. *Documentation*: Complaint/referral log should include the following required information: was the complaint justified, how long to take action, and if referred to another agency that referral information AND lab/investigation reports AND documentation of timely and appropriate action.
30.10	5	The local health department shall make efforts to prohibit the use of tobacco in all areas and grounds within 50 feet of the health department facility. *Documentation*: Correspondence with property owner and/or commissioners.
31.4	6	The local health department shall have current written position descriptions and qualifications for each staff position. *Documentation*: See 23.2

Program Implementation Evaluation

The North Carolina Institute for Public Health's Office of Evaluation Services conducts an annual program review. This review determines if the program is working as intended and identifies areas for program improvement, examines the extent to which accreditation improves local health department capacity to assure services, and identifies preliminary outcomes of the program. Evaluation data are collected from program documents and participants (agency personnel and health directors, site visitors, program administrators, and partners) through surveys and interviews.

Measures to examine if the program is working as intended include agency preparation and performance on the benchmarks and performance of the accreditation administrator. Agency preparation and performance were summarized in the previous sections. Regarding accreditation administration performance, the following indicators have been examined over several years:

- Participant satisfaction with program management—86% of participants (health directors, agency staff, site visitors, Division of Public Health staff) are very satisfied with the Accreditation Administrator management of the program. In particular, 91% of health directors are very satisfied with the Accreditation Administrator management of the program.

- Satisfaction with program output—Among 48 local health department directors, 92% are satisfied with the output of the accreditation program given the time they and their staff expended to prepare for accreditation.

Program Impact

In 2010, the North Carolina Institute for Public Health, Evaluation Services surveyed accredited LHDs to examine agency performance improvement activities after accreditation as well as benefits of accreditation. All 48 agencies accredited under the final rules completed the survey. Among these agencies 96% continue to update policies and 67% percent have conducted quality-improvement activities. The survey focused on the partnership improvement benefits of accreditation. Agencies reported that their relationships with county commissioners, community partners and hospitals, and Boards of Health improved as follows:

- 24% county commissioners

- 54% community partners and hospitals

- 56% Boards of Health

Twenty-two agencies identified specific additional benefits of accreditation that could be organized into 13 themes. The benefit themes identified by most accredited LHDs are listed in Table 15–2.

Table 15–2 Benefit Themes Identified by Most Accredited LHDs	
Benefit	*Number of Agencies Reporting*
Pride at achieving or accomplishing accreditation	7
Improved policies and process to create polices	5
Teambuilding and team work	4
Improved staff appreciation of public health services and functions	4

LINK BETWEEN QUALITY IMPROVEMENT AND ACCREDITATION

What is (or will be) the link between an accreditation process and an LHD's work in quality improvement? That is the question being explored next. One stated purpose of the NC accreditation system is that it will help an agency identify areas for future QI work. The Site Visit and its report point out various areas for improvement in the department. Fifty percent of accredited agencies report engaging in activities to address suggestions for quality improvement identified by site visitors.

Much depends on the attitude or culture of the agency toward quality improvement. One difficulty in gaining acceptance by some health directors has been the perception that the accreditation process does not lead to QI. Some directors have not approached the process with an improvement mindset. Some see the process as one of completing a task and that they are done after the Site Visit and receipt of the report. Accreditation becomes a "to do" that is completed and checked off. Others want to "get all the standards met," instead of looking at how the process will benefit or improve the agency. They may focus on finding or creating as much documentary evidence as possible to show that the agency is able to meet all standards. But a survey of accredited agencies shows that the majority of accredited agencies are conducting QI and 14 agencies have conducted 3 or more QI projects. These QI activities are focused on improving clinic efficiencies, customer satisfaction, and program operations. Previous surveys of these agencies indicated that what the agencies had been reporting as QI activities were actually quality-assurance activities.

Differing opinions still exist among health directors on the role of accreditation in NC. A fundamental difference exists that still must be resolved.

Some think that accreditation is not a path to improvement for all agencies, but should point out local health departments that should not be stand alone agencies. For others the overall goal of accreditation would be improvement in health departments to provide a platform to improve the health status and outcomes of our communities.

Program QI—While the accreditation process strives to bring QI to agencies, the program itself also strives to keep a QI mindset. There are some who feel the process should stay the same without any changes to standards or documentation requirements. Others feel the standards should become increasingly more stringent. During the 09–10 fiscal year, the program completed a comprehensive study to look at elements of QI within the program.

Annual stakeholder reports have been available since 2006 together with reports concerning the pilot phases. Each year, mid-term and annual results are shared with the program staff by Mary Davis and Molly Cannon of Evaluation Services, revised and then presented to the Board. Adjustments are made to current processes and new processes are identified and tested. Future areas for development are also included. David Stone meets monthly with the NCALHD's Accreditation and QI liaison subcommittee to receive feedback on the program and to discuss new ideas regarding changes and future initiatives.

With the start of the NC Center for Public Health Quality (CPHQ) directed by Dr. Greg Randolph, another partner for the Accreditation program was created. Part of the scope of work for the CPHQ is to develop a QI course that all local health departments will complete. CPHQ is a nonprofit agency within the North Carolina Public Health Foundation (NCPHF) and staffed by both the NCPHF and the Division of Public Health (DPH). It collaborates with state and local partners to provide training in quality-improvement methods and tools and develops, leads, and supports strategic QI initiatives for the Division of Public Health and local health departments in North Carolina. While the CPHQ could have been seen as a competitor to the accreditation program, David and Greg had have numerous conversations to link the two organizations together and have their work coordinated to the extent possible. Some ideas are to:

- Suggest health department's staff participate in a QI course either right before or right after accreditation.
  - Determine the right "flow" to the accreditation and QI process and work for integration of those two along with DPH program

requirements. The accreditation process should point out QI opportunities that can be implemented and that will meet the requirements for re-accreditation.

- Train the nurse consultants in QI methods—since the nurse consultants are the primary technical consultants for accreditation.

- Revise standards to promote QI more—and include CPHQ on the standards workgroup.

  - Change both standards and documentation to reflect the priority of QI can help incorporate QI into the everyday work of the agency.

David and Greg also discussed how to ensure that the QI work is meaningful and brings improvements to the agency—not just meets a standard requirement. The key to achievement of this goal is to:

- Have Accreditation Program and CPHQ in regular communication and knowledgeable about each other's processes/objectives so that their work is parallel rather than working against each other. The ultimate goal is to have the two working together to create more efficient and effective agencies—leading to improved health status of our citizens and communities.

NATIONAL VOLUNTARY ACCREDITATION

In 2004, a group of national public health stakeholders came together to study whether a voluntary national accreditation program for state and local public health departments should be developed. The consensus of the group was to move forward with this study, and the Exploring Accreditation project began. The goal of the project was to develop recommendations regarding the feasibility of a voluntary national accreditation program as an appropriate approach to achieve improvement in public health.

The Public Health Accreditation Board (PHAB) was developed as a result of the recommendations of the Exploring Accreditation report and was incorporated in 2007. It is a nonprofit organization created to promote and manage the national accreditation program and is directed by Dr. Kaye Bender, CEO. PHAB has convened public health leaders and practitioners from around the country to develop national standards and processes and has beta tested the assessment process. After public health leaders explored the feasibility of, saw the need for, and understood the value of a national accreditation program, they have advocated for the implementation of a national voluntary program.

The initial PHAB Steering Committee was comprised primarily of state and local public health officials, including boards of health, and their work was informed by existing state-based accreditation programs and accreditation experts from other fields. North Carolina's program has informed the development of the national process. Since the future relationship between a national program and NC's state-based program has yet to be defined, PHAB is currently both a partner and a competitor. Some members of the Public Health Study Commission in NC have questioned the need for a state-based program given the creation of a national public health accreditation system.

In December 2009, NCIPH received a $150,000 grant from the Robert Wood Johnson Foundation to study the national accreditation initiatives currently underway in some 20 states and examine laws and policies supporting public health agency accreditation. "During this serious economic recession, health department accreditation initiatives provide vital tools to measure standards of performance," said Gene Matthews, JD, senior fellow at NCIPH and director of the project. "Knowing how well health agencies are delivering essential public health services to their communities is even more important during hard economic times."

The NCIPH was one of 15 recipients, selected from a field of 235 applicants, of grants from the Foundation's newly established Public Health Law Research program, which aims to build evidence for and strengthen use of effective regulatory, legal, and policy tools to improve public health. To advance the understanding and use of public health law, the Foundation program supports legal analysis and research to learn about the health impacts of specific laws within different communities and settings.

Effective December 1, 2009, this grant enables NCIPH to assess accreditation laws, policies, and regulations in 20 states that have made progress toward accrediting state or local health departments. The Institute also will conduct case studies of six of those states to determine how and why they chose a particular legal structure for accreditation. The case studies will explore the impact of legal structures on accreditation capacity, functions, and outputs. "It is quite an honor to be one of the first handful of organizations selected by the Robert Wood Johnson Foundation to explore this new field of public health law research," Matthews said. "We are indebted to the leadership of North Carolina in being the first state to enact a specific law in 2005 to implement a public health department accreditation program that is now setting an example for other states."

PROGRAM SUSTAINABILITY

Business Plan

During the year of suspension, the program developed a business plan to look at a variety of aspects of the future of accreditation. The business plan had input by program staff and the Accreditation Board. It looks at such elements as partnerships, administration, and funding. The Accreditation Board appointed a subcommittee (including partner members) to review the plan and bring recommendations to the board regarding future funding options and alternative business models that the program may wish to consider.

If the NC accreditation system is to continue, how will the program be sustained? The Accreditation Board has appointed a subcommittee, including stakeholder members, to look at various options for future funding. Options include: seeking nonprofit status for the board, fee-based services, combination of fees and state-appropriated dollars, and foundation support.

CASE ANALYSIS

Inspection has always been a part of quality control and in conjunction with an effective feedback mechanism can be used to drive conformance to process standards and motivate process improvement. The Site Visit has long been a ritual of the healthcare environment, allowing both objective and subjective observations to come together to form a coherent picture of an organization and a project or program. Conformance may be measured against a standard or a protocol. Self-reporting saves observer time and allows pre-visit preparation and a set of reference documents. Over time, accreditation of organizations and certification of individual professionals can involve an increasingly demanding set of standards that lead to improvement, if the collective will is there. Identify and discuss some of these aspects as they play out in the North Carolina program.

ASSIGNMENT QUESTIONS

1. North Carolina Accreditation is mandatory and all local health departments, by statute, must obtain and maintain accreditation status. One argument against this is that the system is semi-regulatory and accreditation should be voluntary. Should the NC system be mandatory? What other approaches could encourage LHDs to seek accreditation? What are the pros and cons of a legislatively mandated system of process improvement?

2. A national voluntary public health accreditation program is under development and is expected to be fully operational in 2011. What are some ways that a state-based system could operate within a national system? Should there be a two-tier system with state systems operating separately from the national system? Can one national system provide standards and benchmarks applicable to all public health agencies?

3. One of the purposes of accreditation is to encourage quality improvement in the department. The report given to local health departments has a section of QI suggestions that the department may choose to use. Many health directors have embraced quality improvement and research shows that many have implemented QI initiatives. Yet, many feel that QI lacks real value to the agency. How do we best use an accreditation system to promote QI initiatives? Should we incorporate QI into the accreditation standards?

4. A future goal of accreditation will be the improvement in health-status indicators for our communities. Since health status can be the result of the full healthcare system, of which the health department is but one component, is accreditation a necessary but not sufficient condition to lead to improved health outcomes?

5. The NC Accreditation program is supported by an allocation by the state legislature. As the only source of funding, this dependence led to a disruption in the program when funding was cut during the 09–10 fiscal year. What type of future business models should be used to ensure that the program is sustainable?

6. Since the NC system is mandatory, it is important to have legislator support and funding. Legislators also have expectations for health outcomes and accountability for local health departments. What approach to legislators is best to persuade their support of funding for accreditation?

CLASS EXERCISE

Follow up on the national effort to develop standards for local public health departments. Compare and contrast those efforts with the North Carolina accreditation process at the time of the case.

The Lewis Blackman Hospital Patient Safety Act: It's Hard to Kill a Healthy 15-Year-Old

Julie K. Johnson, Helen Haskell, and Paul Barach

INTRODUCTION

Lewis Blackman and his parents had a decision to make. Lewis was a healthy, gifted 15-year-old with a bright future. He had been born with a condition called pectus excavatum, which literally means "hollowed chest." It is a congenital deformity of the anterior wall of the chest that results in abnormal growth of the sternum and adjoining sections of ribs. While mild cases may only result in a sunken appearance of the chest, more severe cases may result in impaired cardiac and respiratory function (Shamberger, 1996; Crump, 1992). Many people with pectus excavatum also suffer from negative body image and self-esteem (Medline, 2007), and patients may seek correction for either physical or psychological reasons, which is usually accomplished surgically. In the United States, pectus excavatum occurs in an estimated 1 in 300-400 white male births, with a male-to-female ratio of approximately 5:1. While data are limited, there is reason to believe that the international incidence is approximately the same in most Caucasian and Asian populations. The defect appears to be rare in persons of African descent (Jaroszewski *et al.*, 2010).

The Decision to Operate

In Lewis's case, pectus excavatum did not cause any obvious problems. His pectus defect, while noticeable, was relatively mild. An easygoing boy, Lewis was an avid soccer player who had no evident impairment in stamina, and he was not particularly self-conscious about the concavity in his chest. His parents had never considered seeking surgical correction until they saw a newspaper article promoting a new minimally invasive surgery that was supposed to be safer and quicker than the older method of opening the chest and remodeling the ribs and cartilage. After discussing the options with their family physician, they made an appointment with a surgeon. Ultimately, even though they felt the evidence presented by the surgeon was limited, they decided to go ahead with the minimally invasive surgery because they were told it would become more difficult as Lewis got older. The operation would be performed in a leading academic medical center several hours from their home. The family—Lewis, his parents, and his younger sister—spent the night in a hotel and arrived at the hospital Thursday morning for the surgery.

At the Hospital

Upon arrival at the hospital, the family was surrounded by activity as nurses and residents took Lewis's vital signs, filled out forms, and asked his parents to sign documents. One of the documents, not particularly emphasized, was a one-paragraph consent form for the surgery. By 7:00 a.m., Lewis had been whisked away to surgery. According to the surgeon, the operation went well, but it took longer than Lewis's parents expected—2 and a half hours instead of the anticipated 45 minutes. Figure 16–1 uses process mapping to summarize the tragic series of events that transpired over the next four days.

The first sign of a potential problem occurred in the recovery room when Lewis was observed to be producing abnormally low amounts of urine. In spite of this complication, he was prescribed the standard five-day adult dose of the intravenous NSAID painkiller ketorolac (trade name: Toradol), a medication that should be used with caution in patients with low fluid output. Nevertheless, his condition appeared to be generally stable for the first three days in the hospital. But on the morning of the fourth postoperative day, a Sunday, half an hour after a ketorolac injection, Lewis was suddenly overcome by severe pain in the upper

Lewis' story – "It's hard to kill a healthy 15-year old"

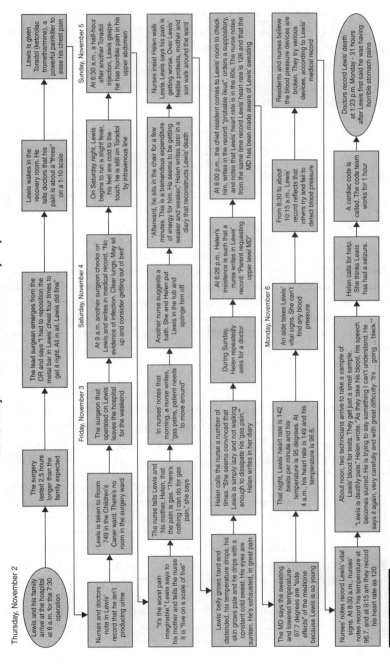

Figure 16-1 Process Map of Events

abdomen. Nurses and a medical intern assured the family that he was suffering from postoperative constipation that would resolve if he got out of bed and began moving around. However, his condition continued to worsen, and his vital signs began to deteriorate. A quote from his mother describes what happened later that day:

> It is now afternoon. Lewis's bowels and urinary system are still not functioning. His belly is hard and distended and he is extremely pale, with a subnormal temperature and a constant cold sweat. His eyes are sunken and surrounded by huge black circles. Lewis is exhausted and in agony. His pain is now radiating to the shoulder. He is also nauseated and often burps, a new symptom. He still tries not to throw up, because he has been told the fruit juice he has drunk will help revitalize his digestive system.
>
> We call the nurse a number of times. She seems to be convinced that Lewis is simply lazy and not walking enough to dissipate his "gas pain." Sometimes no one answers my call. Other times the receptionist answers with weary exasperation, making it clear they consider our concerns a nuisance. They are busy, using this Sunday as a catch-up day for non-medical pursuits. The receptionist is painting decorations on the windows. Another nurse is updating the plates on the doors, including ours. When I go into the kitchen, I find someone has rearranged all the silverware and condiments and stacked them all in new plastic bins. For much of the afternoon, as I hunch over the bed with Lewis gripping my hand in pain, I can hear the nurses chattering and laughing in the break room. [Lewis's mother]

Because of low weekend staffing, there was no attending or upper-level resident surgeon present in the hospital on Sunday. The family's requests for a senior physician in the face of Lewis's increasing pain and weakness were resisted and, when finally honored, were met by a visit from the senior resident who was not identified as such (Monk, 2002).

> Someone calls a doctor. I assume at the time that this is the attending physician I have requested, though I later learn he is a fourth year general surgery resident. It is some time before he arrives and when he does he is clearly coming in from outside, wearing a jacket and bringing with him a whiff of cold air. Apparently the intern is the only pediatric surgeon on duty in the hospital. And somewhere along the line my request for an attending physician has been quietly shelved. I do not know who made this decision.
>
> The doctor is reassuring. He also thinks Lewis's pain is gas pain due to lack of motility in the intestine. Because Lewis has still not uri-

nated, the doctor catheterizes him, thinking that this will also relieve some of the pressure on the bowel. The catheterization produces a relatively small amount (c. 215 cc) of dark, concentrated urine. The doctor is a little surprised: he thinks a full bladder should have produced more urine. I ask him about the pallor, the cold sweat, and the subnormal temperature. He says these are side effects of the medication, because Lewis is so young and "pristine." I wonder why they do not change the medication if it has such terrible side effects. [Lewis's mother]

For the rest of the night, technicians continued to routinely record Lewis's increasingly unstable vital signs on a four-hourly schedule, with no further assessment or intervention. Only when nurses and residents were unable to produce a blood pressure reading on Monday morning and had spent time trying to identify an equipment malfunction was more qualified help sought, a code called, and everything possible done. By then it was too late.

We had been asked to leave the room and wait in the hall. Someone comes to get us. The doctors want to talk to us. I am fearful they will tell us Lewis is brain-damaged. When we go into the room, there are five surgeons in green scrubs. One introduces himself as Dr. Adamson. He is the doctor on call. We have never seen him before. Dr. Adamson says, 'We lost him.' This makes no sense to me. He is speaking as though Lewis has lost a battle with a long illness. He has to repeat it several times before I understand. They say they have no idea what happened. I am stunned. [Lewis's mother]

Autopsy identified the immediate cause of death as an undiagnosed perforated duodenal ulcer, of a type often associated with nonsteroidal anti-inflammatory painkillers (Collen and Chen, 1995).

Lewis's family blamed the devastating outcome on the confusion and poor communication of the teaching hospital hierarchy, and particularly on their inability to determine which caregivers were fully-trained professionals and which were clinical trainees.

When we put it all together, we realized that our son was the victim of a profoundly dysfunctional medical system. We had thought we were sophisticated consumers. But we gradually realized that we had sacrificed our first-born child to a system whose dangers we had almost no way of knowing. [Lewis's mother]

Making a Difference

Following Lewis's death, his parents met with the surgeon who had performed Lewis's surgery. The surgeon listened to their story, apologized, and accepted responsibility for Lewis's death. The hospital later settled with the family without a lawsuit. A physician friend with whom the family had consulted was not surprised the hospital settled out of court. "It's hard to kill a healthy 15-year-old," he said, "Lewis probably could have been saved up through Monday morning." A year and a half later, the attending physicians involved in Lewis's care co-authored an institutional study of complications of the surgical procedure Lewis had. The retrospective study did not include Lewis's case (Fonkalsrud *et al.,* 2002).

Since Lewis's death, his mother, Helen Haskell, has worked on patient safety issues to help reform the system that took his life. She helped organize parents and medical error victims into a mutual support group, Mothers Against Medical Error. They worked with South Carolina hospitals to pass the Lewis Blackman Hospital Patient Safety Act,[1] a state law requiring that hospital personnel wear badges indicating their jobs and professional status, that hospitals give patients information on the role of residents and students in their care, that nurses assist patients in contacting their attending physicians directly, and that hospitals give patients and families a means of calling for immediate help in urgent medical situations. The intent of the South Carolina Department of Health and Environmental Control to enforce the law through inspection is outlined in the memorandum from the Department shown in Exhibit 16–1.

Subsequently, the state of South Carolina endowed the Lewis Blackman chair of Clinical Effectiveness and Patient Safety as a testament to Lewis's remarkable young life and as a commitment to advance the health and safety of all South Carolinians. Seven simulation clinics have been established across the state for training healthcare providers in the teamwork techniques needed for dealing with emergency situations. These simulation clinics use team training exercises and sophisticated

---

[1]For further clarification consult *The Lewis Blackman Hospital Patient Safety Act: Compliance Guide for South Carolina Hospitals* at: http://www.healthstik.com/downloads/SCHA_LBA_Compliance_Guide_100905_1.pdf.

EXHIBIT 16-1

Overview of the Lewis Blackman Hospital Patient Safety Act

The Lewis Blackman Hospital Patient Safety Act (Article 27, Section 44-7-3410 et. seq.,) was added to the SC Code of Laws, effective June 8, 2005. The Act authorized South Carolina Department of Health and Environmental Control (DHEC) to implement and enforce the provisions of the Act, which requires hospitals to, among other things:

A. Identify all clinical staff, clinical trainees, medical students, interns, and resident physicians (as defined in the Act) as such with identification badges that include their names, their departments, and their job or trainee titles. All the above must be clearly visible and explicitly identified as such on their badges and must be stated in terms or abbreviations reasonably understandable;

B. Institute a procedure whereby a patient may request that a nurse call his or her attending physician (as defined in the Act) regarding the patient's personal medical care. If so requested, the nurse shall place the call and notify the physician and or his or her designee of the patient's concerns. If the patient is able to communicate with and desires to call his or her attending physician or designee (as defined in the Act), upon the patient's request, the nurse must provide the patient with the telephone number and assist the patient in placing the call;

C. Provide a mechanism available at all times, and the method for accessing it, through which a patient may access prompt assistance for the resolution of the patient's personal medical care concerns. 'Mechanism' means telephone number, beeper number, or other means of allowing a patient to independently access the patient assistance system. If a patient needs assistance, a clinical staff member or clinical trainee (as defined in the Act) must assist the patient in accessing the mechanism;

(continues)

EXHIBIT 16–1 (continued)

D. Establish procedures for the implementation of the mechanism providing for initiation of contact with administrative or supervisory clinical staff who shall promptly assess the urgent patient care concern and cause the patient care concern to be addressed;

E. Provide to each patient prior to, or at the time of the patient's admission to the hospital for inpatient care or outpatient surgery, written information describing the general role of clinical trainees, medical students, interns, and resident physicians in patient care.

This information must also:

1. State whether medical students, interns, or resident physicians may be participating in a patient's care, may be making treatment decisions for the patient, or may be participating in or performing, in whole or in part, any surgery on the patient;

2. Notify the patient that the attending physician is the person responsible for the patient's care while the patient is in the hospital and that the patient's attending physician may change during the patient's hospitalization;

3. Include a description of the mechanism (see above) providing for initiation of contact with administrative or supervisory clinical staff and the method for accessing it.

For more specific information concerning The Lewis Blackman Hospital Patient Safety Act, please refer to: http://www.scstatehouse.gov/sess116_2005-2006/bills/3832.htm

simulation technology with high-end full-body adult and infant mannequins to simulate patients with various clinical scenarios. A plaque dedicated to Lewis (shown in Figure 16–2) is featured in each of the seven simulation clinics.

Figure 16–2 Dedicatory Plaque for the Lewis Blackman Chair of Clinical
Effectiveness and Patient Safety

Permission for use granted by HealthCare Simulation of South Carolina

CASE ANALYSIS

This case outlines a fatal set of events that led to a legislative requirement requested by a patient advocacy group. It also indicates how regulatory enforcement is expected to be applied. Currently, the Physician's Desk Reference notes that only one dose of ketorolac should be given postoperatively to children. What else could be done to avoid such a result in the future? Your class might well try a Failure Mode Analysis on this situation.

ASSIGNMENT QUESTIONS

1. Where did the system fail Lewis and his family?
2. What were the system failures in Lewis's care process related to:
   a. Preparation?
   b. Organization?
   c. Environment?
   d. Technology?
   e. Work tasks?
   f. Healthcare provider?
3. Where in the process of care did incidents (errors, near misses, adverse events, and harm) occur?
4. What would be the elements of a more transparent informed consent process?
5. Were there opportunities in the process of care to repair physical damage? Relationship damage? Emotional damage?
6. What aspects of this incident will the new legislation cited in the case address? Which aspects does it not address and what else should be done to prevent recurrences of such incidents?
7. If the nurses and residents had checked the references (PDR, for example) for ketorolac, what would they have found and how might it have affected Lewis's treatment?

CLASS EXERCISE

Use the Internet to find out whether any other states have considered or passed similar laws. If so, what do they call for?

Elk Hills Community Medical Center: Revisiting the Baldrige Award

Curtis P. McLaughlin

INTRODUCTION

Martha Hedricks, MHA, was an Assistant Administrator at Elk Hills Community Medical Center (EHCMC), a 225-bed hospital in a Midwestern metropolitan area with a population of about 350,000. It was a true community hospital with many of its medical staff having admitting privileges at multiple hospitals. No one hospital was dominant in the area. In fact, they were all about the same size. Each employed some physicians, but none had tried to develop an integrated system. Each depended on Medicare and Medicaid, the state's Blue Cross affiliate, and the private insurers chosen by the area's largest employers.

The EHCMC board had completed a strategic review of its competitive positions in early 2010 and was searching for a way to differentiate the hospital from its competition. As one component of that search for a competitive edge, management had asked Ms. Hedricks to take another look at reaching Malcolm Baldrige National Quality Award status. Someone had proposed applying several years earlier, and the hospital had gone fairly far with its self-assessment when the Board stopped the process. It had been quite beneficial to the hospital administration, but the medical

313

staff was in turmoil as competing groups of physicians tried to control the hospital resources. That had calmed down after the hospital expanded its facilities, especially its operating room capacity, to meet all the physicians' requirements. That expansion, however, had left the hospital with a somewhat heavy debt burden and cost cutting became the order of the day.

BALDRIGE REVISITED

Because she was familiar with the Malcolm Baldrige Award process from the last time around, Martha decided to start with a look at the latest Baldrige criteria. First, she compared the list of values from the 2009–2010 criteria with those listed in the 2004 criteria. Table 17–1 shows her comparison. The addition of "Management by facts" certainly did not present a problem. The other word changes seemed cosmetic to her, but she planned to investigate further.

Next, she compared the categories and terms used in the two sets of criteria:

- Under Leadership (120 points), 1.2 Social Responsibility had been replaced by 1.2 Governance and Social Responsibility, but the weighting remained the same.

Table 17–1   Comparison of Values from Baldrige Criteria

2004 Criteria	*2009–2010 Criteria*
Visionary leadership	Visionary leadership
Patient-centered excellence	Patient-focused excellence
Organizational and personal learning	Organizational and personal learning
Valuing staff and partners	Valuing workforce members and partners
Agility	Agility
Focus on the future	Focus on the future
Managing for innovation	Managing for innovation
	Managing by facts
Social responsibility and community health	Social responsibility and community health
Focus on results and creating value	Focus on results and creating value
Systems perspective	Systems perspective

- Strategic Planning (85 points) still used the same terms and weightings.

- The third category (85 points) had the same definition of "how requirements, expectations and preferences of publics are determined and responded to" but the new terms were 3.1 Customer Engagement and 3.2 Voice of the Customer.

- The fourth category, "Measurement, Analysis and Knowledge Management," (90 points) was slightly changed by the addition of Information Technology to 4.2 Management of Information, Knowledge and Information Technology.

- Staff Focus had been replaced by Workforce Focus (90 points) with two rather than three categories—5.1 Workforce Engagement and 5.2 Workforce Environment.

- Process Management (85 points) appeared to have changed markedly with 3.1 Work Processes and 3.2 Work Systems having replaced 3.1 Health Care Processes and 3.2 Support Processes.

- The Results category (450 points) seemed to have changed a fair amount with "Outcomes" replacing Results and an increase in the weighting of 7.1 Health Care Outcomes from 75 to 100 points with a reduction from 75 to 70 for each of the others:

  - 7.2 Customer-Focused Outcomes

  - 7.3 Financial and Market Outcomes

  - 7.4 Workforce Focused Outcomes

  - 7.5 Process Effectiveness Outcomes

  - 7.6 Leadership Outcomes

These did not seem to be really major changes, although greater emphasis of clinical outcomes was clearly intended. The Baldrige Web site indicated that the most important changes from the 2008 criteria were in the emphasis on customer engagement, organizational core competencies in relation to strategic planning, emphasis on managing information technology, and leadership focus on sustainability and social responsibility. The scoring criteria reproduced in Table 17–2 appeared to have change relatively little over the last several years.

Table 17–2	Excerpts from Baldrige Appendix

Malcolm Baldrige Award 2009–2010 Health Care—Item Scoring

Each item is scored either on (1) Process or (2) Results. Tables A1 and A2 show the scoring for each of these items. The tables show the process criteria for each range using four factors—Approach (A), Deployment (D), Learning (L), and Integration (I). The selection within the range is based on the best fit of the overall item response. Scoring within those limits is up to Examiner discretion based on closeness to the next higher or next lower range.

Score	*Process Categories (1–6)*
0% or 5%	• No systematic approach to Item requirements is evident, information is anecdotal • Little or no deployment of any systematic approach is evident • An improvement orientation is not evident; improvement is achieved through reaction to problems • No organizational alignment is evident, individual areas or work units operate independently
10%, 15%, 20% or 25%	• The beginnings of a systematic approach to the basic requirements of the item is evident • The approach is in the early stages of deployment in many areas or work units, inhibiting progress in achieving basic requirements of the item • Early stages of a transition from reacting to problems to a general improvement orientation is evident • The approach is aligned with other areas or work units largely through joint problem solving
30%, 35%, 40% or 45%	• An effective, systematic approach, responsive to the basic requirements of the item • The approach is deployed, although some areas or work units are in early stages of deployment • The beginning of a systematic approach to evaluation and improvement of key processes is evident • The approach is in the early stages of alignment with your basic organizational needs identified in response to the Organizational Profile and other Process Items
50%, 55%, 60% or 65%	• An effective, systematic approach, responsive to the overall requirements of the item, is evident • The approach is well-deployed, although deployment may vary in some areas or work units

Table 17–2	Continued

Score	Process Categories (1–6)
	• A fact-based, systematic evaluation and improvement process and some organizational learning, including innovation, are in place for improving efficiency and effectiveness of key processes • The approach is aligned with your organizational needs identified in response to the Organizational Profile and other Process Items
70%, 75%, 80% or 85%	• An effective, systematic approach, responsive to the multiple requirements of the item is evident • The approach is well-deployed with no significant gaps • Fact-based, systematic evaluation and improvement and organizational learning, including innovation, are key management tools; there is clear evidence of refinement as the result of organizational-level analysis and sharing • The approach is integrated with your organizational needs identified in response to the Organizational Profile and other Process Items
90%, 95% or 100%	• An effective, systematic approach, fully responsive to the multiple requirements of the item, is evident • The approach is fully deployed without significant weaknesses or gaps in any areas or work units • Fact-based, systematic evaluation and improvement process and extensive organizational learning, through innovation, are key organization-wide tools; refinement and innovation, backed by analysis and sharing, are evident throughout the organization • The approach is well-integrated with your organizational needs identified in response to the Organizational Profile and other Process Items

Score	Results Category (7)
0% or 5%	• No organizational performance results and/or poor results in areas reported • Trend data either are not reported or show mainly adverse results • Comparative information is not reported • Results not reported for any areas of importance to the accomplishment of your organization's mission. No performance projections are reported

(continues)

Table 17-2	Continued

Score	Results Category (7)
10%, 15%, 20% or 25%	• A few organizational performance results reported and early good performance levels in a few areas • Some trend data are reported, with some adverse trends evident • Little or no comparative information is reported • Results reported for a few areas of importance to the accomplishment of your organization's mission. Limited or no performance projections are reported
30%, 35%, 40% or 45%	• Good organizational performance levels are reported for some areas of importance to item requirements • Some trend data are reported, and a majority of the trends presented are beneficial • Early stages of obtaining comparative information are evident • Results are reported for many areas of importance to the accomplishment of your organization's mission. Limited performance projections are reported
50%, 55%, 60% or 65%	• Good organizational performance levels are reported for most areas of importance to item requirements • Beneficial trends are evident in areas of importance to the accomplishment of your organization's mission • Some current performance levels have been evaluated against relevant comparisons *and/or* benchmarks and show areas of good relative performance • Organizational performance results are reported for most key patients and stakeholder, market, process, and action plan requirements. Performance projections for some high-priority results are reported
70%, 75%, 80% or 85%	• Good to excellent organizational performance levels are reported for most areas of importance to Item requirements • Beneficial trends have been sustained over time in most areas of importance to the accomplishment of your organization's mission • Many to most trends and current performance levels have been evaluated against relevant comparisons *and/or* benchmarks and show areas of leadership and very good relative performance • Organizational performance results are reported for most key patient and stakeholder, market, process, and action plan requirements. Performance projections for some high-priority results are reported

Table 17-2	Continued
Score	**Results Category (7)**
90%, 95% or 100%	• Excellent organizational performance levels are reported for most areas of importance to Item requirements • Beneficial trends have been sustained over time in all areas of importance to the accomplishment of your organization's mission • Evidence of health care sector and benchmark leadership is demonstrated in many areas • Organizational performance results fully address key patient and stakeholder, market, process, and action plan requirements, and they include projections of your future performance

Source: www.nist.gov/baldrige/publications/upload/2009_2010_HealthCare_Criteria.pdf, pp. 70–71.

SUCCESSFUL APPLICATIONS

Perhaps she would get a better idea from reviewing the applications of recent winners. She was surprised to find only two winners in 2007, one in 2008 and one in 2009. The 2009 winner was Heartland Health of St. Joseph, MO; the 2008 winner was Poudre Valley Health System of Fort Collins, CO; and the 2007 winners were Sharp HealthCare of San Diego, CA and Mercy Health System of Janesville, WI. The first thing that struck her about their applications was that all four were effectively integrated delivery systems which had an insurance arm and a number of employed physicians. Each presented a broad view of their role in the community and cited activities that went well beyond the usual clinical activities of a community hospital. Perhaps reflecting the increased emphasis on community involvement, the Heartland Health application devoted a lot of attention to its community development foundation and activities. Elk Hills had undertaken relatively few efforts in the community beyond some outreach and screening efforts initiated by community and patient groups.

Heartland Health also showed a consistent level of clinical indicator improvement going back at least five years and reported (as of 2008) "being in the top 0.5% of hospitals in the nation in sustaining exceptional performance for 5 consecutive years" based on HealthGrades Best Hospitals 12–13 patient safety scores. It reported recent decubitus ulcer and ventilator-associated pneumonia rates of zero and zero surgical site infections for CABG and knee and hip replacements.

Ms. Hedricks had no way of knowing whether these were make or break requirements for future awards, but she knew that Elk Hills had yet to get a reliable integrating electronic medical record system working effectively and many of the clinic sites were not yet linked electronically for billing or results reporting.

Reporting Back

She took her findings back to the Board and found several points of view among the Board and senior administrators:

- Several board members remembered the last exercise and preparing for the Baldrige examiners visits that never happened. They variously commented on the positive effects of the preparation process and the self-assessments that were completed, but also the time, cost and effort that had gone into that exercise. Some doubted whether there was much incremental to be gained at this point in time.

- Staff had gotten wind of what she was doing and some argued that the hospital was now gathering and reporting so much data that was now available to the public that the competitive benefits of winning the Baldrige Award would now be quite limited. The public could already go to the Web and get very specific comparison data on the hospital and its local competitors.

- Those in favor of proceeding further with an application argued that with only one or two winners nationally in a given year, a successful submission would certainly differentiate Elk Hills from the rest of the pack.

- Others suggested that Elk Hills would be better off putting that energy into implementing already successful protocols or bundles for known quality problems that would immediately show up in the statistics available to the buying publics.

Next Steps

Ms. Hedricks knew that the Board would soon want a formal recommendation from her. She could research the matter further or she could recommend what she saw as one of three basic options:

1. Recommend not dealing with the Baldrige option and putting the organization's energies elsewhere.

2. Recommend going and completing the Baldrige self-assessment to find out what improvements should be made in the short run.

3. Prepare a Baldrige application and learn what can be gleaned from the examiners' visits.

One proponent of the Baldrige process had pointed out that while all the measurement and reporting showed what was happening, it said relatively little about why the organization was getting those results.

CASE ANALYSIS

The Baldrige Award process had been of great interest to some as a way of improving the whole industry. Now with so many efforts going on there is the question of its incremental value as a diagnostic tool and a performance motivator. It is focused on a broad definition of organizational excellence. Most other programs have focused on relatively narrow clinical and administrative areas. Class discussion needs to focus, in part, on the specifics of narrowly focused issues versus across the board achievement of organizational excellence.

ASSIGNMENT QUESTIONS

1. How does the Baldrige Award process seem to mesh with all the other healthcare quality efforts reported in the cases in this book?

2. What benefits would specifically accrue to an integrated delivery system in preparing for and competing for the Baldrige Award?

3. What trends in health care would you expect to see reflected in the next set of Baldrige criteria?

4. How are the changes in health-information technology supported by recent legislation and funding likely to influence the quality-improvement movement in general and the Baldrige Award process in particular?

5. Have Ms. Hedricks and the Elk Hills Board been asking the right questions? If not, what would you offer as an alternative framing of the issues?

CLASS EXERCISE

Go to the Web sites of recent Baldrige Award healthcare winners and conduct your own analysis of their applications. What does it seem to take to be a winner today?

PROCESS IMPROVEMENT RESEARCH

Improvement and innovation can come from many sources, some new and some old. Part V gives three illustrations of research aimed at process and system improvement. The gold standard for research in health care has been the randomized, double-blind clinical trial, a component of the evaluation strategy to measure the impact of stents and bypass surgery in Case 18. However, these studies often raise more questions, while trying to provide answers. For all of our faith in evidence-based medicine we must recognize that evidence is often equivocal when applied to specific clinical situations, and this is especially true with the ever-increasing role of patient preferences and patient-specific care in "personalized medicine." This lack of clear information for decision-making may be due to lack of dominance of one choice over the others, or lack of correspondence between the sample population and the specific patients faced in practice, or not representing the skill levels of the local practitioners who may be trained differently or may be ahead of others due to learning-by-doing.

The other two cases in this section show other professionals at work in areas relevant to process improvement. One applies classical statistics to planned experiments with delivery-system strategies (Case 19), and the other displays the efforts of building designers to improve the performance of those who must work within that built environment (Case 20). Both areas offer opportunities for planned experimentation and also observation and analysis of natural experiments. Sharing these results with professional peers can lead to the adoption of improvements to the delivery system. Healthcare professionals need to respect what these other professionals bring to the improvement table, and thereby broaden the teamwork concept that has been a cornerstone of successful quality improvement in health care.

Stents vs. Bypass: Expanding the Evidence Base

Curtis P. McLaughlin and Craig D. McLaughlin

INTRODUCTION

Researchers at Dartmouth Medical School have studied small area variations using the Medicare database. Reporting in August 2006, for example, they cited the example of cardiac revascularization in Elyria, Ohio. Medicare patients in this city of 55,953 (2000 Census), the county seat of Lorain County, received angioplasty at a rate nearly four times the national average. Thirty-one of the area's 33 cardiologists belonged to the North Ohio Heart Center and performed 3,400 angioplasties in 2004. The Elyria rate in 2003 was 42 angioplasties per 1,000 Medicare enrollees versus 13.5 for all of Ohio and 11.3 nationwide (Abelson, 2006).

All three treatment approaches to blocked coronary arteries—drugs, bypass surgery, and unblocking procedures such as angioplasty with or without stents are used there. In Elyria, however, cardiologists rely heavily on angioplasty. There is open debate on where and when to use which procedure—"some experts say that they are concerned that Elyria is an example, albeit an extreme one, of how medical decisions in this country can be influenced by financial incentives and professional training more than by solid evidence of what works best for a particular patient" (Abelson, 2006, p. 1). Both angioplasties and bypass surgery are considered to be highly profitable procedures, so profitable that Medicare has been trying to lower payment rates markedly but has been forced through lobbying to enact only a very small cut. At Elyria's community hospital, Medicare pays the hospital about $11,000 for an angioplasty with a coated stent and up to $25,000 for bypass operations. The cardiologist receives about $800 for the angioplasty and the surgeon up to $2,200 for bypass surgery. The bypass surgery in Elyria is done by surgeons from the Cleveland Clinic who have privileges at the community hospital (Abelson, 2006).

Outcomes

The founder and president of the North Ohio Heart Center responded to reports of these findings by noting that the clinic had good results and outcomes with its patients and attributed the high use of angioplasty to early diagnostic interventions and aggressive treatment of the coronary artery disease and to concern about patient safety, which led them to practice staging of their patients (doing more than one admission and procedure on many patients whereas other cardiologists might do multiple arteries at the same time). Thirty-one percent of the patients underwent multiple admissions and procedures, about three times the rate in Cleveland. Insurers reported that the hospital's results were good, and UnitedHealth designated it a center of excellence for heart care.

At a December 2006 conference on "Pay-for-Performance: A Critical Examination," Dr. Margaret O'Kane, head of the National Committee for Quality Assurance (NCQA), observed in her welcoming address:

> How many of you saw the *New York Times* article about the use of stents in Elyria, Ohio? It was from the *Dartmouth Atlas*. Elyria Ohio happens to be the stent capital of the United States. They use about four times the national average and our national average is higher than anybody else's. Guess what, they happen to be in everyone's centers of excellence. Because, if you put stents in people who don't really need them, they're probably less risky patients and they have good outcomes (Kaisernetwork.org, 2006).

Trends

Stents have become increasingly popular. Faced with choices between the two procedures most patients seemed to prefer the stents. Over the ten years preceding 2006, bypass surgeries had fallen by about a third to

365,000, while that year nearly a million patients received stents. The incomes of cardiac surgeons had fallen from an inflation-adjusted $1.02 million in 1990 to $425,000 in 2006, while the comparable incomes of interventional cardiologists had risen from $392,000 to $550,000 (Feder, 2007).

Then in 2006 and 2007 there was an increasing shift from stents back toward surgery, especially where multiple blockages were involved. This may have been related to reports that patients who had received drug-coated stents had a slight long-run risk of clots forming in the stents and blocking the arteries (Feder, 2007). Neither procedure reduces the rate of plaque buildup, but surgery may have the added benefit of permanently removing known sites of narrowing. Guidelines from the American Heart Association and the American College of Cardiology at that time called for referring for surgery patients with blockages in two or more arteries and other complications. However, one eminent cardiologist estimated that as much as 20% of the patients receiving stents should have been referred and were not, especially as the surgical procedures had become less invasive. Feder (2007) cites two possible contributing factors: (1) in some states where surgical outcomes were publicly reported, surgeons were referring high-risk patients back to cardiologists to avoid bad numbers on their record, and (2) there were now enough stents in place for long enough to increase the demand for replacement surgeries.

Concerns about the long-term risks of stents were sufficient to warrant at least two clinical trials. However, definitive results on the longer-term effects are not expected until 2012.

HOLDING OFF ON STENTS

In April 2007, Bowden *et al.* published an article titled "Optimal medical therapy with or without PCI for stable coronary disease." It reported what was considered to be "blockbuster" results from randomized clinical trial of the effectiveness of stents in patients with relatively mild, but persistent heart disease (Winstein, 2010). It was called the COURAGE (Clinical Outcomes Utilizing Revascularization and Aggressive Drug Evaluation) and reported that percutaneous coronary intervention (PCI) with optimal medical treatment (generic drugs) produced no better outcomes than optimal medical treatment alone. The study involved 2,287 patients who were followed for two to seven years (median 4.6). The study concluded that "as an initial management strategy in patients with stable coronary artery disease, PCI did not reduce the risk of death, myocardial infarction, or other major cardiovascular events when added to optimal medical therapy."

Despite the confirmation of these findings in subsequent studies, what transpired was an immediate 13% drop in the use of stents but their usage returned to prior levels by the end of 2008.

Responses from Interventional Cardiologists

The responses from other cardiologists varied widely with some agreeing with the study and some saying that it confirmed current guidelines to others calling it "rigged to fail." Dr. Gregory Denher, president of the Society for Cardiovascular Angiography and Intervention (SCAI), commented that the results were not "a huge revelation, but more a penetrating glimpse at the obvious" (Stent News, 2007).

James Trippi, MD, FACC, interventional cardiologist with the large Indianapolis-based The Care Group LLC, reacted to the release of the study on April 12[1] in an April 18 press release from the Group:

> It is important to remember that this study does not include the newer medicated stents and only used bare metal stents in patients with chronic stable angina. Medical studies select patients with very defined problems. Applying the results of these studies to individual patients with different characteristics and complexities may not be appropriate. Stable angina is defined as few episodes of pain easily controlled with medication.

According to Dr. Trippi:

> A patient with a 70% lesion, few symptoms and good cardiac functional ability might do just as well with or without a bare metal stent provided the patient adheres to an intense regimen of medications. It should be noted that many of the medically treated patients in the study eventually ended up with stents or coronary artery bypass because of increasing symptoms. Patients who are getting bare metal stents when they have a moderately tight blockage with controlled symptoms don't have heart

---

[1]Released on the Internet as early as March 26 at http://www.thecaregroup.com/amod/Media/Press%20Release/Courage%20Research%204_18%202007.pdf. Accessed December 10, 2010.

attacks or die any less because they get good medical treatment for all the other less severe lesions that are just as likely to thrombose causing a heart attack as the stented lesion. This study confirms that state of the art medical treatment is effective. (The Care Group, 2007)

The *Stent News* of May 28, 2007, a service of Angioplasty.org, offered "Answers to Top Ten Questions About Stents and Angioplasty vs. Drug Therapy." This article noted that the patients involved were at low risk of heart attack and that both approaches seemed equally safe. It stated that:

> Under current practice guidelines, it is recommended that patients with stable angina first be given a trial of medical therapy, along with lifestyle changes and risk factor reduction. They are candidates for stents if they continue to experience problems. What is unknown is how often these guidelines have not been followed, and whether cardiologists have in fact recommended stents as a first treatment option for this patient population. There is significant controversy as to how often this occurs. Estimates of how many angioplasty procedures are done in patients with stable coronary artery disease range from 25% to 85%.

It further observed that:

> This initial report did show that the scores for physical limitation, angina frequency, and quality of life were significantly better for patients in the angioplasty group: in fact *1/3 of the patients in the medication-only group switched over to angioplasty during the course of the trial because their angina was not relieved by medication alone.*

Looking Back from 2010

A *Wall Street Journal* article entitled "A simple health-care fix fizzles out" (Winstein, 2010) suggested that the lack of change based on the COURAGE trial showed that comparative effectiveness research might not produce the results claimed for it by the Obama Administration:

> Doctors and health-care watchers point to several reasons Courage didn't move the needle. Patients have little incentive to decline costly care when insurers are paying. Interventional cardiologists, on the other hand, have a financial incentive to use stents—they receive $900 per stenting procedure, roughly nine times the amount they get for an office visit. . . . Over the past 10 years, improvements in stents have coincided with an explosion in their use, as the hour long procedure edged out bypass surgery as the preferred treatment for clogged arteries in all but the sickest patients. The average cardiologist who installs

stents made about $500,000 in 2008, up 22% from 10 years prior, adjusted for inflation . . . (Winstein, 2010, p. A18)

This article cites one estimate of the unnecessary cost at $5 billion.

CASE ANALYSIS

This case is intended to focus your thoughts on the nature of scientific evidence in health care both in terms of stability and strength of evidence. Continuous clinical quality improvement will have to take into account the changing nature of evidence, the importance of learning-by-doing, and the adjustments that need to be made to individual patient differences including comorbidity and genetic variability in responses to treatment. Almost any given set of evidence can be interpreted in multiple ways. As we strive for improved clinical performance, these will be key variables and frequent distractions to our efforts to win over the professionals and the public. Remember too that the development of new types of stents has continued as well. However, we cannot ignore the importance of learning-by-doing along with our concerns about the influences of economic rewards and the influences of vendors on clinical choices.

ASSIGNMENT QUESTIONS

1. What do you think of using small area studies based on large Medicare databases to identify outliers like the cardiology treatment in Elyria, Ohio?

2. Contrast the information from such a study with the knowledge available from a double-blind clinical trial comparing the same two interventions.

3. Salaried cardiologists at Kaiser Permanente in northern Ohio tended to use drugs more and cardiac procedures at a rate slightly below the national average. Analyze the role that differing financial incentives might be playing here.

4. If you were Anthem Blue Cross and Blue Shield in Ohio, what studies would you conduct to attempt to explain and/or deal with these striking local differences in treatments and costs?

5. How would the findings of the COURAGE study affect your strategy as an Ohio insurer?

6. What do you think of the *Wall Street Journal's* concerns about the effectiveness of comparative effectiveness research?

CLASS EXERCISE

Research the current literature on stents vs. drugs vs. surgery. Have things changed since early 2010? What is the strength of the evidence base that is developing? What does this say about the future of evidence-based medicine?

Cal Mason, COO, Metro Children's Hospital: Planned Experimentation in CQI

Lloyd P. Provost

INTRODUCTION

Calvin Mason, MBA, reflected on his first nine months as Chief Operating Officer (COO) at Metro Children's Hospital. He was attracted to the position at Metro because of their reputation for the use of quality improvement in all aspects of their work and throughout the organization. Calvin had studied quality improvement methods when getting his undergraduate engineering degree at Purdue, but had not had an opportunity to apply that learning in his previous jobs. While other organizations he worked with gave lip-service to quality, his work day in previous jobs had been filled with administrative tasks, information system firefighting, and supply-chain activities. Almost all his projects were financially focused, so he had not had a chance to explore his interest in quality improvement.

THE IMPROVEMENT PROJECT

During his second month at Metro, Calvin joined a development program in quality improvement that had been in place for the past three years. All managers and clinician leaders at Metro were expected to participate in this three-month program which included the basic approach to quality improvement. Participation in this program required an improvement project, so Cal met with his staff to help scope out a project to focus on for the class. Based on these discussions, he chose a project to consolidate the learning from the hospital's recent emphasis on access to clinical appointments and to do some follow-on improvement in areas identified during this early work. One specific concern was the high rate of no-shows to appointments.

The quality-improvement training program was built around the Model for Improvement (that Metro had adopted from Associates in Process Improvement). This roadmap for improvement is shown in Figure 19–1.

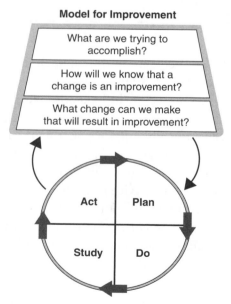

Figure 19–1 Model for Improvement

Following this model, Cal used the knowledge he gained from his background research to frame his improvement project by attempting to answer the three fundamental questions:

What are we trying to accomplish? Develop, test, and implement strategies to reduce the no-show rate for pediatric outpatient clinic appointments by 5% or more from current levels. The focus for the project would be on all the outpatient clinics associated with Metro's hospital.

How will we know that a change is an improvement?

- Reduction in no-show rate by 5% or more (goal = current rate – 5%);

- Increased patient or parent satisfaction with the appointment process; and

- Business case: The benefit from the reduction in no-shows at least pays for the cost of the change strategies.

What change can we make that will result in improvement? Cal's discussion with staff had provided a lot of ideas and information about current practices. He planned a literature review to see what others had learned about the specifics of conducting effective reminder calls.

Initial Work on Project

Cal began his work by obtaining information on the current performance of the outpatient clinics. He had an analyst pull monthly data from the last two years and developed a Shewhart p-chart using the no-show data from all clinics subgrouped by month. Figure 19–2 shows this p-chart.

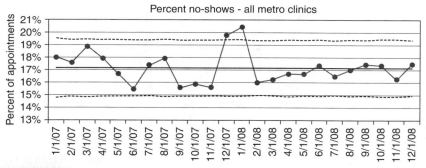

Figure 19–2 P-chart for No-shows by Month from All Metro Outpatient Clinics

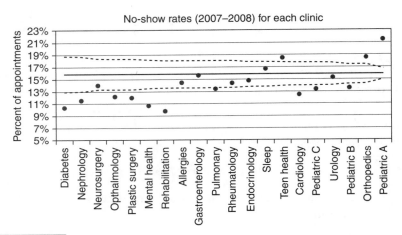

Figure 19-3   No-show Rates for Each Metro Outpatient Clinic

This chart showed special causes on the high side in December 2007 and January 2008. Cal's investigation of these data discovered that the high no-show rates for that period had been attributed to two snow storms that stopped traffic for multiple days and the holidays during that period. A plan had been put in place to be proactive in planning for no-shows during future holiday periods. It seemed to have worked for the next year. The snow story incident had not yet repeated itself.

The rest of the chart indicated a stable system with about a 16% to 17% no-show rate. This was similar to values reported in the literature that ran from 10% to 25%. Cal also prepared a chart to compare the performance of each of the clinics during the two-year period. Figure 19-3 shows this p-chart with each clinic representing a subgroup. The clinics are ordered from the smallest to the largest based on the average number of monthly appointments, which gives the limits on the p-chart a funnel shape.

The Shewhart p-chart for the clinics showed a very unstable system with many clinics above and below the limits of common cause variation. The order on the chart provided one theory for the special causes—the clinics with the most appointments tended to have higher no-show rates. In a meeting with the clinic managers, they agreed that the staff was able to better manage no-shows in the smaller clinics. Three of the clinics with high volumes and low no-show rates had used a strategy of aggressive over-booking, but this often resulted in long wait times and patient or parent dissatisfaction.

Background Learning

Cal felt that the general stability of the system-wide chart over the past two years showed that it was practical to work on changes that could improve all the clinics—even the ones with already low rates. A number of articles in the literature suggested using reminder calls the week before the appointment to reduce no-shows. Metro had a call center to manage outpatient appointments for all the clinics, so they were a possible resource for this concept. Another suggested strategy dealt with follow-up appointments—instead of booking the appointment for the patient at the time of the previous visit, ask the patient to make an appointment at a time convenient for them. Cal arranged a meeting with the clinic managers and the call center leader to discuss these ideas.

Cal presented his charts at the meeting and asked the participants to work with him as a formal quality-improvement (QI) team to reduce the no-show rate. They all agreed and began to share their knowledge and experience. Some of the clinics had tried reminder calls over the past years. While they generally felt the calls helped reduce no-shows, they were resource intensive and often were skipped during busy times. With staff turnover, they often got dropped. None of the clinics had useful data on the benefit of these calls in the past. The call center was a possible resource to centralize the calls, but that would require additional resources. Cal had read that one hospital had a computer system to make follow-up calls. The call center leader agreed to look into using the computer to make calls, but some of the clinic managers were concerned that their patients would not like being called this way and it would affect patient satisfaction.

There was a lively discussion about Cal's second idea for change. A few vocal managers said they had an obligation to give the patient an appointment, because many patients would not take the initiative to do so and follow-up was essential to good care. Cal referenced an article on this topic and asked everyone to read it before the meeting they scheduled for next week. Cal also said he would ask a financial analyst to join the team to work on the business case for improving no-shows.

At that next meeting, they discussed the two ideas proposed for reducing the no-show rate. The call center leader reported that they could use temporary help to do some reminder calls during a test period. She shared a number of scripts that other centers had used for similar calls and circulated copies for review and suggestions. She also reported that the center already had the technology to do computer calls and walked through an example of how the flow of a call would work. One option was to allow the patient to cancel the appointment and request another date and time if they would not be able to make the scheduled appointment. The financial analyst who had joined the team said that there would definitely be a cost benefit if the computer was used to do the reminder calls. He also suggested that they do the calls far enough ahead of time so that cancelled appointments could be refilled. This led to a debate about the ideal lead time and time of day for the reminder call. The literature was not clear about these decision variables.

Cal next led the team in a discussion of the idea to let the patient or parents schedule his/her own follow-up appointments. Based on the success in the article they had read, one of the clinic managers had already piloted this idea in his clinic and found patients to be receptive and appreciative of the opportunity to review their schedule. He was optimistic about pursuing this idea. Another manager suggested that they create reminder files for patients who forgot to re-schedule within a month before their time for follow-up.

Cal agreed to come to the next meeting with a plan to begin testing the ideas that they were discussing. Based on all the discussions, he had agreed to look into patient-selected appointment times, doing computer and personal reminder calls, and selecting the appropriate timing of reminder calls. The call center leader would finalize standard scripts and flows for both personal and computer calls based on feedback from the other managers.

Cal left the meeting pleased with the participation but concerned about how to test all these ideas about reducing no-shows. His training on the Model for Improvement had emphasized small-scale PDSA tests, but he felt he needed a more comprehensive study to investigate the proposed change ideas. He had the support of the clinic managers. So how should he utilize the 20 outpatient clinics in the test? How could the team discover the optimum options and combinations of these ideas that would lead to the best reduction in no-show rates?

DESIGNING THE STUDY

The night after the team meeting, Cal pulled out his old undergraduate text on experimental design and reviewed some principles he had studied what now seemed like years ago (Moen, Nolan, and Provost, 2000). He quickly remembered the advantages of factorial designs to study multiple changes in one study to gain efficiency and discover interactions among the changes. He copied a form from the book and began to organize his thoughts around a study design. Exhibit 19–1 shows his proposed plan, which would require participation of 16 of the 20 clinics. He hoped the design matrix shown in Table 19–1 would help the team understand how each of the proposed changes and their interaction impacted their no-show rates.

Cal presented his proposal to run a PDSA cycle based on this study design during the next month at the improvement team meeting. The clinic managers had agreed on a standard script for the reminder calls. One of the managers agreed to draft two questions to collect feedback on the reminder calls and about the overall appointment process. Sixteen of the clinic managers agreed to have their clinics participate in the experiment. The other four clinic managers agreed to do a follow-up PDSA test in their clinics to validate the best combination of the changes learned from the experiment. Cal would randomly assign each of the clinics to one of the test combinations in the design matrix. Since the majority of follow-up appointments were within 60 days, the clinics that were assigned to have patients make their own appointments would begin that process the next week. Then the call clinics would conduct the two-week study beginning two months from the meeting. This would also allow the call center leader to get procedures in place and train the staff to conduct the reminder call tests.

During that meeting a number of questions were raised. Some thought the literature was conclusive enough to rule out parts of the test. Others

Table 19–1 Design Matrix for No-show Factorial Design

Source of Reminder Call	Timing of Call before Appointment	Clinic with Low Number of Appointments (Block 1)		Clinic with High Number of Appointments (Block 2)	
		Office Makes Follow-up Appointment	*Patient Makes Follow-up Appointment*	*Office Makes Follow-up Appointment*	*Patient Makes Follow-up Appointment*
Human Call	2 days	Clinic 1	Clinic 2	Clinic 3	Clinic 4
	4 days	Clinic 5	Clinic 6	Clinic 7	Clinic 8
Computer Call	2 days	Clinic 9	Clinic 10	Clinic 11	Clinic 12
	4 days	Clinic 13	Clinic 14	Clinic 15	Clinic 16

EXHIBIT 19–1

Experimental Plan for No-show Study

Experimental Unit—Clinic: Select 16 of the 20 outpatient clinics, for a two-week period.

Response Variables	*Method of Measurement*
1. No-show rate	Use data routinely collected—Change from baseline
2. Patient satisfaction	Add two questions to reminder call script

Factors of Interest	*Levels to Study Factor*
1. Follow-up appointment scheduling	a. Current systems used by clinics
	b. Patient schedules own follow-up visit
2. Source of reminder calls	a. Call center personnel do call
	b. Computer does call
3. Timing of reminder call	a. 2 days before appointment
	b. 4 days before appointment

Background Variables	*Method of Control*
1. Seasonal or weather effects	Hold constant (same two-week period)
2. Script for reminders call	Get consensus and hold constant
3. Baseline no-show rate	Form 2 blocks of 8 clinics
4. Size of clinics	Same 2 blocks of 8 clinics

Replication—Implement the specific factor/level combination for all patients during a two-week period in each selected clinic. This will range from an expected 30 to 300 patient visits.

Randomization—After assigning clinic to a block (by baseline rate and size of clinic), randomly assign clinics to the eight specific factor combinations.

Planned Grouping—Use two blocks of eight clinics each to isolate impact of baseline no-show rate and size of the clinic (related based on P-chart of clinics).

Experimental Pattern—2^3 factorial replicated in two blocks (total of 16 tests involving 16 of the outpatient clinics).

thought the design a bit complex and suggested trying things one at a time. They noted a number of things that might go wrong and that sample sizes in some cells might be too small. After discussion, however, they all agreed to support the experiment. After all, Cal was the new COO and he seemed to know what he was talking about.

CONDUCTING THE FACTORIAL EXPERIMENT

Two months later in March, the PDSA cycle to run the factorial experiment began. The final test plan used, with the clinics assigned to each test combination, is shown in Table 19–2.

For example, the Nephrology clinic was one with a lower number of appointments and a low baseline no-show rate. For the two-week test period, this clinic would have patients (or families) schedule their follow-up visits, and their reminder calls would be made two days before the appointment with a human doing the calls.

The study was completed without any major interruptions during the scheduled two-week period in March. The change in no-show rates for each clinic during this period is shown in Table 19–3. Cal analyzed the data using simple graphical methods to estimate and display the effects of each of the changes and interactions in the study (Exhibit 19–2 and Figure 19–7).

While the clinics with higher baseline no-show rates tended to show bigger improvements during the study, the effects of the factors and interactions were consistent across the two blocks of clinics.

Table 19–2 Test Plan: No-show Factorial Design

Source of Reminder Call	Timing of Call before Appointment	Clinic with Low Number of Appointments (Block 1)		Clinic with High Number of Appointments (Block 2)	
		Office Makes Follow-up Appointment	*Patient Makes Follow-up Appointment*	*Office Makes Follow-up Appointment*	*Patient Makes Follow-up Appointment*
Human Call	2 days	Ophthalmology	Nephrology	Pediatric B	Sleep
	4 days	Rehabilitation	Plastic Surgery	Cardiology	Urology
Computer Call	2 days	Pulmonary	Neurosurgery	Endocrinology	Orthopedics
	4 days	Mental Health	Allergies	Pediatric C	Teen Health

Table 19–3		Change in No-show Rates from Factorial Study				
		Clinic with Low Number of Appointments (Block 1)		**Clinic with High Number of Appointments (Block 2)**		
Source of Reminder Call	*Timing of Call before Appointment*	*Office Makes Follow-up Appointment*	*Patient Makes Follow-up Appointment*	*Office Makes Follow-up Appointment*	*Patient Makes Follow-up Appointment*
Human Call	2 days	Ophthalmology −2.6	Nephrology −4.2	Pediatric B −2.4	Sleep −6.1
	4 days	Rehabilitation 0.2	Plastic Surgery −1.6	Cardiology 0.1	Urology −3.3
Computer Call	2 days	Pulmonary −2.2	Neurosurgery −2.3	Endocrinology −2.2	Orthopedics −4.2
	4 days	Mental Health −0.4	Allergies −3.2	Pediatric C −0.2	Teen Health −5.8

EXHIBIT 19–2

Analysis of Data from Factorial No-show Study: Analysis of Effects

Dot-diagram for Clinics with Low Number of Appointments
Important effects: Follow-up approach (F)= −1.6% no-show
Source of reminder call (S) = 1.6% no-show
Source/Timing interaction (SxT) = −1.1% no-show

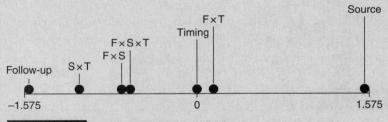

Figure 19–4 Dot-diagram for Clinics with Low Number of Appointments

(continues)

EXHIBIT 19–2 *(continued)*

Dot-diagram for Clinics with High Number of Appointments

Important effects: Follow-up approach (F) = –2.6% no-show
Source of reminder call (S) = 1.5% no-show
Source/Timing interaction (SxT) = –1.2% no-show

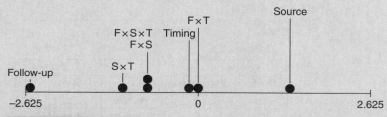

Figure 19–5   Dot-diagram for Clinics with High Number of Appointments

Dot-diagram for All Clinics (Average of Low and High Number of Appointments)

Important effects: Follow-up approach (F) = –3.7% no-show
Source of reminder call (S) = 1.4% no-show
Source/Timing interaction (SxT) = –1.2% no-show

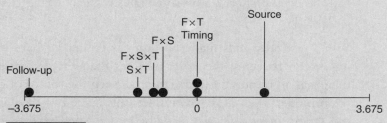

Figure 19–6   Dot-diagram for All Clinics (Average of Low and High Number of Appointments)

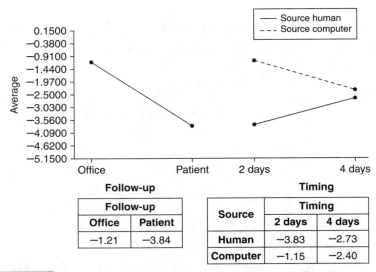

Follow-up	
Office	Patient
−1.21	−3.84

Source	Timing	
	2 days	4 days
Human	−3.83	−2.73
Computer	−1.15	−2.40

Figure 19–7 Analysis of Data from Factorial No-show Study: Response Plot of Important Effects for All Clinics

Cal combined the results of the two blocks of clinics to summarize the key results from the study:

1. Letting the patients schedule their own follow-up appointments had the biggest effect on no-show rates with an average reduction of 2.6%.

2. While reminder calls made by humans tended to have a bigger impact on reducing the no-show rates than the computer calls, there was an important interaction between the source of call and the timing of the call. For reminder calls made two days ahead of the appointment, the calls made by humans had resulted in a big reduction in no-show rates (−4.3% for humans vs. −1.6% for computer calls). But for reminder calls made four days ahead, both methods resulted in a similar reduction (about −3.1%).

3. Patient (parent) satisfaction scores for satisfaction with the appointment process increased from 73% to 86% when the patients made their own appointments.

4. Patient (parent) satisfaction scores for satisfaction with the reminder call averaged about 91% regardless of the source of the call or the number of days ahead the call was made.

Cal assigned Miriam Bernardi, his administrative intern, to do a further analysis of the no-show results in the factorial study. He asked her to present to him any further insights she had and to interpret each of the graphs that he prepared. He was especially concerned about how best to present the final results of the study to the rest of the improvement team and then to his quality-improvement class.

Implementing the Results of the Study

Cal presented the results of the study at the QI team meeting in the last week of March. First, the clinic managers shared their feedback and observations from the tests in their clinic. A number of patients in the clinics that had been tested by letting them make their own follow-up appointments had spontaneously offered their appreciation for this change. Some patients thanked the receptionist for the reminder call when they arrived for their appointment. After Cal presented the results, there was a lot of discussion about the advantages of the two-day vs. four-day reminder call. For clinics with very high demand, the four-day window for cancellations offered a good opportunity to fill the appointment slot with other patients. The financial analyst agreed to consider this opportunity cost in his analysis of the business case.

The four clinics that did not participate in the study were anxious to try out the changes. For the next two weeks, everyone agreed to test the combination of patient scheduled follow-up appointments with reminder calls made by computer four days prior to the appointment date. They predicted an average reduction of about 5% no-shows (overall from 17% to 12%) for all the clinics combined. Because human staff was not required for the reminder calls, the call center had no problem in supporting these changes. When the team met again in two weeks, they would review the results of these confirmation tests and the business case for the changes they were testing.

At the next meeting, Cal presented an updated Shewhart P-chart for no-shows (Figure 19–8). The March data showed a special cause indicating an important change in the no-show rate.

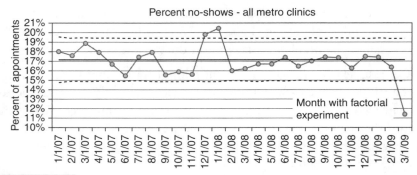

Figure 19–8 Updated P-chart with Month of Factorial Experiment

The business case for these changes in the appointment process had a number of components:

1. Letting patients schedule their own appointments resulted in a cost of about $1/appointment to manage the process of reviewing follow-up scheduling and sending out reminder cards for patients that did not schedule an appointment within two weeks of the desired time.

2. The call center's administrative costs to manage the reminder calls were about $2/appointment.

3. The net revenue gain from reduced no-shows was about $74 per appointment. This assumes that 70% of canceled appointment slots could be refilled with another waiting patient.

On a monthly basis, for each reduction of 1% no-shows the net revenue minus cost gain amounted to about $1,775 ($71 × average number of appointments of 2,500 × 1%). So the predicted 5% reduction in no-show rate would yield a net monthly savings of $8,875.

All of the clinic managers agreed to continue with the patient scheduling and the computer-generated reminder calls four days prior to the scheduled appointment. They expected the overall no-show rate to continue at about 11% to 12%. They were interested in doing another factorial design to work on some refinements to their access work. One of the clinic managers agreed to lead this effort and asked to borrow Cal's reference book on planned experimentation. Cal recommended a recent article on factorial designs in health care that all the managers could read

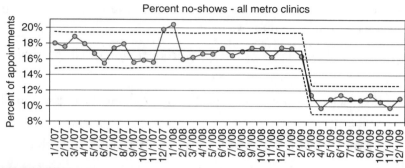

Figure 19–9 Updated P-chart for No-shows with Limits for Improved Process

("The One-Person Randomized Controlled Trial," J. Olsson *et al., Quality Management in Health Care.* 14:4, 2005).

Cal continued to update the no-show chart each month. At the end of the year, he updated the chart (Figure 19–9) with new limits to reflect the improved system of scheduling appointments. With that success in hand, he looked forward to beginning to work on an improvement project on flow in the hospital.

CASE ANALYSIS

Statistical techniques may come in handy during the course of a continuous improvement effort. The most frequently used one is the control chart, but there is a wide variety of options available. This case illustrates the use of a more sophisticated approach that can be used to design a study or to analyze a naturally-occurring experiment. It can be very useful to have statistical support if you and your team are not doing statistical analysis regularly. Those skills are likely to be available from someone in the organization trained in epidemiology, biostatistics, or economics.

ASSIGNMENT QUESTIONS

1. How did Cal's approach to this quality-improvement project differ from your experiences with quality-improvement initiatives?

2. What alternative approaches could Cal have used to accomplish this system-wide improvement?

3. What was the key to gaining the cooperation of all the clinics in this study?

4. As you looked at Cal's plan for the factorial test, what questions did you have?

5. Complete Miriam Bernardi's assignment as outlined in the case.

6. How important was the role of the financial analyst to the quality-improvement team?

CLASS EXERCISE

Use the individuals in your group with a statistical background to identify alternative statistical analyses that might have been used to design a study of the factors behind the no-show problems experienced at Metro Children's Hospital. What statistical techniques have been used in the literature to study that and similar behavioral problems?

ACKNOWLEDGMENTS

This case is adapted from improvement activities at Cincinnati Children's Medical Center coordinated by Terri Byczkowski.

The Houston Medical Center Bed Tower: Quality and the Built Environment

Debajyoti Pati, Thomas E. Harvey Jr., and Paul Barach

INTRODUCTION

When Houston Medical Center in Warner Robins, Georgia, decided to add a new bed tower to their hospital, medication errors and nursing time spent in getting medication received one of the top priorities in their performance matrix. Nurses spend considerable time in medication related activities—17.2% according to a recent Ascension Health study (Hendrich, Chow, Skierczynski, and Lu, 2008), which does not include time spent walking between the medication room and patient rooms nor time spent queuing in the medication room. Anecdotal evidence suggests that multiple trips to the medication room, environmental chaos, and distractions while preparing medications or on the way, among others, cause regular distractions, and contribute to medication errors. In addition, time spent on trips to the medication room constitutes time away from patient care—time which could have been spent at the bedside.

In a typical medication room, medications are stored in AMDs (Automated Medication Dispensers)—the ATMs of the pharmaceutical world. Nurses make several trips to the medication room depending on the number of patients assigned to them. It is considered safe practice to get medications for only one patient at a time on a single trip to the AMD instead of "batching" by collecting and delivering medications for several patients. With unit footprints increasing in size (Latimer, Gutknecht, and Hardesty, 2008), a trip to the medication room could constitute a long, time-consuming, and distraction-laden process. Moreover, walking to the medication room is only one of numerous other trips nurses make as part of the care-delivery process including trips for supplies, equipment linens, and patient charts. (Even with the implementation of electronic documentation, most hospitals still rely on paper-based documentation.)

THE ROLE OF THE BUILT ENVIRONMENT IN QUALITY AND SAFETY

A number of reports from the Agency for Healthcare Research and Quality (AHRQ) have cited the physical environment as an area warranting particular attention in healthcare quality research (AHRQ, 2001, 2003, 2005). The design of hospital physical environments can contribute to medical errors, increase rates of infections and injuries from falls, slow patient recovery, and contribute to high nurse turnover. These conclusions are supported by both anecdotal evidence as well as by two extensive reviews of research literature funded by the Robert Wood Johnson Foundation to understand the role of the physical environment in enhancing the safety and efficiency of patient care (Ulrich, Zimring, Quan, and Joseph, 2004; Ulrich *et al.*, 2008).

There are a number of domains of universal impact, where the physical design influences occupants irrespective of the setting type. These domains include light, noise, friction, and thermal comfort. The influence of these physical environment factors can become magnified several fold in healthcare settings owing to the physical and/or mental condition of the patients and the psychological pressures on both patients and caregivers. For instance, noise has been shown to be a stressor of such significance that it affects patients physiologically—increased blood pressure, heart rate—as well as psychologically—sleep deprivation, pain, ICU psychosis, self-reported stress, and annoyance (Baker, 1984; Morrison *et al.*, 2003; Topf and Thompson, 2001). Similarly, improper visual and/or auditory conditions could lead to clinician errors. For instance, noise impacts communication, concentration, and cognitive performance, leading to stress and fatigue in staff (AHRQ, 2005).

The built environment can also affect individuals' efficiency and safety indirectly by influencing group dynamics and teamwork (Pati, Evans, Waggener, and Harvey, 2008). Environmental phenomena associated with a patient's individual culture, family, and friends have a bearing on the healing process and are impacted by both the built environment and model of care. Caregivers respond to organizational culture, peer relationships, and professional relationships, which are affected by the physical environment and operational policies.

The built environment has an important role in facilitating or impeding process optimization. Impediments due to the built environment can result in workarounds, which lead to sub-optimal process optimization. For example, central cores of operating-room suites are designed to be semi-sterile, but when the path to other ORs goes through the semi-sterile core, foot traffic heightens the bacterial load and ultimately can cause peri-operative infections. Figure 20–1 is a schematic representation of the complex relationship between the caregiver, built environment,

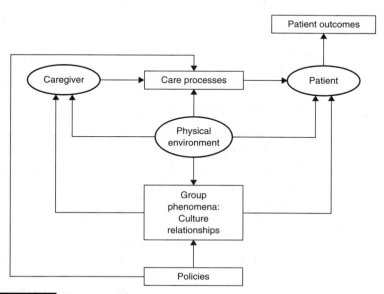

Figure 20–1 Factors Influencing Health Care Delivery

group phenomena, and organizational policies that directly and indirectly influence care process, patient quality, and safety.

THE EFFECT OF DESIGN ON THE CARE PROCESS

When considering the effect of the built environment on patient care, it helps to imagine the physical space a patient moves through the care environment as part of the hospital stay. Patient admission and discharge are not the only events when patients are physically moved during a hospital stay. A typical stay in an American hospital involves 3 to 6 intra-hospital transfers or patient hand-offs (Hendrich, Fay, and Sorrells, 2004). Such transfers may move a patient to a different unit with an appropriate level of life-support provisions or adequate skills of clinical staff. Since the cost of stay depends on the acuity level of the unit in which a patient is admitted, moving patients constitutes a standard protocol to maximize bed usage and keep costs low. Patient transfers, however, can be associated with a number of negative events, including loss of information during clinician hand-offs, patient injury, infections, and staff injury, all contributing to an increase in the length of stay for the patient and substantial hospital costs. (Hendrich, Fay, and Sorrells, 2004; Ulrich and Zhu, 2007; Sharit, McCane, Thevenin, and Barach, 2008; Johnson and Barach, 2009).

The Effect of Design on Caregivers

Design of the built environment also has an impact on nursing efficiency. Moving nurses around due to workforce limits remains a big challenge to care quality. While patient care tasks take caregivers legitimately away from the bedside, the time RNs lose in hunting and gathering supplies and documents and walking to various destinations related to patient care tasks is enormous and does not add value to the process. Studies show that nurses in American hospitals spend a considerable amount of time in non-value added activities (Hendrick, Fay, and Sorrells, 2004). Reducing some or all of the time wasted in such activities could add valuable time at the bedside or to other productive activities such as mentoring, peer support, and process improvement.

Joint Efforts in Design and Improvement

While the domains of direct impact of the physical environment on patients and caregivers are important, those pertaining to process improvements and supporting group phenomena represent high-impact areas in health quality improvement. They are best addressed jointly through working closely with clinicians in designing the physical environment, care processes, and policy interventions. The Houston Medical Center example illustrates the potential role of improvements in the built environment shaping nursing care.

POTENTIAL SOLUTIONS THROUGH DESIGN

At Houston Medical Center, the impact that the two alternative design choices—medication rooms vs. medication servers inside patient rooms—would have on nurse walking and time at bedside was considered an important performance criteria but one of unknown magnitude. The distances nurses walk to perform activities are a function of five factors:

1. Actual distance between various origins and destinations on a unit—a function of unit design attributes

2. Operational processes

3. Staffing model

4. Shift type and length

5. Type and acuity of patient population

There are several potential design solutions to reduce the amount of time and distance nurses spend walking. One solution is to bring the supplies and medications closer to the nurses. Some inpatient units incorporate supply cabinets on the corridors that are designed to be shared between two or more rooms. Another solution is to provide "nurse servers"—cabinets on the corridor walls of patient rooms, typically with a door from the corridor and another from the room interior. Supplies are delivered to the nurse server, and caregivers access the supplies from inside the room. Nurse servers can be designed to stock both supplies and medications. Although this appears to be a simple solution to the nurse walking problem, operational issues pertaining to inventory management, control and rotation, charge capture, and restocking responsibility pose challenges for management. Moreover, supplies and medications are then the responsibility of two separate departments in hospitals, thus adding to the complexity of operational planning and enhancing the risk for medical errors and patient harm.

Qualitative research methods—specifically ethnographic observations, process mapping, and interviews—are used to ascertain the factors that affect nursing staff efficiency (Barach and Johnson, 2006; Mohr and Barach, 2008). This might include the daily average number of trips needed to the medication room and to nurse servers for medical and surgical patients, average time to access and transport medication, and average time required to deliver medications to the patient. A simulation strategy was used to assess nursing performance in the two alternative scenarios. Med-Model is a process simulation tool that provides a powerful analytical technique for aiding decision-making (available from ProModel Corporation).

In MedModel, different types of patients, caregivers, and administrative personnel are arranged in locations according to a given predetermined rationale. The interactions between the different elements in the model result in generally reliable estimates of time and expense. The comparison of the alternative options of medication room or nurse servers was based on the new Houston Medical Center medical and surgical neurological/orthopedic unit layout.

Modeling the Decision—Medication Rooms vs. Nurse Servers

Key factors considered for the model were the time it required nurses to administer medications to the patients, patient type and diagnosis, and walking distance to deliver the medication. The results from the models were determined in the number of feet the caregiver walked for every minute of care delivered. Since nursing trips related to a medical patient are different than for a surgical patient, the variation in the number of trips for these two types of patients were coded into the simulation model. When considering nurse servers, the number of trips needed for a medical patient was found to be five times greater than for a surgical patient. Also, the number of trips needed to retrieve medications from the medication room for a surgical patient is seven times that of a medical patient. Without nurse servers, a medical patient needs 28% fewer trips

Table 20–1 Number of Trips Needed per Patient Type According to Each Design Alternative

Number of Trips/Patient Type	Medical	Surgical
Avg. number of trips needed to the nurse server	05	01
Avg. number of trips needed to the medication room if there is nurse server in the patient room	01	07
Avg. number of trips needed to the medication room if there is no nurse server	05	07

to the medication room when compared to a surgical patient. Table 20–1 summarizes the trip characteristics. Note that a surgical patient requires a similar number of trips to the medication room, even if there is a nurse server in the patient room, owing to the fact that surgical patients need narcotics and/or controlled medications that cannot be stocked in the nurse servers for security reasons.

The nursing staff efficiency determinants include the time to access and transport the medications and the time to deliver the medications to the patient. The time to access and transport is a function of the distance from the source (i.e., medication room or nurse server) to the patient. The distances that the nurses walked in the model were only between patient rooms and the medication room. Because the nurse server is located in the patient's room, its distance was not computed. Also, the nurse server design option still contained a central medication room for controlled drugs.

The nurses in the models were programmed to walk and deliver medications during 12-hour shifts. The nurses' walking speed was assumed to be uniform and equal to 150 feet per minute (fpm) (approximately 50 meters/minute), which is a conservative estimate for comfortable human walking speed. It is also the default value used by MedModel. Multiplying the average walking time by this number, allows one to determine the distance walked in feet. Consequently, the efficiency is calculated as the ratio of the distance walked per one minute of care delivered. Figure 20–2 shows the floor plan of the proposed ortho/neuro unit in Houston Medical Center.

The result of the simulation suggested that on average nurse servers in patient rooms will reduce nurse walking by 576 feet over a 12-hour shift (note that reduction in walking will vary depending on the patient population being served, number of beds on a unit, type of patient accommodation—private or semi-private, the level of decentralization,

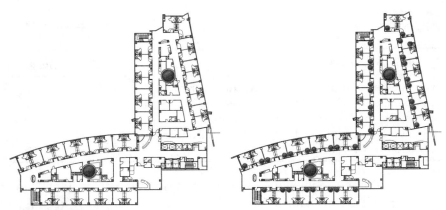

Figure 20–2	Proposed Ortho/Neuro Unit in Houston Medical Center on Which the Nurse Server Study Was Conducted (Left: Centralized Medication Rooms; Right: Medication in Nurse Servers and Smaller Central Medication Rooms)

and staffing model). The average predicted reduction in time spent on retrieving medication was 30 minutes per nurse, per shift. This translates on an average size unit (at 30 beds, 5 nurses per shift) to savings of 6 hours/per 24 hours shift or about 2 days FTE/per week per unit. The result of this simulation was sufficient for the hospital to adopt the nurse server option.

Generally, nurse working conditions have been treated as an operational issue and addressed through operational interventions. The model developed in this study included only medication tasks, with the 30 minutes reduction resulting from medication related activities alone. That raises the issue regarding the role facility designs play in improving staff conditions. The physical design of the environment in which nurses work are not typically considered as instrumental in affecting positive changes in working conditions and efficiencies. This simulation exercise demonstrated that facility design and operations interact in meaningful ways by determining the nursing workload, and that physical design can play a major role in addressing operational issues.

The Nurse Walking Distance Study

If bringing medications to the bedside reduced wasted time by 30 minutes on average per nurse, what kind of improvement could one realize if other activities are also brought as close to the patient as possible? What role could the facility design play in this combined intervention strategy?

To examine the question, a study was designed that included other frequent activities conducted by Registered Nurses (RNs) in the United States (Pati, Ritchey, and Harvey 2008). Data were collected from a nationwide stratified random sample of RNs, representing 46 states in the United States. Nurses volunteered to collect data using an online survey at the end of their typical shift. Eight hundred and twelve nurses responded to questions on task frequencies (i.e., frequencies of various activities that they conducted on that shift) as well as questions on their unit attributes and operational model. Table 20–2 lists the frequency of activities related to a traditional activity location that the nurses conducted on their shift. It should be noted that the table presents the number of times a certain activity was conducted as a percentage of all such activities that were included in the survey. It is not a reflection of the time spent on each activity. The survey focused on tasks that take a nurse away from a patient rather than documenting the time spent on various activities (direct patient-care activities are not on the list since such activities were not included in the survey questions). All the activities listed in Table 20–2 were conducted in the context of patient care.

Table 20–2	Frequencies of Activities RNs Conducted on a Typical Shift

Activity Type	Percentage of Total Number of Times Conducted on Medical Surgical Units
Nurse/Documentation Station	15.37%
Telephone	15.26%
Meds	15.18%
Clean Supply	13.42%
Nourishment	10.25%
Clean Linen	9.60%
Soiled Utility	5.37%
Equipment	5.24%
Elevator	3.14%
Another Place	2.45%
Lounge	2.11%
Off-Unit Transport	1.40%
Off-Unit Supply	1.20%
Conference	0.00%
Supervisor	0.00%

Note: 0.00% represents negligible number of trips compared to other destinations, and not absence of trips.

The frequency data gathered from the survey was subsequently used to simulate a 12-hour day shift to examine the implications of operational and design interventions on the distance nurses walk and time spent in walking on a hypothetical unit. A 30-bed medical surgical unit was adopted for the study. The 30-bed unit size represented the modal category of the medical units where the respondents worked. A 1:6 nurse-to-patient ratio was used, which was one of the modal categories (1:5 being the other) of the nurses' responses to the question on patient load. The frequency data from the survey was filtered to isolate subsets of data representing medical-surgical units and 12-hour day shifts. The floor layout used in the study represented a typical rectangular, racetrack circulation configuration from the HKS inpatient unit design portfolio shown in Figure 20–3.

Two key assumptions were made to reduce the complexity in comparing various scenarios: a) the nurses were not assisted by nursing aides, and b) the nurses were not combining trips. These two factors are important

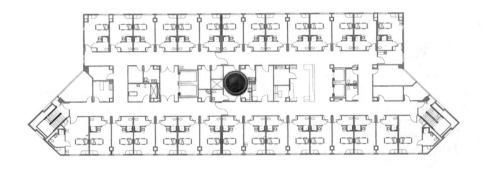

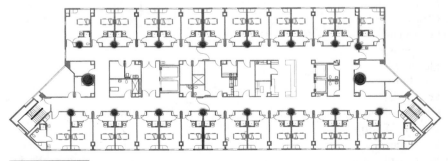

Figure 20–3 Floor Layout of the Medical-Surgical Unit Used in the Study (Top: Centralized Model; Bottom: Decentralized Model)

factors that influence the actual distances walked. Instead of incorporating these factors that vary substantially between hospitals as well as units, such corrections were considered in the specific context of the operational design. Two additional assumptions were also made to reduce the complexity in conducting the simulation: c) all patients assigned to a RN were located in contiguous rooms, and, d) the unit was fully occupied. Assigning adjoining rooms to patients, if possible, has the potential of reducing walking distances, and hence was considered. One hundred percent occupancy was assumed to reduce any noise from occupancy rate. The unit occupancy rate could impact walking depending on the rooms that are occupied first during low census.

Layout IQ (Rapid Modeling Corporation), a software specifically developed to automate walking distance calculations, was subsequently used to simulate a number of different scenarios, against a baseline scenario. The baseline scenario involved a completely centralized unit, where all nursing support spaces were collocated at one location at the center of the support core. From this baseline (centralized) scenario, singular aspects of the nursing activities were pulled closer to the patients, one at a time, while keeping the remaining activities centrally located. As in the Houston Medical Center study, the objective was to examine the degree of impact a single change in nursing activity bears on walking distance and nursing time availability.

In each of the scenarios, a 12-hour day shift was simulated with five nurses and 30 patients. Without adjusting for nursing aides and combined trips, the mean walking distance of a RN in the baseline scenario aggregated to 33,935 ft per shift (6.43 miles). Adopting the industry standard of 150 feet per minute, 33,935 feet translates to about 3.8 hours of a 12-hour shift. Against this baseline case the subsequent scenario manipulations calculated distance and time that would be reduced if one individual aspect of the care process is brought closer to the patient. Table 20–3 provides a summary of the potential savings associated with each individual intervention.

A subsequent simulation scenario combined all the individual decentralization interventions into one model and repeated the analyses. The difference in mean walking distances between a centralized model and a centralized model on the 30-bed unit adopted for the study was a staggering 67.9% (not adjusting for nursing aides and combined trips). The reduction in walking translates to 154 minutes of potential time diverted

Table 20–3	Summary of Potential Reduction Associated with Each Individual Intervention-in-care Process		
Activity Type	**Intervention**	**Walking Distance Reduction (%) Compared to Baseline**	**Time Diverted (minutes, per RN, per 12-hour day shift)**
Charting	Two distributed inside central core + at room side alcoves	15.00	34.0
Telephone	Handheld Device	14.00	32.0
Medication	Bedside Server	14.00	32.0
Clean Supply	Bedside Server	12.50	28.0
Telephone	At room side alcoves	12.00	28.0
Charting	Two distributed in central core	9.79	22.0
Clean Linen	At room side alcoves	7.70	17.5
Nourishment	Two distributed in central core	2.16	5.0
Equipment	Four distributed in central core	1.25	3.0
Soiled Utility	Two distributed in central core	1.18	3.0

back to patient care for a single nurse during a 12-hour day shift (assuming 5 hours/24 hours/per shift or 1.5 FTE days/week/nurse).

The 154 minutes potential time savings in the specific context of this study could have meaningful implications for quality improvement. Note that the 154 minutes reduction is in the context of a staffing ratio of 1:6. Thus, the mean reduction per patient is 25.67 minutes per shift. For the 30 patients on the unit, the total patient time lost associated with all five RNs is 770 minutes—or 12.8 hours per shift.

The diversion of 12.8 hours of combined time away from waste and towards value added activities could be viewed as the equivalent of adding one FTE (full-time equivalent) RN without actually hiring one. From another perspective, it could be seen as the equivalent of reducing the patient load from 1:6 to 1:5 without the costs associated with adding another nurse. The literature suggests that a reduction in one patient load is associated with a 7% reduction in the risk of patient death, 23%

decrease in RN burnout, and a 15% increase in RN job satisfaction (Aiken *et al.*, 2002). While the actual time diversion may marginally vary owing to the degree of contiguity of patient rooms (upward), number of trips that are combined (downward), and the availability of a nursing aide (downward), the implications on care could be quite significant.

CASE ANALYSIS

Healthcare facilities designed for safety and improved working conditions for health providers are resulting in the need for new types of space. There are many ways that the planning and design processes can be improved. Often the built environment is a process constraint that is hard to improve without major capital expenditures. Process analysis and process-improvement techniques, such as time and distance layout studies and computer simulations, can be used to analyze the impact of alternative designs that cannot be tested directly in the work setting. Such techniques adapted from industrial engineering, management science, or systems analysis offer important gains for transforming healthcare settings and enhancing the safety of patients and the well-being of providers.

ASSIGNMENT QUESTIONS

1. What are the potential impacts of the physical environment on patient- and provider-care and well-being?

2. The studies undertaken here were not conducted by teams of hospital staff. How can these non-healthcare teams fit the CQI model?

3. What are the conditions for success imposed by senior management by accepting a design with decentralized activity locations?

4. The decisions in this case are essentially capital investment decisions. So what additional information would be necessary to complete the justification of either alternative at the Houston Medical Center?

5. What other solutions might be evaluated to alleviate the nurse walking problem?

6. We hear a lot about tradeoffs between cost and quality. How does this case enlighten these ongoing tradeoff discussions? Keep in mind the time dimension of capital investment decisions vs. operational cost implications and patient-care quality impact (maximizing the time a nurse on the job actually spends in direct patient-care activities).

7. The method of gathering data about nursing activities used here is called work sampling. It is used to establish the ratio of frequency (or time spent) in various productive and non-productive component activities of a task or time period. Is it something that should be included in CQI training programs?

8. How should the study findings be factored into new hospital design plans?

CLASS EXERCISE

Search the literature for further examples of ways in which the built environment can be improved to enhance patient safety, quality of care, or cost of care delivery.

ACKNOWLEDGMENTS

The research studies presented in this chapter were made possible by cash and in-kind contributions from HKS Architects, Inc., and Herman Miller. Clarissa Lima conducted the MedModel simulation for the Houston Medical Center data.

REFERENCES

Abelson, R. 2006. Heart procedure is off the charts in an Ohio city. *New York Times.* Available at: http://www.nytimes.com/2006/08/18/business/18stent.html. Accessed August 18, 2006.

Adams, O. and V. Hicks. 2000. Pay and Non-Pay incentives, Performance and Motivation. Prepared for WHO's December 2000 Global Health Workforce Strategy Group, Geneva. Department of Organization of Health Services Delivery, World Health Organization, Geneva

Afrol News. 2009. Malaria cripples Ghana's health budget. Available at: http://www.afrol.com/articles/27317. Accessed November 22, 2010.

Aiken, L. *et al.* 2002. Hospital nurse staffing and patient mortality, nurse burnout, and job dissatisfaction. *JAMA*, 288(16), 1987–1993.

Agency for Healthcare Research and Quality. 2001. *Making Health Care Safer: A Critical Analysis of Patient Safety Practices.* Rockville, MD.

Agency for Healthcare Research and Quality. 2003. *The Effect of Health Care Working Conditions on Patient Safety.* Rockville, MD.

Agency for Healthcare Research and Quality. 2005. *Creating a Culture of Patient Safety through Innovative Hospital Design.* In Advances in Patient Safety (Vol. 2). Rockville, MD.

Agyepong I.A., M. Gyapong, and E.K.Wellington. 1998. Can We Reform the Health Sector from Bottom Up? Evaluation of the Impact of the Health Workers for Change Manual in a Rural Health Facility in the Dangme East district of the Greater Accra region of Ghana. Unpublished research report. Obtainable from the Ghana Health Service Research Unit, P.O. Box 184, Adabraka, GHANA or from the Dangme West District Health Administration and Research Centre library, Ghana Health Service, P.O. Box 1, Dodowa, GHANA.

Agyepong I.A. 2000. An Implementation Model for a District Management System to Achieve Continuous Quality Improvement in Malaria Control as part of Primary Health Care in Ghana. A dissertation submitted to the faculty of the University of North Carolina at Chapel Hill in partial fulfillment of the requirements of the degree of Doctor of Public Health in the Department of Health Policy and Administration, School of Public Health.

Agyepong I.A., W.A. Sollecito, S. Adjei, and J.E. Veney. 2001. Continuous quality improvement in public health in Ghana: CQI as a model for primary health care management and delivery. *QualManag Health Care*, 9(4): 1–10.

Agyepong, I.A. *et al.* 2003. Evaluation of the Impact of Continuous Quality Improvement on Malaria Control in Greater Accra Region. Unpublished research report. Obtainable from the Ghana Health Service Research Unit, P.O. Box 184, Adabraka, GHANA or from the Dangme West District Health Administration and Research Centre library, Ghana Health Service, P.O. Box 1, Dodowa, GHANA.

Aldrete, J.A. 1995. The post-anesthesia recovery score revisited. *J Clin Anesth*, 7:89–91.

Al Hussein, *et al.* 1993. Should the nurse be blamed? *IntNurs Rev*, 40(1):27–28.

Anekwe, L. 2008. QOF points docked at PCTs turn the screw. *Pulse*. Available at: http://www.accessmylibrary.com/article-1G1180628795/qof-points-docked-pcts.html. Accessed December 2, 2009.

Appleby, J., N. Devlin, and D. Parkin. 2007. NICE's cost effectiveness threshold: How high should it be? *British Medical Journal*, 335:358–359.

Baker, C.F. 1984. Sensory overload and noise in the ICU: Sources of environmental stress. *Crit Care Q*, 6(4):66–80.

Baker, G.R. *et al.* 2008. "Intermountain Healthcare." *High Performing Healthcare Systems: Delivering Quality by Design.* pp. 151–178. Toronto: Longwoods Publishing.

Barach P. and J. Johnson. 2006. Safety by Design: Understanding the dynamic complexity of redesigning care around the clinical microsystem. *Qual Saf Health Care*, 15 (Suppl 1): i10–i16.

Bhattacharyya, T. *et al.* 2009. Measuring the report card: the validity of pay-for-performance metrics in orthopedic surgery. *Health Affairs*, 28 (2):526–532.

Boden, W.E. *et al.* 2007. Optimal medical therapy with or without PCI for stable coronary disease. *N Eng JMed*, 356(15):1503–1516.

Bohmer, R.M.J. 2009. *Designing Care, Aligning the Nature and Management of Health Care*, Boston, MA: Harvard Business Press.

Bohmer, R.M.J. and A.C. Edmondson. 2003. Intermountain Healthcare. Boston, MA: Harvard Business School Publishing, Case 9-603–066.

Bohmer, R.M.J. and E.M. Ferlins, 2006. Clinical Change at Intermountain Healthcare. Boston, MA: Harvard Business School Publishing, Case 9-607–023, Revised, 2008.

Bohmer, R.M.J. and A.C. Romney, 2009. Performance Management at Intermountain Healthcare. Boston, MA: Harvard Business School Publishing, Case 9-609–103.

Byington, C.L *et al.* 2004. Serious bacterial infections in febrile infants 1 to 90 days old with and without viral infections. *Pediatrics*, 113(6):1662–6.

Campbell, D. 2007 (May 8). Support grows to boost bread for healthy babies. *Guardian*. Available at: http://www.guardian.co.uk/society/2007/May/06/health.food. Accessed January 14, 2011.

Campbell, S.M. *et al.* 2009. Effects of pay for performance on the quality of primary care in England. *N Eng J Med*, 361:368–378.

Cassels, A. and K. Janovsky. 1995. Strengthening Health Management in Districts and Provinces. World Health Organization, Geneva.

Centers for Disease Control and Prevention. 1991. Effectiveness in disease and injury prevention use of folic acid for prevention of spina bifida and other neural tube defects: 1983–1991. *MMWR Weekly*, 40:513–516.

Centers for Disease Control and Prevention. 1999. Folate status in women of childbearing age: United States 1999. *MMWR Weekly*, 49:962–965.

Centers for Disease Control and Prevention. 2004. Spina bifida and anencephaly before and after folic acid mandate: United States, 1995–1996 and 1999–2000. *MMWR Weekly*, 53:362–365.

Centers for Disease Control and Prevention. 2007. Folate Status in Women of Childbearing Age, by Race/Ethnicity—United States, 1999–2000, 2001–2002, and 2003–2004. *MMWR Weekly*, 55: 1377–1390.

CIA (Central Intelligence Agency). 2010. The World Factbook: Africa: Ghana. Available at: https://www.cia.gov/library/publications/the-world-factbook/geos/gh.html. Accessed September 9, 2010.

Collen, M.J. and Y.K. Chen. 1995. Giant duodenal ulcer and nonsteroidal anti-inflammatory drug use. *Am J Gastroenterol* 90:162.

CMS. 2004. CMS HQI Demonstration Project Composite Quality Score Methodology Overview Available at: http://www.cms.gov/HospitalQualityInits/download/HospitalCompositeScoring MethodologyOverview.pdf. Accessed September 8, 2010.

CMS. 2007. Terms and Conditions between Premier, Inc. and CMS of the Hospital Quality Incentives Demonstration, First Amendment. Available at: http://www.cms.gov/HospitalQualityInits/35_HospitalPremier.asp. Accessed Sept. 8, 2010.

Crump, H. 1992. Pectus excavatum. *Am Fam Physician*, 46(1):173–179.

Deming, W. E. 1993. *The New Economics for Industry, Government, Education.* Cambridge: Massachusetts Institute of Technology Center for Advanced Engineering Study.

Denham, C. R. 2006. Leaders need dashboards, dashboards need leaders. *J Patient Saf*, 2(1):45–53.

DoH (Department of Health). 2008. *NHS Next Stage Review: Our Vision for Primary and Community Care*. Available at www.dh.gov.uk/prod_consum_dh/groups/dh_digital assets/@dh/@en/documents/digitalasset/dh_085947.pdf.

DoH (Department of Health). 2009. General Medical Service Statement of Financial Entitlements-NI, 4th edition. Available at: http://www.dhsspsni.gov.uk/the_general_medical_service_statements_of_financial_entitlements_ni_4th_edition_final_29_01_09__3___3_.pdf. Accessed December 10, 2010.

Dopson, S. and L. Fitzgerald. 2005. *Knowledge to Action: Evidence-Based Health Care in Context*, New York, NY: Oxford University Press.

Doran, T. *et al.* 2006. Pay-for-performance programs in family practices in the United Kingdom. *N Eng J Med*, 355(4):375–384.

Doran, T. *et al.* 2008. Effect of financial incentives on inequalities in the delivery of primary care in England: analysis of clinical activity indicators for the quality and outcomes framework. *Lancet*, 372:728–736.

Ebbing, M. *et al.* 2009. Cancer incidence and mortality after treatment with folic acid and vitamin B_{12}. *JAMA*, 302 (19): 2119–2126.

European Food Safety Authority. 2009. ESCO Report on Analysis of Risks and Benefits of Fortification of Food with Folic Acid. Available at: http://www.efsa.europa.eu/EFSA/ efsa_locale-1178620753812_1211902990971.htm. Accessed November 10, 2009.

Feder, B.J. 2007. In the stent era, heart bypasses get a new look. *New York Times.* Available at: http://www.nytimes.com/2007/02/25/health/25bypass.html. Accessed October 17, 2009.

Food and Drug Administration. 1993. Food standards: Amendment of the standards of identity for enriched grain products to require addition of folic acid. *Federal Register,* 58:53305–53312.

The Food Standards Agency Board. 2006. Consultation on options to increase folate intakes of young women. Available at: http://www.food.gov.uk/consultations/ ukwideconsults/2006/folate.

Food Standards Australia New Zealand (FSANZ). 2009. Mandatory folic acid fortification and health outcomes. Available at: http://www.foodstandards .gov.au/scienceandeducation/factsheets/factsheets2009/mandatoryfolicacidfo4460 .cfm. Accessed: December 10, 2010.

Fonkalsrud, E.W. *et al.* 2002. Comparison of minimally invasive and modified Ravitch pectus excavatum repair. *J Pediatr Surg.* 37(3): 413–417.

Gaull, G. E., C.A.Testa, P.R.Thomas and D.A.Weinrich. 1996. Fortification of the food supply with folic acid to prevent neural tube defects is not yet warranted (fortifying policy with science—the case of folate). *J Nutr,* 126:773S–780S.

Gawande, A. 2004. The Bell Curve: What happens when patients find out how good their doctors really are? *The New Yorker,* 6:82–91.

GSS (Ghana Statistical Service). 2005. *2000 Population and Housing Census.* Accra, Ghana: Office of the President.

GSS (Ghana Statistical Service (GSS), Ghana Health Service and ICF Macro). 2009 *Ghana Demographic and Health Survey 2008.* Accra, Ghana: Office of the President.

Grosse, S. D., *et al.* 2005. Reevaluating the benefits of folic acid fortification in the United States: economic analysis, regulation and public health. *Am J Public Health,* 95:1917–1922.

Haynes, A.B. *et al.* 2009. A surgical safety checklist to reduce morbidity and mortality in a global population. *N Eng J Med,* 360:491–499.

Health and Social Care Information Centre. 2009. Diabetes mellitus QOF for April 2008–March 2009, Achievement by Indictor, England. Available at: http:// www.ic.nhs.uk/statistics-and-data-collections/supporting-information/audits-and-performance/the-quality-and-outcomes-framework/qof-2008–2009/data-tables/ england-level-data-tables/QOF0809_national_clinical.xls. Accessed Nov. 15, 2010.

Health Select Committee. 2007. House of Commons Health Committee, *National Institute for Health and Clinical Excellence, First Report of Session 2007–2008.* Available at: http://www.publications.parliament.uk/pa/cm200708/cmselect/ cmhealth/27/27.pdf. Accessed November 19, 2009.

Hendrich, A., M. Chow, B.A. Skierczynski, and Z. Lu. 2008. A 36-hospital time and motion study: How do medical-surgical nurses spend their time? *The Permanente Journal*, 12(3):25–34.

Hendrich, A., J. Fay, and A.K. Sorrels. 2004. Effects of acuity-adaptable rooms on flow of patients and delivery of care. *Am J Crit Care*, 13(1):35–45.

Hertkampf, E. 2004. *Folic acid fortification: Current knowledge and future priorities (discussion paper)*. Santiago, Chile: Institute of Nutrition and Food Technology, University of Santiago.

Hibbard, E. D., and Smithells, R. W. 1965. Folic acid metabolism and human embryopathy. *Lancet*, 1:1254–1256.

Honoré, P., R. Clarke, D. Meade, and S. Meditto. 2007. Creating Financial Transparency in Public Health. *J Public Health Manag Pract*, 13(2):121–129.

Honoré, P. and C. Lesneski. 2009. Presentation at American Public Health Association, Philadelphia, PA. November 8, 2009, Learning Institute #2013: Strategies for Local and State Public Health Agencies to Reduce the Negative of a Distressed Economy.

Institute of Medicine. 2001. *Crossing the Quality Chasm: A New Health System for the 21st Century*. Washington, DC: The National Academies Press.

Intermountain Healthcare. 2008. Independent Contract Agreements for Physician Administrative Services. Available at: http://intermountainhealthcare.org/quality/Pages/. Accessed February 9, 2010.

Intermountain Healthcare. 2009. Clinical Programs: Improving Healthcare Delivery. Available at: http://intermountainhealthcare.org/quality/Pages/ClinicalPrograms.aspx. Accessed February 9, 2010.

James, B.C and J.S. Lazar. 2007. Sustaining and Extending Clinical Improvements: A Health System's Use of Clinical Programs to Build Quality Infrastructure. Chapter 7 in Nelson, E.C., P.B. Batalden and J.S. Lazar, Eds., *Practice-Based Learning and Improvement: A Clinical Improvement Action Guide*. Oakbrook Terrace, IL: Joint Commission on Accreditation of Healthcare Organizations, Joint Commission Resources, Inc.

Jaroszewski, D. *et al.* 2010. Current management of pectus excavatum: a review and update of therapy and treatment recommendations. *J Am Board Fam Med.* 23(2):230–239.

Jha, A. and A. Epstein. 2010. Hospital Governance and the quality of care. *Health Affairs*, 29(1): 182–187.

Johnson, J. and P. Barach. 2009. Handovers of patient care: what will it take to ensure quality and safety during times of transition? *Med J Aust*, 190(11): S110–S112.

Junod, S.W. 2006. Folic acid fortification: Fact and folly. U.S. Food and Drug Administration. Available at: http://www.fda.gov/oc/history/makinghistory/folicacid.html. Accessed January 7, 2006.

Kaisernetwork.org. 2006. Pay-for-Performance: A Critical Examination: Welcome and Keynote, National Committee for Quality Assurance, December 1, 2006. Available at: http://www.kaisernetwork.org. Accessed Jan. 14, 2010.

Kroch, E. *et al.* 2006. Hospital boards and quality dashboards. *J Pat Saf*, 2(1):10–19.

Langley, G. J. *et al*. 1996. *Improvement Guide: A Practical Approach to Enhancing Organizational Performance*. San Francisco: Jossey-Bass.

Latimer, H., H. Gutknecht, and K. Hardesty. 2008. Analysis of hospital facility growth: are we super-sizing healthcare. *Health Environments Research and Design J*, 1(4):70–88.

Leonhardt, D. 2009. Making Health Care Better. *New York Times*. Available at: http://www.nytimes.com/2009/11/08/magazine/08Healthcare-t.html. Accessed November 5, 2009.

Lynch, P. 2009. Whatever happened to Ireland's plans for mandatory folic acid fortification? *Irish Medical News*. Available at: http://www.irishmedicalnews.ie/index.php/current_issue/2393-whatever-happened-to-irelands-mandated-folic-acid-fortification. Accessed November 9, 2009.

Margolis, P. *et al*. 2004. Practice based education to improve delivery systems for prevention in primary care: Randomised trial. *BMJ*, 328:388–92.

Mason, J.B. *et al*. 2007. A temporal association between folic acid fortification and a rise in colorectal cancer rates may be illuminating important biological principles: a hypothesis. *Cancer Epidemioly, Biomarkers Prev,* 16(7):1–5.

McDonald, R. and M. Roland. 2008. Pay for performance in primary care in England and California: Comparison of unintended consequences. *Ann Internal Med*, 7:121–127.

Medicare.gov (2011). Nursing Home Compare. Available at: http://www.medicare.gov/NHCompare/Include/DataSection/Questions/SearchCriteriaNEW.asp?version=default&browser=IE%7C8%7CWindows+7&language=English&defaultstatus=0&pagelist=Home&CookiesEnabledStatus=True. Accessed January 20, 2011.

Medline. 2007. Pectus excavatum. *MedLine Plus Medical Encyclopedia:* U.S. National Library of Medicine and the National Institutes of Health, 2007. pp. 11–12.

Moen, R., T. Nolan, and L. Provost. 2000. *Quality Improvement through Planned Experiment*, 2nd Ed., New York, NY: McGraw-Hill.

MOH. 2001. Ministry of Health, Government of Ghana, August 2001. The Health of the Nation. Reflections on the First Five Year Health Sector Program of Work. 1997–2001.

Mohr, J. and P. Barach. 2008. Understanding the design of health care organizations: the role of qualitative research methods. *Environment and Behavior,* 40:191–205.

Mohr, J.J. and P.B. Batalden. 2002. Improving safety on the front lines: the role of clinical microsystems. *Qual Saf Health Care*. 11(1): 45–50.

Monk, J. 2002. How a hospital failed a boy who didn't have to die. *The State*. Available at: http://www.lewisblackman.net. Accessed October 16, 2009.

Morris, A.H. *et al*. 2008. A replicable method for blood glucose control in critically Ill patients. *Crit Care Med*, 36(6):1787–95.

Morrison, W. E. *et al*. 2003. Noise, stress, and annoyance in a pediatric intensive care unit. *Crit Care Med*, 31(1):113–119.

MRC Vitamin Study Research Group. 1991. Prevention of neural tube defects: Results of the Medical Research Council Vitamin Study. *Lancet,* 338:131–137.

NACHRI. 2010. Pediatric Intensive Care Medicine: Eradicating Catheter-associated Blood Stream Infections: A Proven Initiative for Sustainable Change. Available at: http://www.childrenshospitals.net/AM/Template.cfm?Section=CA_Blood_Stream_Infections&TEMPLATE=ContentDisplay.cfm&CONTENTID=53939. Accessed December 22, 2010.

NHS. 2008. Available at: http://www.sehd.scot.nhs.uk/pca/PCA2008(M)01.pdf. Accessed December 22, 2010.

NICE. 2009. QOF Indicator Programme process guide. Interim issue, May 2009. Available at: http://www.nice.org.uk/media/742/32/QOFProcessGuide.pdf. Accessed November 20, 2009.

Noble, D. 2008. Edelman Analysis of Health Select Committee Inquiry into NICE, January, 2008. Available at: http://edelman.co.uk/files/Edelman_analysis_of_HSC_inquiry_into_NICE_-_10_Jan_2008/pdf. Accessed November 20, 2009.

Nolan, T. and D.M. Berwick, 2006. All-or-none measurement raises the bar on performance, *JAMA*, 295:1168–1170.

Olsson, J. and Terris, D. (2005). The One-Person Randomized Controlled Trial. *Quality Management in Health Care*, 14(4), 206-216.

Palca, J. 1992. Agencies split on nutrition advice. *Science, 257*:1857.

Pati, D., J. Evans, L. Waggener, and T. Harvey. 2008. An exploratory examination of medical gas booms versus traditional headwalls in intensive care unit design. *Crit Care Nurs Q*, 31(4):340–356.

Pati, D., T. Ritchey, and T. Harvey. 2008. *Towards Optimizing Inpatient Unit Design and Care Model: A Measure to Predict Nurse Walking Distance on Hospital Bed Units.* Ongoing study at HKS, Inc.

Romano, P.S. *et al.* 1995. Folic acid fortification of grain: An economic analysis. *Am J Public Health*, 85:667–676.

SACN (Scientific Advisory Committee on Nutrition). 2008. Paper for information. Briefing for review of SACN recommendation for mandatory fortification. SACN/08/00, 21/01/08. Available at: http://www.sacn.gov.uk/pdfs/sacn_08_00.pdf. Accessed November 9, 2009.

Saminu, Z.R. 2010. Ghana: Malaria is Threatening Survival of the Economy—Aidoo, *Ghanaian Chronicle*, February 26. Available at: http://allafrica.com/stories/printable/201002260719.html. Accessed March 3, 2010.

Schechter, M. and P. Margolis. 2004. *Improving Healthcare in Subspecialty Healthcare: The Example of Cystic Fibrosis.* Unpublished manuscript.

Scheffler, R.M. *et al.* 2009. Estimates of Health Professional Shortages in Sub-Saharan Africa by 2015. *Health Affairs Web Exclusive*, 6 August, w849-w862 (10.1377/hltaff.28.52849)

SerVaas, S. and Perry, P. 1999. A flaming failure. *Saturday Evening Post,* 27(5),62–ff.

Shamberger, R. 1996. Congenital chest wall deformities. *Curr Probl Surg,* 33(6):469–542.

Sharit, J., L. McCane, D.M. Thevenin, and P. Barach. 2008. Examining Links Between Sign-Out Reporting During Shift Changeovers and Patient Management Risks. *Risk Anal,* 28(4):983–1001.

Staines, A. 2009. Institutional Strategies for Holistic Improvement, presentation at the Institute for Health Care Delivery, Salt Lake City, Utah on July 29, 2009. (First presented at the IHI National Forum in December, 2007.)

Steinbrook, R. 2008. Saying No isn't NICE—The Travails of Britain's National Institute for Health and Clinical Excellence, *N Eng J Med*, 359:1977–1981.

Stent News. 2007. Answers to Top Ten Questions About Stents and Angioplasty vs. Drug Therapy: COURAGE Trial Results Breed Confusion. Available at: http://www.ptca.org/new/2007/0328.html. Accessed February 14, 2010.

Tedstone, A. 2007. Folic acid: UK Position, Nutrition Division, Food Standards Agency, January 11, 2007. Available at: http://www.fbr.bund.de/cm/232/folic_acid_uk_position.pdf. Accessed November 1, 2009.

The Care Group. 2007. The Care Group Cardiologists Comments on Stents vs Medication (The COURAGE Study). Available at: http://www.thecaregroup.com/amod/Press%20Release%20/Courage%20Release%204_18%202007.pdf. Accessed August12, 2010.

Topf, M. and S. Thompson. 2001. Interactive relationships between hospital patients' noise-induced stress and other stress with sleep. *Heart Lung*, 30(4):237–243.

Ulrich, R. and X. Zhu. 2007. Medical complications of intra-hospital patient transport: implications for architectural design and research. *Health Environments Research and Design J*, 1(1):31–43.

Ulrich, R., C. Zimring, X. Quan, and A. Joseph. 2004. *The Role of the Physical Environment in the Hospital of the 21st Century: A Once-in-a-Lifetime Opportunity*. Concord, CA: The Center for Health Design.

Ulrich, R. *et al.* 2008. A Review of the Research Literature on Evidence-Based Healthcare Design. *Health Environments Research and Design J*, 1(3):61–125.

UNICEF. 2007. UNICEF Ghana Fact Sheet Malaria, July 2007. Available at: http://www.unicef.org/wcaro/WCARO_Ghana_Factsheet_malaria.html. Accessed September 9, 2009.

Urbach, J. and J. Harris. 2008. Ghana: Malaria—Killing With Kindness. Accra: Public Agenda. Available at: http://allafrica.com/stories/printable/200810061508.html. Accessed March 3, 2010.

Van Matre, J.G. 2006. All-or-none measurement of health care quality. *JAMA*, 296:392.

Wachter, R.M. and P.J. Pronovost. 2006. The 100,000 Lives campaign: A scientific and policy review. *Jt Comm J Qual Patient Saf*, 32(11):621–627.

Wang, X. *et al.* 2007. Efficacy of folic acid supplementation in stroke prevention: a meta-analysis. *Lancet*, 369 (9576):1876–82.

Winstein, K.J. 2010. A simple health-care fix fizzles out. *Wall Street Journal*, February 11, pp. A1, A18.

WHO. 2008. *World Alliance for Patient Safety, Implementation Manual Surgical Safety Checklist (First Edition): Safe Surgery Saves Lives*. Geneva: World Health Organization.

WHO. 2010. *Ghana: Country health profile*. Regional Office for Africa. Available at: http://www.afro.who.int/en/ghana/country-health-profile.html. Accessed December 15, 2010.

INDEX